GOTHICK MEDITATIONS at MIDNIGHT

Gothick Meditations at Midnight: Esoteric Commentaries on Classic Horror Literature and Film, 1919–1975

Copyright © 2023 Stephen E. Flowers

ISBN 9781885972859

Interior design by Michael Moynihan
Cover design by Michael Moynihan & Antumnos Studio
Cover art by Albin Grau (detail from a poster for F. W. Murnau's *Nosferatu*, 1922)

Special thanks to Claus Laufenburg for assistance with H. H. Ewers images and permission to include the Atelier Eburth portrait from his personal collection.

All rights reserved. No part of this book, either in part or in whole, may be reproduced, transmitted, or utilized in any form or by any means electronic, photographic, or mechanical, including photocopying, recording, or by any information storage and retrieval system, without the permission in writing from the Publisher, except for brief quotations embodied in literary articles and reviews.

For permissions or inquiries regarding the serialization, condensation, or adaptation of this work, write to the publisher, Lodestar, at: tilruna72@gmail.com

Lodestar
www.seekthemysteries.com

GOTHICK MEDITATIONS at MIDNIGHT

Esoteric Commentaries on
Classic Horror Literature and Film
1919–1975

Stephen E. Flowers

LODESTAR
2023

Acknowledgments

The author thanks Michael Moynihan for his tireless editorial work and invaluable artistic eye, as well as: Michael A. Aquino, Lilith Aquino, Don Webb, Sheila Walters, Stephen Wehmeyer, Crystal Flowers, Tom Seymore, Ralph Tegtmeier, Adam Parfrey, Blanche Nonken, Albo Südekum, Leon Wild, Lothar Tuppan, John Hagen-Brenner, Toby Chappell, Joshua Buckley, Claus Laufenburg, and James A. Chisholm.

CONTENTS

Preface
vii

Foreword: A Warning to the Reader
ix

Recollections of Gothick Horror &
Memories of Being a Monster Kid
xv

Grimm Tales of the Page and Screen:
A Theoretical Introduction
xxxiii

I. Hidden Dimensions of Dracula:
Occult, Psychological, Political, and Historical
1

II. The Mythology of the Mummy:
Anankê and Kharis
33

III. Phantom of the Opera: The Ghost in the Machine
51

IV. The Wolf Man and the Rites of Passage
73

V. Frankenstein: A Man-made Creation
91

VI. H. P. Lovecraft and the Shadows Out of Time
117

VII. The Mysteries of Edgar A. Poe
141

VIII. Zombies: From the Cane Fields to Cosmic Ghouls
169

IX. Cults and Covens
189

X. Hanns Heinz Ewers: Horror from the Inside
217

XI. William Castle:
Moviegoing as Ritual and Rite of Passage
243

XII. Caligarism and the Trapezoidal Cinema
261

XIII. Ed Wood's Plan Nine from Inner Space:
The Visions of the Outsider
275

XIV. Sci-Fi Theater (Preview of a Coming Attraction?)
291

Afterword: The Light Grows Dimmer
315

———

Appendix A: Best Classic Horror Films, 1913–1975
321

Appendix B: Best of the Rest, 1976–2022
325

Appendix C: Twenty Guilty Pleasures
327

Appendix D: Fifty Must-see Classic (Pre-1975)
Science-Fiction Films
329

Bibliography
331

PREFACE

In Plato's "Myth of the Cave," part of his dialogue *The Republic*, the Greek philosopher shows men bound in chairs viewing shadows of real objects reflected on the flat surface of a subterranean cave. The point was to discover what these real objects were, and to look beyond the shadows to gain true knowledge. These two-dimensional reflections of reality have come to dominate our consciousness more than Plato could have imagined. The task of discovering the meaning behind the images, however, remains eternal.

During my youth in the early 1960s, I often descended into the cave of the Casa Linda Movie Theater in Dallas, Texas to view wondrous images projected onto the screen. These images brought to vivid life the things I read about in my favorite magazines, such as *Famous Monsters of Filmland* or *The Castle of Frankenstein*.

I always remained curious as to the meanings that lurked below the surface of these images. The present book grew out of that curiosity, finally to be expressed in print a half-century after it was first implanted in my childhood brain. This book is an exploration of the times, the films, and the literature in which the archetypes of the human imagination were allowed to run free under the guise of the "scary movie." You will also find out quite a bit more about what made the average "Monster Kid" of the early 1960s "tick" than you might have wished for.

More seems to be simmering beneath the surface of these films than even their creators may have realized when they made them. Here I try to awaken to our conscious minds what once slumbered in darkness. This book contains thousands of little sparks, any one of which might bring the reader to a moment of greater insight.

I have penned over fifty books in my life so far, and I have never had more fun writing one than the present volume. I hope the reader will find it almost as much fun to read.

Stephen E. Flowers
Woodharrow
Halloween, 2018

Foreword
A Warning to the Reader

Let this be a warning to the reader to beware—*beware*—that much of what you are about to read is meant ironically. Some of it is made up of inside jokes and references, much of it is meant in dire earnestness, other parts are sublime philosophical principles, while the remainder is just plain fun. I will leave it to the reader to decide which is which, and what is what. *We knows what we knows and we keeps it to ourselves.*

After setting the stage for the essays with a couple of introductory pieces (one is a quasi-autobiographical sketch of my boyhood interest in horror movies and how they affected the course of my life, and the other outlines the theory of the book) you will have before you a series of independent essays that deal with certain films (or, better said, groups of films), personalities, and themes, which have been chosen simply for the level of inspiration and interest they have for me.

These essays, or meditations, are generally stand-alone compositions. For this reason, there will be the occasional repeated material or points here and there. The pieces are intended to be enjoyed individually. The thread that stiches them all together is explicitly outlined in the introductory essay and more implicitly in the autobiographical one.

The title of this book, *Gothick Meditations at Midnight*, needs some explanation. The essays take the form at one point or another of meditations, or esoteric commentaries, inspired by the literary and/or cinematic material under our lens at the moment. As an exercise, I started reviewing these films in a nightly ritual of the midnight viewing of a choice DVD, which acted as a catalyst and "mood setter" for my writing exercise.

It is the word *Gothick* in the title that is perhaps most mysterious. Originally, the term "Gothic" was derived from a self-designation of an ancient Germanic tribe, the Goths, who were a powerful and influential group of people in antiquity, but who faded from history in the Middle Ages. In the eighteenth century, "Gothic" was used as a blanket designation for *all* the ancient Germanic peoples. (Another term, "Teutonic," was also used for this, but in modern times the technical term has become "Germanic," which can be confusing because it is *not* synonymous with "German.") In the Anglophone world of the British Isles and America, "Gothic" took on broader connotations, conjuring images of deep antiquity, atavistic traits (as the English, and hence Americans, had historically emerged from northern Germany), dark forests, and crumbling castles. This inspired the use of the term to describe a new type of literature both in Germany and in the Anglo-American world: the Gothic Romance was created in parallel with Gothic horror. My use of the stylized form *Gothick* is meant to encompass all of these senses.

The book concludes with a series of appendices, the first of which lists the "Best Classic Horror Films" according to myself, the author. As with all lists of this sort, it is mainly intended as a discussion-starter and a device to entertain the reader. What I do hope this list will convey is a sort of canon of horror films compiled from the perspective that the reader will come to understand better in the course of reading the essays. For *some* younger people, who may have trouble even watching the black-and-white Universal classics, much less the silent greats (I have to work at some of them as well), this list may act as a registry of "must-views" in order to become a true aficionado of the early or

Foreword: A Warning to the Reader

classic horror genre.

It might well be asked: *Why the pre-1975 time frame?* The reason is that just about before that time horror films were made with a certain level of naiveté, so they can be seen as more akin to esoteric cultural Rorschach tests. Therefore, they become subject to inner interpretations that bring out and make explicit what would otherwise only be hidden or implicit. After about 1975 (certainly post-*Exorcist*), more and more of the Monster Kid Generation started to actually *make* the films.

And what is a Monster Kid? Monster Kids are people, mainly boys, who were born between 1945 and 1960, and grew up on horror movies on television and at the Saturday matinees. To the core of the generation belong those who were between six and twelve years of age in the heart of the "monster craze" (1958–1968).

Some of these Monster Kids grew up and became filmmakers themselves. Often they made explicit what the previous generation had only expressed or suggested in hidden ways. Things that would have been left to the imagination of the viewer in the earlier era of filmmaking were now shown in gory detail.

It is the hidden dimension of the older films that opens them to deeper psychological and even esoteric examination. The so-called Hayes Code (which lasted from 1934–1968), which restricted what could be depicted on the screen, had also added a level of "rules" to the art form. Many films made after 1975 do have a hidden component, but it does not dominate. Also, it must be said that while many truly great films have been made in the more recent period, they are just "different."

An important and recurring theme in this book—both with regard to the narratives of the literature and films themselves, as well as the constitutions of those who love and admire them— is that of the *Outsider*. One of H. P. Lovecraft's most important short stories was entitled "The Outsider" (1926). This reads almost like a folk tale and is pregnant with symbolic power. It tells the story of an unnamed entity who breaks free of a tomblike estate where he has dwelt for ages and makes his way toward a home where a party is going on; he enters and the guests are shocked and dismayed by his arrival. He does not understand until he gazes upon a horrible figure standing before him in a gilded frame, and he comes to know, in his own words that:

> I am an outsider; a stranger in this century and among those who are still men. I have known ever since I stretched out my fingers to the abomination within that great gilded frame; stretched out my fingers and touched *a cold and unyielding surface of polished glass.* (Lovecraft 1963, 59)

This idea of the Outsider was developed much further by Colin Wilson in his landmark philosophical book entitled *The Outsider* (1956). What characterizes the Outsider?

—The Outsider wants to cease to be an Outsider.
—He wants to be integrated as a human being, achieving a fusion between mind and heart.
—He seeks vivid sense perception.
—He wants to understand the soul and its workings.
—He wants to get beyond the trivial.
—He wants to express himself so he can better understand himself. He sees a way out via intensity, through extremes of experience.

We will see how these features play certain roles in the culture and literature that feed the Gothick Meditations.

As an example of awareness of this principle, we can quote the words of one of the filmmakers studied in this book, William Castle, who, when he heard of people looking of hidden meanings in his films, said:

> It's a very strange thing. I definitely feel that possibly in my unconscious I was trying to say something . . . I never expected that they would put under a microscope pictures that I made in the fifties and sixties and look for hidden meanings.

Foreword: A Warning to the Reader

... And I think about inner meaning, truly, it is possible that deeply buried within my unconscious was the feeling of trying to say something. (Law 2000, 201)

Recollections of Gothick Horror & Memories of Being a Monster Kid

In my early childhood my family—my mother, father, and myself—lived in a small North Texas town called Denison. Both of my parents had been born in that town on the Red River near the Texas-Oklahoma border. My grandmother lived next door, and next door to her lived my great aunt and uncle. I was an only child and things were pretty idyllic.

My first conscious memory of becoming a Monster Kid was when one afternoon Janice, an older girl whom my grandmother regularly took care of, and who had become a sort of "sister figure" to me, came over to the house and lent me a copy of the Classics Illustrated comic-book version of *Frankenstein*. I was not able to read at the time, but was fascinated with the pictures and the quasi-forbidden nature of the subject matter. This was around 1958 and the teenage-based monster culture was already in full swing. That afternoon I was probably eating lunch while watching Soupy Sales on TV. The seed was planted, and the soil was ready.

With our newly acquired television set, I was able to see some bits and pieces of horror movies. Two that I remember making an impact were *Frankenstein Meets the Wolf Man* and *The*

Werewolf of London. The overall atmosphere of these films was unforgettable to me.

I started first grade the next year and it was at that time that I started to get my father to take me to horror movies after school. (In fact, it may have been his idea originally.) The first one I saw was *Brides of Dracula* (1960). Others I saw at the same time were *Leech Woman* and *13 Ghosts*, both of which also came out in 1960. My father got a big kick out of getting up and going to the back of the theater to watch me duck behind the seats and then peer between them when the scary parts rolled around. I think he saw it as a test of his boy's courage. Of course, the *13 Ghosts* was good that way, because with Mr. Castle's "ghost viewer"—a piece of cardboard with a strip of blue and a strip of red cellophane to look at the screen through—one part allowed you to see the ghosts, while the other made them disappear. Thank goodness for that invention.

I also loved dinosaurs (as many boys did in those days) and remember seeing *Dinosaurus!* (1960) around the same time. Other films that made a big impact in that period of my young life were *Journey to the Center of the Earth* (1959) and *The Lost World* (1960). Everything fired my imagination toward the sense of the *unknown* and the urge to discover things that felt like they were hidden from me in everyday life. The landscape around my house became mythologized into an inner world made visible. These movies formed a backdrop for scenarios with my favorite plastic dinosaurs—the great Marx Company versions.

In the summer of 1960 my family moved to Dallas. My father changed jobs. Before this he had been a railroad man with irregular hours, which allowed him to be with me much of the time, and now he became a traveling salesman of office supplies—in those days, mainly typewriter ribbons and carbon paper. Suddenly, he was away half the time on business trips. I went from being a pretty well-adjusted kid in a small town to being quite frightened of the new and unfamiliar surroundings in "Big D." We lived in a cookie-cutter suburban neighborhood with a lot of kids on the block to play with. But there was an undercurrent of strangeness to it all. The possibility of nuclear annihilation hung over our heads. As time went on, I also slowly discovered that there were often real horrors going on behind the closed doors of those little houses on San Paula Avenue from 1960 to 1967. In many respects, it was a labyrinth of the weird and dysfunctional, and in a twisted way the Monsters helped me get through it all.

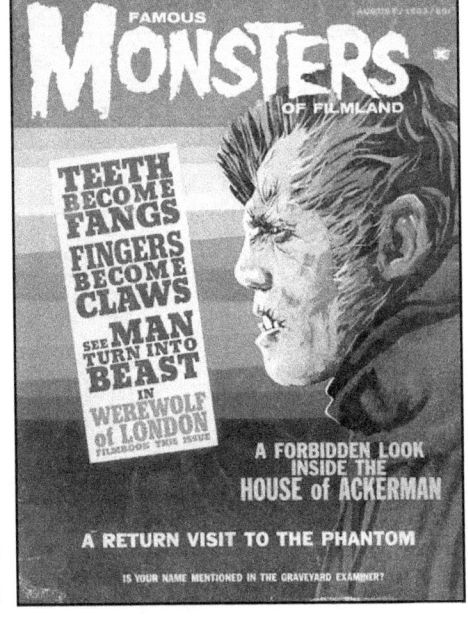

One day in a local Rexall drugstore I was looking at the magazine rack and saw a copy of something startling: an issue of *Famous Monsters of Filmland*. I asked my mother to buy it; she glanced at it and said: "No! This is trash." I was upset. It looked wonderful to me. It was issue no. 24 with a picture of Henry Hull's portrayal of the werewolf on the cover. The next night, when my mother and I were alone in the house, she came out of the other room and into the kitchen with something behind her back. She pulled it out and handed me—the coveted issue of *FM*! (As an only child, I was often spoiled in this way by both my parents. They might say no at first, but usually indulged me soon enough.)

I was ecstatic. Monster movies would become a sort of ersatz religion for me, and *Famous Monsters* was a kind of bible of that newfound faith. Karloff, Lugosi, and Chaney were its gods and soon the Casa Linda movie theater became its temple. More regular "church services" were held every Saturday evening on *Nightmare Theater* on Channel 11. It came on after the truly horrible *Porter Waggoner Show*, and I would have to suffer through Porter and some buxom blond named Dolly hawking laundry soap (every box came with a towel) before the *real* show could begin.

In the 1960s every town had a horror movie show on television. These were spawned when Screen Gems released its "Shock Package" of old horror films and even told the local stations, usually independent ones, how to put together a show built around the movies. This involved the use of a "horror host" to introduce the films. In most cases these horror hosts made a good deal of sport of the films. In the Dallas–Fort Worth area, we were blessed by the work of Bill Camfield—known as Gorgon on his Saturday-night presentation called *Nightmare*. He took his role as horror host quite

The Casa Linda theater, Dallas

Recollections and Memories xix

The opening credits to Channel 11's *Nightmare* program (1964).

seriously and showed considerable respect for the films. I appreciated this very much, as I too took them very seriously. Camfield was not all seriousness, though: he also played one Icky Twerp on Channel 11 who, during his *Slam-Bang Theater*, would introduce *Three Stooges* episodes in the afternoons. The Stooges were another cultural fixture of the generation of the Monster Kids. But it was *Nightmare* that introduced us North Texas kids to all the classics. *Nightmare* was the Dallas/Ft. Worth area's iteration of that Shock Theater package of pre-1948 Universal and Columbia Pictures productions released to television in two waves in 1957 and 1958. The release of this package of old horror movies triggered the publication of Forrest J Ackerman's magazine *Famous Monsters of Filmland* (in February of 1958), which snowballed together with the many science-fiction suspense television shows of the time to help shape the particular generation of Monster Kids to which I belonged.

The monster craze of the early 1960s had its immediate roots in the more general fascination with monsters and science fiction that had been generated in the 1950s. But whereas the fad in the 1950s was mainly focused on new films produced for teenagers and developed a high level of interest in the science fiction genre, the 1960s phase, supported by that television Shock Package, was a blend of the old (i.e., Universal Pictures productions of the 1930s and 1940s) coupled with new films that were very often heavily influenced by these older classics (e.g., the Hammer films from England reviving Dracula, Frankenstein's Monster, and the Mummy, and Roger Corman's Poe series). But most loyal Monster Kids loved any and all of these movies, regardless of the time period.

Famous Monsters of Filmland (1958–1983) was the best-known magazine. For a brief period it had a companion publication, *Monster World*, which only lasted for one year (1964). In addition to these we had *The Castle of Frankenstein* (1962–1975). *Castle* provided an aura of seriousness and respect, which I again much appreciated. James Warren, the publisher of *Famous Monsters*, insisted on the magazine being aimed at eleven-year-olds. This was a smart business move that ensured a long term of success. Ackerman would have preferred a more mature approach, but the boss called the shots.

At one point the Saturday night *Nightmare* programs became the context for what I called my "Monster Parties." In these parties the neighborhood kids and I would create a sort of house of horrors in my home (or that of my good friend John Hagen) based on the theme of the movie to be shown on *Nightmare* that night. It was a sort of forerunner to the kind of shows that are now common in elaborate Halloween houses of horror. Mine were obviously the kind of thing a nine- or ten-year-old would think up. I discovered dry ice and used makeup tips found in Dick Smith's book (published in conjunction with *Famous Monsters*) called the *Do-It-Yourself Monster Make-Up Handbook* (1965).

I also sometimes led friends off into some odd adventures. One day I got my buddy David Brown to don a cape and he let me wrap his head in some linen toweling (the kind that used to be put in hand-drying dispensers before the advent of disposable versions!). We went down to the nearby Casa View shopping center and rode around on our bikes, getting off periodically to go inside the stores. He would walk around and scare the hell out of people—just by walking around the store and saying nothing. (Nota Bene: People were easier to scare in those days.) Then we would depart the store. It was all great fun. But then we were nabbed by a couple of big men wearing guns, who took us off to an office above the J. C. Penney store. They sat us down and started to interrogate us. David, in his cool sort of way, just sat there with his mummified head. When the mall cops asked him what the deal was with the bandages, David calmly told

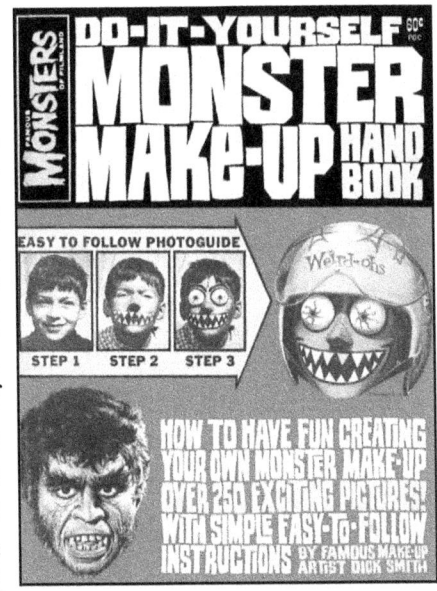

them that he had worn them "ever since the accident." When the mall fuzz got tired of being made to appear foolish, they told him to unwrap the bandages. I don't know what they expected, but all they got was a freckle-faced kid. We were sent packing and told to stop scaring people.

From a time long before all of this, I was fascinated with images that portrayed torture and pain. These abounded in the popular entertainment during late 1950s and early 1960s. Films and television programs, and perhaps especially the Westerns (which seemed to be every other show on TV in the 1950s) showed scenes of women being tied to posts for their whippings or guys being staked out on ant hills by the cruel Indians, the usual stuff. In retrospect, it seems that these scenes were certainly calculated to arouse some sort of sexual feeling, although it was easily masked by "innocent" plot devices. Sometimes such depictions occurred in the context of horror scenarios. They could, if done well, be effective and, lacking the erotic spice, also cause a child to become unsettled or even disturbed on some level. For myself, at least, these led to my playing out some of these scenarios with certain of my playmates. This was done, I suppose, as a way of exorcising some uneasy feelings deep within my child's psyche. I remember one episode in particular in the summer of 1962 when the "DuPont Show of the Week" presented *The Richest Man in Bogota* (based on H. G. Wells's short story *In the Country of the Blind*). This production starred Lee Marvin, if I remember correctly. The idea of the story is that there are people who have lost their eyes because they live in darkness. Sight is seen as a "disease" by them. The Marvin character stumbles upon their world and thus has to be healed of his affliction of sight, so they try to burn away his eyes with a flaming torch. The priest-like figure approaches, saying: "I hold here the fire of healing!" The next day I remember vividly having my playmates re-enact this scene. It exorcised the bad feelings I had from viewing the images. We took turns being tied to a post and then approached by one kid holding a make-believe torch and speaking the words: "I hold here the fire of healing!" It may be a general function of ritual play to bring various human anxieties, hopes, fears, and inspirations into a controlled and predictable scenario. Come to think of it, this is probably why so many boys of the time loved above all other things to "play army." We played out the violent scenarios of the war(s) that had in one way or another impaired so many of our fathers. Few learned anything directly from their fathers about this world they had experienced; we got our images from the same source as the monsters—television and movies. Whatever the symbols, the ritual of physical play had its important healing function.

The Monster-Kid Craze

The overall monster craze is graphically documented in a 2015 book called *Monster Mash* by Mark Voger, which shows the wide range of monster-related media for the period covered of 1958–1972. Much of it, including the popular song of the time called "The Monster Mash" by Bobby Pickett, was extremely silly and meant to appeal to a broad range of kids—mostly pubescent and prepubescent boys. At the time, I certainly could not have articulated to anyone why I was interested in it all, but it did seem, even then, to go beyond a fad and a nonsensical diversion. The "monster world" represented an alternative universe, which accepted the horror of real existence but provided an imaginative way out of the labyrinth of real-life horrors: the threat of nuclear annihilation, missile crises, the assassination of our president, and so on. In the monster world, the horrors were not denied, but they were ritualized, mythologized, and thus brought under the conscious control of the Monster Kid.

At the zenith of the monster craze of the early 1960s, a kid living in the Dallas–Fort Worth area could see a great deal of his favorite programming on many of the network television channels. For example, every afternoon after school the "Dialing for Dollars" movie on Channel 8 often featured a horror or science-fiction film. At one point, they had a large box which was suspected to contain some sort of monster. After a period of time, the space-monster inside was revealed as "Creech"—a local disc jockey, part-time reporter, and pitch man named Ted Cassidy in some pretty schlocky makeup. (Mr. Cassidy was apparently "discovered" by this means and was subsequently cast as Lurch in the *Addams Family* TV program.) Early Saturday night there was the great *Nightmare* offering already described, and then after the ten o'clock news on Channel 5 there was *Sci-Fi Theater*. The other channels tried to compete as best they could. I remember one weekend when some channel showed *The House of Wax* three times over a twenty-four-hour period. I watched it all three times.

Another feature of the monster craze of the 1960s was the production of "Monster Cards." Whereas other kids collected baseball cards, the Monster Kid collected cards that came with very bad bubble gum that was more like a sheet of plastic than anything edible by normal human beings. But we didn't buy them for the gum. One kind of these cards was issued with images from Universal films and another kind had American International images. They were not quite to my liking because they had comical captions. I often snipped these silly sayings off of my cards. None of my mutilated collection survived beyond childhood.

The late 1950s and early 1960s were also a golden age for television horror and sci-fi shows. Among the best were: *Men into*

Space (1959–1960); *Thriller* (1960–1961), introduced by Boris Karloff; *Alfred Hitchcock Presents* (1955–1965); *The Twilight Zone* (1959–1964); *One Step Beyond* (1959–1961); *Science Fiction Theatre* (1955–1957); and *The Outer Limits* (1963–1965). The craze went so far that a classic episode of the popular program *Route 66* was produced for Halloween of 1962 entitled "Lizard's Leg and Owlet's Wing," starring Lon Chaney, Jr., Boris Karloff, and Peter Lorre ... it seemed everyone was getting in on the monster mash. Even the absurd world of American television sitcoms was invaded by the monster craze when, between 1964 and 1966, we had two competing monster-themed programs on rival networks: the *Addams Family* (ABC) and *The Munsters* (CBS).

In my virtual *religion* of monsters and horror, if *Famous Monsters* was its bible, then the series of monster models put out by the Aurora model company between 1961 and 1966 were its *icons*. At one point, I had a complete set of these thirteen models which had been bought the minute they came out and meticulously preserved over the years: Frankenstein's Monster (1961), Dracula (1962), The Wolf Man (1962), The Mummy (1963), Phantom of the Opera (1963), The Creature from the Black Lagoon (1963). The Hunchback of Notre Dame (1964), King Kong (1964), Godzilla (1964), Dr. Jekyll as Mr. Hyde (1965), The Bride of Frankenstein (1965), The Witch (1965), and the Forgotten Prisoner of Castel Mare (1966). Many of these were actually built and painted by my mother, Betty Flowers. She was a professional arts-and-crafts person, so they were extraordinarily well done. Only half of these have survived

Recollections and Memories

The Midway at the 1966 State Fair of Texas. Photographer unknown. (University of North Texas Libraries, Special Collections)

the years, while the other half of them was destroyed as the result of a wildfire which swept our property in October of 2015. I remember later my mother telling me that it was while painting the face of the Phantom of the Opera that she heard the news that President Kennedy had been assassinated just ten miles from where she was sitting in our home on the eastern edge of Dallas.

Of course, one of the greatest of all horror films of all time is Todd Browning's *Freaks* (1932). I never saw this film until adulthood, largely because it was effectively banned from shortly after its release until the 1970s, when it began to be shown again. But in Dallas, during the mid-1960s, we had our own real-life annual Freak Show. This was made up of the various human oddity attractions on the midway at the State Fair of Texas. Like some of the scarier amusement rides on that same midway, going to the freak shows served us kids as little rites of passage, just as horror films did. Every year in October when the State Fair was in operation, the various schools in town got what was called a "Fair Day." School was out and we could go to the Fair for free that day. What a deal! But a kid would have to work up his courage to pay the extra money to go behind the curtain and see such human oddities as the "Lobster Boy," "Ronnie and Donnie" the Siamese twins (alive! alive!), or the "Two-Faced Boy," and so on. I said work up *his* courage because I don't think I ever saw a girl at one of these. If I had, I suppose I would have fallen in love on the spot. All of these magical venues—the Casa Linda Movie Theater, the Freak Shows at the State Fair, and the rides on the midway—were tests of courage to us prepubescent boys out on the lone prairie.

In the labyrinth of suburban Dallas in the early 1960s, among elementary school age kids, almost all of our fathers were veterans of World War Two. Nowadays we are more familiar with the effect of war on the minds of people, but in the world of the 1960s these men were generally thought to be paragons of strength and manly virtue. Indeed, most of them were, and looking back I can appreciate why my parents' generation came to be called the Greatest Generation. It is a shame that they managed to build a world that has in many respects been squandered by subsequent generations. We "Boomer kids" were often a spoiled and indulged generation. These men in our neighborhoods had something "*other*" about them. They had seen and experienced things which made them different. Only later would some of their sons see the same things in the rice paddies of Vietnam. For the most part, kids seemed to see their fathers as various sorts of "monsters." They left home in the early morning (often before we got up) and usually did not return until after dark. As kids, we were left alone and in the company of women. In some real way, I think the old horror stars—who were men of our fathers' generation, or actors who played in movies that our fathers themselves had watched as kids—formed a link between contemporary sons and fathers. These old men such as Karloff, Lugosi, Chaney, Lorre, and Price made the older generation, as monstrous and "other" as it seemed to us, nevertheless safe and friendly on some level. This basic idea is something akin to the way in which stories such as the Grimm's Tales, as frightening as they were meant to be to children, nevertheless functioned in a therapeutic way because they introduced horrors in a friendly and safe context.

As a kid my interest in monsters waned a bit in the later 1960s. I got all into the "Beautiful Losers" of Dallas—the Cowboys of Dandy Don. This brief obsession was soon replaced with one more characteristically strange for a boy of *that* time—*professional wrestling*. I attended matches to see the great Fritz Von Erich applying his bloody Iron Claw. The carny atmosphere of the wrestling world was far more akin to the world of monsters than were the North Dallas Forty.

But as I matured, I returned to monsters. In my final year of high school, I was required—like every other kid—to write a "major research paper" for senior English class. In my junior and senior years, I had focused on two things: first, a planned journey to Germany to go to the Goethe Institut to learn some German language, travel around Europe for a while, and "find myself"; and, secondly, to read as many of the classic examples of Gothic horror literature as I could. I devoured Shelley's *Frankenstein*, Leroux's *The Phantom of the Opera*, Lewis's *The Monk*, and Stoker's *Dracula*, for example. When the time came to write the research paper, I settled on the topic of "The Fact, Superstition and Imagination in *Dracula*." Obviously, the high school library would be of no help in doing my research. So, I made my first forays into the world of the occult sections of bookstores at the mall. The year was 1971. The occult revival was in full swing—even in Dallas, Texas. I found several books, including *The Supernatural* by Hill and Williams. That and other books—such as W. B. Crow's *A Fascinating History of Magic, Witchcraft, and the Occult* and an interesting period piece called *Inside the Cults* by Tracy Cabot—opened my eyes to a strange new world. This was before the McNally and Florescu book *In Search of Dracula* had appeared (it was published the following year). I cobbled together some interesting material and wrote an almost fifty-page paper on the subject, when most students' papers were only about ten pages long. In many ways, it was the beginning of my writing career.

In the process of researching this senior paper I became reacquainted with a man I had seen once on the *Joe Pyne Show* a few years earlier—Anton Szandor LaVey. In my high school research paper, I wrote the following about him (errors in interpretation and historical accuracy must be chalked up to my extreme youth):

> Within the borders of the United Sates there is an open organization, established for the purpose of worshiping the Master of Hell and to ask Satan and the other demons to bless the members with their favor. This cult has its center in San Francisco and it is called the Church of Satan. The "Pope" of this church of Evil, Anton LaVey, is of Russian-Hungarian background; the influence of this ancestry and the tales of vampires and other supernatural beings related to Anton by the Transylvanian branch of the LaVey family should not be discounted. The grandparents of the Satanic leader were true believers in the legends of their homeland. The Scholomance which Dracula was supposed to have attended and the modern Church of Satan have the same general purpose, which is an attempt to gain the favor, blessings, and power of Hell. The Scholomance was, however, of a more serious nature—contacting the dead, demons, and the Lord Satan. Anton LaVey is similar to the character of the "living" Dracula whom Stoker outlines in the novel; both worship Satan and wish for immortality. The "Pope" of Satan states: "I'll never die because I've arranged it. My conscious ego will survive because I don't want to miss what will happen after my shell dies. I will come back." The worship of demons, witchcraft, and related beliefs are not as distant from this

Forrest J Ackerman at a 1972 press conference.
(Dutch National Archives)

modern world as the simple Balkan folk of four centuries ago; much of these supernatural practices are performed within a few miles of our own homes and with a purpose closely associated with that of Count Dracula's Scholomance.

I will come back to my exploration of the Dracula archetype in the first essay of this book. For now, it is only important to see that as my interests (first stimulated at least in part by my fascination with monsters and horror films and the things they represented) matured, I too began to delve deep into the forbidden areas of human knowledge. After high school, I departed for an extended adventure in Europe. When I returned to the USA, I went to visit my favorite aunt in San Antonio, Texas. She took me to see her Baptist minister, very famous in that town at that time. I picked up their church magazine. What did it have in it? An article about the Church of Satan and Anton LaVey! In those days, the early 1970s, people tended not to *lie* about their opponents as much as they do today. The Baptist church magazine just laid out LaVey's philosophy, one that I had seen a good deal of already, but it was the moment that inspired me to try to join this organization. If there was anything ever akin to a formalized "church of horror movies" it would have been the early Church of Satan. As I later discovered, Forrest J Ackerman, whom I later met both at the Magic Castle in Los Angeles as well as at his home, the infamous Ackermansion, was an associate of Anton LaVey's, as well as of my own mentor, Michael A. Aquino. The web of wyrd is complex.

That was many years ago. Since then my own philosophies and spiritual explorations have matured considerably. But it must be said that nothing I experienced or learned in connection with these "dark dimensions" was remotely immoral or criminal in any context. In many ways, these more adult organizations were extensions of the spirit I first evoked in my monster parties and in reenacting the disturbing scenes from horror films in order to render them harmless—under the control of my own will and creativity.

I consider this book another extension of that same spirit. Here I muse on the deeper meanings of the words and images that inspired me as a child and young man. Revisiting them with a more developed mind and heart has been a tremendous pleasure and I just hope I can convey some of the remarkable Zeitgeist of that phase of American cultural history when the

Monster Kid was in his element and the seeds of wonder were first sown in the minds of many children and youngsters. But the contents of this book go well beyond all of that, deep into the esoteric fields of the human mind to uncover the gems of meaning hidden—whether consciously or unconsciously—in the art of the horror film from 1919–1975.

Grimm Tales of the Page and Screen

A Theoretical Introduction

Although each of the essays in the book more or less stands alone and can be read separately and in no particular order, there is a theoretical framework that holds the essays together. That theoretical underpinning is useful to know at the outset. One aspect is that of the *function* of the horror film and tale: how does it work and what purpose does it fulfill in our present-day culture? Another dimension is the use of the horror narrative and imagery as a mode of interpreting or analyzing the culture (or individual) who produced it. Finally, what is the role of such stories in the formation of a modern mythology? Exploring all of these angles with our object of observation being a given work, or series of works, of horror film or literature will reveal some hidden meanings that may be useful to the understanding of ourselves and our society. In the end these essays are meant for fun and as mediations yielding insight into our individual psyches.

Perhaps the oldest prototype of the horror tale are stories such as those presented by the Brothers Grimm in their volume of *Kinder- und Hausmärchen* published in the first of many editions in Germany in 1812 and translated into English as *Children's and Household Stories* (later *Grimms' Fairy Tales*) in 1844. These were not strictly fictional tales; they were folktales that had been somewhat edited aesthetically for general publication. Filled with cruelty and magic, they usually have children as their victims and heroes—or, more often, heroines. These stories were representative of the kinds of tales grandmothers told to their grandchildren to scare them into doing the right thing, and to frighten them with the supernatural rooted in the soil of their homeland. Because they were told by a close relative (or later, read aloud from a book such as the Grimms produced), the tales also served as a *safe* way to be frightened. In fact, children living in the times when these stories were told were exposed to a fair amount of *real* horror—horrible diseases, war, and sometimes grinding poverty. From these roots, we can see that experiencing horror tales has always been intended as a therapeutic exercise.

Older horror films are often akin to cultural Rorschach (or "ink blot") tests in the sense that they present images and messages which may appear to be one thing, but this message can be something dredged up from the unconscious of the collective psyche of the film industry. No art form is more collective in its approach or more collaborative in its execution than filmmaking: the producer, director, screenwriter, and editor are all among the individuals involved who can make or break a film and who contribute substantively to its content. The final product of their group effort then becomes an art object to be interpreted and received by the individual viewer throughout all of history. The horror and science-fiction film is also akin to a modern mythology that has the ring of *syncretic truth* to it. Syncretic truth, a term pioneered by the Soviet scholar M. I. Steblin-Kaminskij, refers to the concept that narratives, to be credible to an audience, must accord with what their minds are willing to accept as plausible. The plausibility—no matter how utterly implausible a horror-film narrative is on the surface—lies in the *surreal* dimension. The surreal is that which appears unreal to our conscious minds, but which actually expresses a hyper-real dimension, thus bringing a hidden reality into the view of our conscious minds. What is syncretically true expresses what is possible on a subjective level, and also often exploits for artistic purposes what is frightening on a psychological level. In a culture that has been deprived of the mythic dimension by the adoption of a dogmatic religion and a superficial value system, the power of myth has generally been lost—but not entirely forgotten. Myth is eternal, myth is real, myth is persistent and will come to the surface where it is given the opportunity through the exercise of imagination, unbridled by the limitations of conventionality. In the horror and science-fiction genre this state of liberation is the norm, and so it is only natural that these factors should surface in this context. And so it does. This type of literature and film fills a cultural need for the expression of an inner truth that is far more eternal than mere facts.

By whatever means, great *arcana* can and do find their ways into even the most popular forms of entertainment—in the collective dreams and nightmares of a culture. The way to test *arcana* found in popular culture is through knowledge of the archetypal patterns from which it is drawn—either consciously or unconsciously.

In the thirteenth essay, I will address the topic of science fiction and science-fiction films. I love, or loved, these as well, again especially those made from within the older mindset. It should, however, be noted that some of the films discussed and some on the list of the hundred greatest horror films, might also have been classified as science fiction. The most glaring example of this is *Frankenstein*. Both the book and the films have equal parts science fiction and Gothick horror. *Frankenstein* is classified as horror as much out of tradition as anything else. Another defense of *Frankenstein* as horror rather than science fiction is that the author does not dwell on, or much discuss, the ideas of science or technology. It is, however, a story of how a scientist made something for which he was unprepared to take responsibility. But the question of abandonment of responsibility is not limited to the scientist as far as the importance of the story is concerned.

In theory it appears quite easy to understand the distinction between horror and science fiction: horror is supernatural or mythic in its basis, whereas science fiction is grounded in a natural context (even if imaginary or exaggerated). So vampires, werewolves, and living mummies tend to be in the supernatural realm, whereas corpses reanimated by electricity or prehistoric creatures surviving in a lagoon generally fall into the technical or natural context. The "problem" is that the *stories* themselves—the atmospheres they evoke as well as the manner in which they are recounted—often blend these categories in a freewheeling way. Any Monster Kid could have told you that *Frankenstein* is horror and *Godzilla* is science fiction. One was shown on the horror-movie show "Nightmare" in my neck of the woods, and the other might be on "Sci-Fi Theater." The difference is clear, but both tend to be equally loved by the same people (until more recently, perhaps). Both genres were well represented in the pages of *Famous Monsters of Filmland* in the 1960s, for example. In fact, there seems to be a spectrum along which the narratives fall with *Dracula* or *The Exorcist* at one end and *The Day the Earth Stood Still* and *The Time Machine* at the other. In the middle is the all-too-human horror of homicidal (or matricidal) madness: *Psycho*.

The Gothick Dimension

This particular volume tends to be dedicated toward the tales and films that are more purely horror, often based in the supernatural. I classify them as Gothick. (Another volume is contemplated, which would be dedicated to the science-fiction genre over a similar span of years.) It is perhaps good at this point to explain what is meant by "Gothick." Obviously, I have used an idiosyncratic and archaic spelling of the word Gothic for this volume. By adding the "-k" I am indicating a distinction between the linguistic and ethnological use of the word to indicate the ancient Germanic group known as the Goths, who flourished in the Migration Age (200–600 CE) throughout Europe, and the movement in art and literature which made use of the term "Gothic" in later times. It is interesting that there is a link between these two usages, however. The word Gothic(k) was used by early historians as a term synonymous with "Germanic," meant to designate all of the Germanic peoples of antiquity—not only the Germans, but the Scandinavians and Anglo-Saxons as well. It connoted the dim, dark past out of which we emerged, but of which we knew little. It is filled with mystery and fraught with fate. Our unknown past is ever present, and ever ready to come back and haunt our dreams and realities. This mood was translated to literature on a smaller scale in works such as *The Castle of Otranto* (1764), *Mysteries of Udolpho* (1794), and *The Monk* (1796). These are stories in which gloomy ancestral mansions or castles, often with strange architecture, are used as settings for events. There are revelations of secret relationships (e.g., that Ambrosio and his lover Antonia are brother and sister in *The Monk*). Innocent young women go to lonely places where mystery (usually involving a powerful man) awaits. There is passion, insanity and romance. Often there are supernatural beings (ghosts, vampires, etc.) and an element of the occult.

Each film, and each piece of literature, is best approached on its own terms, with little or no further attempt to analyze the genre into which it falls. My own meditations have no "agenda" other than to look at the films and literature in terms of esoteric connections and links to the individual human soul. Many other "interpreters" have had sociopolitical agendas—"gender studies," Marxist criticism, *ad nauseam*. These I find sterile and impotent. They are written from a shallow viewpoint of professional whining. Among current academics this "professional" dimension can be quite concrete. We are presently in an academic environment reminiscent of Soviet Russia or Nazi Germany as far as the ideological purity that is expected of writers in the academy. I reject this utterly. Film and literature in the horror genre are visceral, cultural, and psychological expressions of things *hidden* from everyday consciousness. Cookie-cutter interpretive templates based on (often historically discredited) socioeconomic and political theories are the furthest thing from a tool for discovering any worthwhile truth in this venture.

The time span of the films considered for my meditations is from 1919 to 1975—from *The Cabinet of Dr. Caligari* to the *Texas Chainsaw Massacre*. For me, the classic era of horror films ends somewhere around *The Exorcist* and *Texas Chainsaw*

Massacre. I would not deny that a number of very good horror films were made *after* that time, and certainly some have been produced in recent years that are of superb cinematographic quality. Generally speaking, though, I no longer seek out horror films, so I cannot comment too much.

However, as I have already alluded to, what I believe is that the earlier period possessed, and the later period lost, a certain psychological and cultural naiveté that allowed the horror film to act as a sort of cultural Rorschach test. For the older period these elements can often only be teased out with exercises such as my midnight meditations. In the final analysis, I did not want to have to wade through a bunch of Freddy Kruger or Jason films to complete my exercise.

Another enormous loss has been the lack of great horror actors. In the old days we had Lon Chaney, Bela Lugosi, Boris Karloff, Peter Lorre, and Lon Chaney, Jr., then Christopher Lee. The last of the greats was Vincent Price. These actors have achieved a level of immortality beyond what they would have if they had not devoted their careers to the genre. Each would have been just another minor character actor in Hollywood had they not have been immortalized as horror stars.

One set of critics commenting on the Weimar Era cinematic obsession with horror, the uncanny, and the fantastic has suggested that such an unwholesome trend was merely a precursor to the real-life horrors of the Nazi Era. But if interest in the interior world, sexual experimentation, adventurism, and in the artistic license of this period in German cinema history is somehow seen as a precursor to the political excesses of Nazism, then we might also wonder what even more horrific future awaits us today, given the nature of early twenty-first-century "culture" and the films it is producing. Of course, the reality of how cultural forces and predelictions interact is hardly as linear as this sort of theorizing might imply.

The Reform-minded Germans of the late nineteenth and early twentieth centuries—those who participated actively in the Reform Movements from about 1880 to 1933—had a kaleidoscope of possibilities open to their future;[1] it was just a matter of the wrong, ineffective, and shortsighted options being chosen.

This book is based on the idea that horror films, as well as many science-fiction films—made in an era when the artists who created them were largely unconscious of, or uninterested in, the forces lurking in the images and myths they were both using (as they welled up from their unconscious minds) and creating (often from the same source)—can be examined in order to discover and discuss the hidden or esoteric meanings that lie underneath these works. This requires a meditative and contemplative approach akin to that used by magicians and mystics when contemplating the myths and symbols of antiquity.

The element of empathy is one of the most important keys that will allow one to gain insight into the underlying meanings of this modern mythology. The great founder of hermeneutics—the art of making valid interpretations—was Friedrich Schleiermacher, who made it a sort of rule of his new art that the interpreter must have sympathy or even empathy with the object of his interpretation in order to have any hope of discovering the truth that lies beneath. This is an especially important and conspicuous aspect when it comes to the understanding of horror movies.

Because the Monster-Kid craze was built around the irreverent mentalities of most eleven-year-old boys, the films were more often than not made the butt of jokes and derisive ridicule—even by many of the "horror hosts" who introduced us to the films in the 1960s.[2] All of that is suitable for the immature mind, but it can never be the attitude by which one will ever be able to unlock the secrets of these contemporary myths—unless one has become one of those unfortunate souls who think that "life is but a joke." I, for one, always tried to look a bit deeper into

---

1. For a general introduction to this world of the Reform Movements, see my forthcoming book *The Reform of Life* (2023).

2. There is even the well-known current series known as *Mystery Science Theater 3000* (1988–1996; revived 2017–present) that is built on this premise as some form of entertainment.

the monster world in the belief that there was something more to it than met the eye.

I
Hidden Dimensions of Dracula
Occult, Psychological, Political, and Historical

As the reader will have noticed in my introductory essay, I first began my juvenile writing career by researching and writing about *Dracula*. My first theatrical horror-film experience was with *The Brides of Dracula*. So, clearly, I have held a deep and abiding interest in the *nosferatu*. However, when I undertook this project of the *Gothick Meditations at Midnight*, I originally had no real place for vampires or Dracula other than frequent asides. I felt that by now "it had all been said" and I would have nothing original or insightful to offer to the field. There exist today people who have devoted their whole spiritual and erotic lives to the archetype of the vampire. Then Crystal, my wife, pointed out that such a project as the *Gothick Meditations* could *not* do *without* an essay devoted to the vampire for just this reason. After some soul-searching, I determined to revisit the contents of my first paper written on the subject when I was a mere lad of seventeen years of age: my high school senior writing project entitled "The Fact, Superstition and Imagination in Dracula" in 1971.

As mentioned before, during the last two years of

Brides of Dracula (1960)

high school I was preparing for an adventure in Europe. It was my plan to go to Germany, attend the Goethe Institut to better learn the German language, and travel around Europe to see what would happen. Such adventures were not all that uncommon in 1971. For years, a poster of the Bavarian castle of Neuschwanstein, built by the "Mad King" Ludwig II, had hung on my bedroom wall at home. In my travels I, of course, had a visit to this edifice on my list of things to do. In those days, for an American traveling abroad, the only regular contact one would have to news on the home front was the English-language daily newspaper *The International Herald Tribune*. One early morning in Munich, as I prepared to board the train to Füssen, the town nearest to where the castle of Neuschwanstein was situated, I bought a copy of the newspaper to read on the way. In it was an article about the recent publication of the book by Raymond T. McNally and Radu Florescu, *In Search of Dracula*, which "revealed" that Dracula was based on the historical personage of Vlad the Impaler (Romanian *Țepeș* [pron. tsep-esh]). My amateur researches of just ten months earlier seemed to be expanded and corroborated in ways I could never have imagined up to then. When I returned home to Texas a few months later, I soon discovered there had been an explosion of vampire-related non-fiction literature: besides the McNally-Florescu book, there were other books dedicated to the history and study of vampires, such as Anthony Masters's *The Natural History of the Vampire*, Donald Glut's *True Vampires of History*, and Gabriel Ronay's *The Truth about Dracula*. Additionally, it was in those months between returning from Germany and beginning my college life at Eastfield Community College in Dallas that I actually joined the infamous Church of Satan. (This turned out to be nothing more than a membership by mail, as I never ended up meeting an actual living Satanist as a result of it at the time.)

For me the meaning of all this was the discovery of my own willingness to plumb the depths of the unknown and seek intellectual adventure wherever I could find it. Fantasies and dreams born of childhood would become realities—eventually.

Vampire Literature

In the case of the mythology surrounding the figure of Dracula and the modern vampire, we have fairly well-documented ideas about its origins and early development. Interestingly, it is historically linked to the same haunted summer that gave rise to the novel *Frankenstein*.

In European folklore, the vampire has a venerable and ancient history. But few, if any, of the vampires of (mainly Slavic) folklore approach the noble air and sophisticated power of the Count we have all come to know so well. The vampires of Slavic folklore were usually lumbering bloated corpses, barely recognizable as human.

The secret of the appearance of the aristocratic vampire lies in the sensibilities of English Romantics in the Byron Circle, especially one Dr. William Polidori. This traveling companion of Byron was in the company of the Byron-Shelley entourage during that summer of 1816, and participated in the "ghost story" arrangement that I will discuss in Essay IV (Frankenstein). Polidori published his short story "The Vampyre" in 1819,

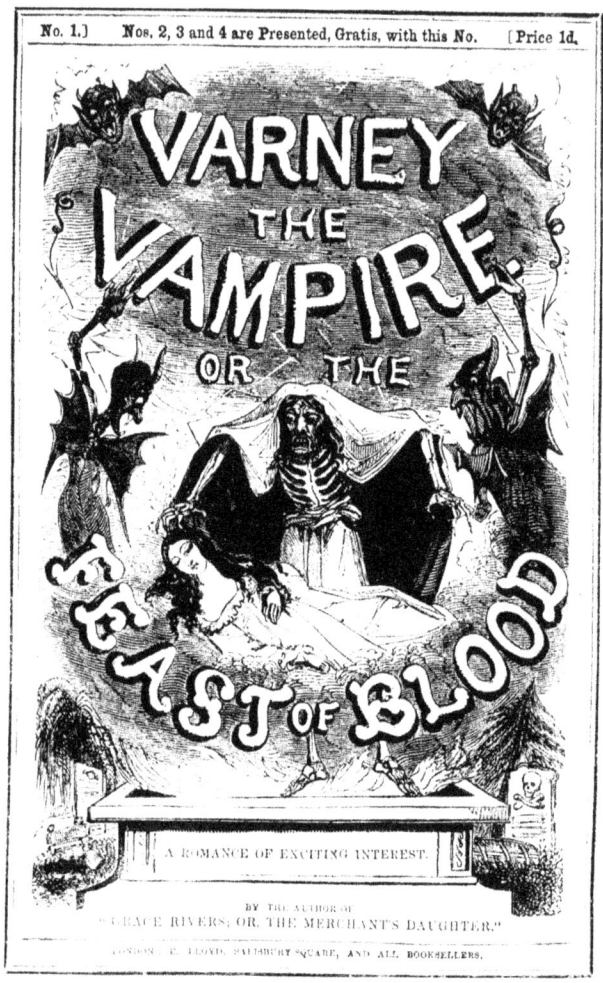

although for a long time it was attributed to Byron himself. It tells the story of a dominant, magnetic, and cruel Lord Ruthven who is accompanied by a young traveling companion, Aubrey, on the grand tour of Europe. Aubrey leaves Ruthven when the older man dishonors the daughter of a family in Rome. Aubrey goes to Greece and falls in love with a young girl, Ianthe, who tells him of vampire legends. Ianthe is then killed by a vampire and Ruthven appears shortly after. They join up again and are soon attacked by bandits. Ruthven is mortally wounded and, as he is dying, swears Aubrey to an oath to say nothing about the Lord for a year and a day. Aubrey returns to London and is shocked to discover Lord Ruthven apparently alive and ever reminding Aubrey of his oath. Ruthven then sets about seducing Aubrey's sister while the brother is helpless to do anything about it as he undergoes a general breakdown. Aubrey dies on the day the oath expires, which is also the day of the wedding of Ruthven and Aubrey's sister. Aubrey tried to warn the family, so after the wedding night they rushed to try to save her, ". . . but when they arrived, it was too late. Lord Ruthven had disappeared, and Aubrey's sister had glutted the thirst of a VAMPYRE!"

Significant literary bridges exist between Polidori and Stoker during a time span of three quarters of a century. Most significant are the compendious (900-page) *Varney the Vampire, or The Feast of Blood*, originally published as a "penny dreadful" between 1845 and 1847 by James Malcom Rymer and Thomas Peckett Prest, as well as Joseph Sheridan Le Fanu's short work *Carmilla* (1871–1872). Lord Francis Varney is an upper-class man who victimizes beautiful young women; he is possessed of superhuman strength and hypnotic powers, has fangs that leave two marks on the victims' necks, and so on. Le Fanu's work adds elements of erotic power we will discuss later.

The vampire novels of the French writer Paul Féval (1816–1887) should not go unmentioned here. He wrote three essential vampire tales: *Le Chevalier Ténèbre* (1860), *La Vampire* (1865), and *La Ville Vampire* (1874). *Le Chevalier Ténèbre* is translated into English as *Nightshade*. It tells the story of two graves in the midst of Hungary which are covered by black stones bearing inscriptions in French. The larger of the two belongs to one Jean Ténèbre ("Darkness"), who was a knight, and the smaller one to Ange Ténèbre, who had been a priest. They had lived some four hundred years before the narrative of the novel takes place. The graves had occasionally been opened over the years, and each time the countryside was visited by a vampiric plague. It is thought by scholars that Féval actually wrote *La Vampire* in 1856, but it was not published until 1865. This narrative deals with a perverse and charismatic Countess Addhema. Her vampiric lust involved her being able to restore her youth and beauty by

The First America edition of Stoker's *Dracula* (1899).

applying the scalped head of hair of young female victims to her own undead skull. Her tomb is discovered and found to be full of the skulls of girls. When the countess is finally destroyed, she is seen to be the bald cadaver, crumbling to dust. Féval's third and last novel with a vampiric theme was *La Ville Vampire* (Vampire City, 1867). Here Féval uses the persona of the English pioneer of Gothic fiction, Ann Radcliffe, as the female vampire-hunter. She determines to save her friends from the clutches of the noble vampire, Otto Goetzi. She and her companions (male and female) set out to discover the vampiric stronghold of the city of Selene, and destroy the vampires dwelling there. Féval's stories, written in French, could have been read by the educated class in England even before they were translated. Themes he developed became seminal to the vampiric mythology.

Bram Stoker (1847–1912) published his famous book *Dracula*

in 1897. It is a distillation of a tradition of vampire folklore and literary vampire figures going back to Polidori, but also contains a great number of mysteries of its own. The image of the aristocratic vampire was pioneered by Polidori who is said to have based many of the characteristics of the "vampyre," Lord Ruthven, on his friend and mentor, Lord Byron. In a similar fashion, it is also said that Stoker based many of the traits of Dracula on his employer and idol, Henry Irving. Irving was a renowned actor in Victorian England who specialized in portraying villainous characters such as Shylock and Mephistopheles.

Besides Stoker, the man most responsible for popularizing the vampire and vampiric lore, especially in connection with the occult and Satanism, is the eccentric English lay-scholar Montague Summers (1880–1948). His book *The Vampire, His Kith and Kin* (1928) is a classic in the field. He also popularized lore surrounding werewolves and witches, and appears to have professed to actually believe in the existence of things such as vampires, so his work is especially intense.

Dracula on Stage and Screen

Dracula in particular and the vampire in general have been the topic of hundreds of stage plays and cinematic films from around the world for a very long time. The powerful story of Count Dracula was used from a very early date in the making of films due to the fact that Stoker's book was still in its early stage of popularity when the art of filmmaking was still in its infancy. The earliest cinematic efforts stem, interestingly enough, from Eastern Europe: a Russian film, *Drakula* (1920), and a Hungarian one, *Dracula's Death* (1921). Both of these films are listed as being "lost." The oldest extant version of the Dracula story is the 1922 German film *Nosferatu* produced by the Prana Studio. Famously, the makers of the film were sued by Bram Stoker's widow and the judgment ordered that all copies of the film be destroyed. This was despite the fact that the German film *Nosferatu* changed the name of the vampire to Count Orlok. Lucky for the world, some prints of the movie survived. It was directed by the great German filmmaker F. W. Murnau and conceptualized and

Poster illustration by Albin Grau for *Nosferatu* (1922).

envisioned by its producer, Albin Grau. It remains a critically acclaimed masterpiece of the German expressionist era. As a result of the lawsuit over copyright violation and subsequent court order that the prints be destroyed, the film was condemned to a period of extreme obscurity. Despite this, however, the film has long garnered the highest praise from the critics and also inspired several later tributes: Werner Herzog's homage/remake (1979) and the imaginative *Shadow of the Vampire* (2000). I delve more into the world out of which this particular film emerged in Essay XI. The best overall view of the history of the *Dracula* material from the Stoker novel to the latest films is contained in David Skal's *Hollywood Gothic* (2004).

As Stoker was the business manager of the great stage actor Henry Irving, it might be expected that there would be some interest in a stage version of *Dracula*. This is the case, of course, but it is noteworthy that Bram Stoker himself wrote a stage play version of the novel even before the novel itself was published. On May 18, 1897, there was a reading of his dramatic version—which took six hours to complete—at the Lyceum Theater in London. The novel appeared in print eight days later. The play written by Stoker was not "stage friendly." Irving was uninterested in the idea and so the project was forgotten. The

F. W. Murnau

writing of dialog was not a strong suit of Stoker's, which is one of the reasons for its documentarian style, the narrative being made up of the characters' journals and even wax-cylinder voice recordings (high technology in the 1890s).

The novel became an international bestseller. The first licensed version of *Dracula* appeared on the stage in London in 1924, written by Hamilton Deane. In 1927 this was revised for an American audience by John L. Balderston and premiered in New York on October 5, 1927, starring the Hungarian actor Bela Lugosi in the title role. The pivotal character, Texan Quincey Morris, was first transformed into a female character by Deane and then eliminated altogether by Balderston. The 1927 version of the play became the basis for the screenplay of the 1931 Universal Pictures production of *Dracula*. Lugosi's characterization of the count made him an immortal of Hollywood. In connection with the London stage production there was the gimmick of having a real nurse on duty to administer smelling salts to the faint-hearted audience members. A foreshadowing of William Castle!

The film against which all other vampire films are measured is *Dracula* (1931) starring the Hungarian actor Bela Lugosi (= Béla Ferenc Dezõ Blaskó [1882–1956]). This Universal production tells the story of Renfield, an English solicitor, who travels to Transylvania to arrange for Count Dracula to purchase land in England. Local villagers warn him against going, but he carries on. When Renfield enters the castle, he is greeted by the mysterious Count and after doing their business dealings, Dracula victimizes the solicitor and infects him with vampirism and makes him his pathetic minion. We then see the ship bearing Dracula and his cargo across the sea. Renfield is now a raving lunatic and the crew members are all killed on the journey. When the schooner reaches England, the madman, Renfield, is taken to Dr. Seward's sanatorium next to Carfax Abbey. We next meet Dracula as he is roaming the city streets, plying his vampiric trade. He enters a theater and meets the Seward family, including the doctor's daughter, Mina, her fiancée John Harker, and a family friend, Lucy. Lucy is smitten by the Count. That night he enters her room and takes her blood. The next day Lucy dies. (It is later revealed that she has risen as a vampire and is roaming the streets by night.) Back at the sanatorium, we find Renfield demonstrating his obsession with eating flies and consuming small lives. Professor Van Helsing analyzes his blood and discovers vampirism. Dracula can communicate telepathically with Renfield, although the "fly-eater" remains confined. At night Dracula comes to visit Mina as she sleeps and begins to feed from her. The next evening Dracula visits the Seward home where he is confronted by Van Helsing, as the professor shows Dracula that he casts no reflection in the mirror. Dracula leaves the house and Mina runs to him and is once

Bela Lugosi in *Dracula* (1931).

more fed upon. Mina is entrusted to nurse Briggs for her safety and a wreath of wolfsbane is put around her neck as she sleeps. Renfield gets out of his cell and eavesdrops on a discussion about vampires, and then he recounts to them how Dracula had used him to gain entrance into the sanatorium. Dracula then enters and confronts Van Helsing, telling him that Mina now belongs to him. The vampire attempts to hypnotize Van Helsing, but his will is too strong to succumb, and the professor finally repels Dracula with a crucifix.

That night Dracula hypnotizes nurse Briggs into removing Mina's protective wolfsbane and opening the windows to her room. She is spirited away to Carfax Abbey by Dracula and Renfield follows. Van Helsing and Harker observe Renfield as he makes his way toward the abbey, and they discover Dracula and Mina going down into its crypt. John calls to Mina and Dracula kills Renfield for leading them to the hideout. The sun is rising, so Dracula must seek his coffin. Van Helsing finds him, drives a stake through his heart, and Mina is thus released from his control.

The 1931 film version is itself an icon of vampiric cinema. The themes, characterizations, and ambiance all cast long shadows into the future of not only vampire movies, but all horror movies. A good deal of credit for this is due to cinematographer Karl Freund, who is reported to have actually directed much of the picture. For whatever reason, the Dracula "franchise" was not nearly as exploited at that of Frankenstein. Such serial exploitation would have to wait for Hammer's contributions.

During the late 1950s, when the English film production company Hammer was "re-vamping" the Gothic Universal classics, the most successful character by far in the Hammer ensemble was Dracula as played (usually) by Christopher Lee. In a manner of speaking, Lee's version of Count Dracula owed its external appearance to Bela Lugosi's version, but his characterization was more based on the primitive nature of the vampire of Slavic folklore. He did not often speak, although in later films Lee would end up quoting at least one passage from the original novel. For the most part he only stalked his prey and forcefully attempted to feed on his victims (yet he did oddly retain a penchant for beautiful brides and fine abodes and clothing . . .). Hammer produced a series of nine Dracula films between 1958 and 1974.

A major breakthrough in conceptualization of the Dracula saga was made in 1973 when producer Dan Curtis employed the brilliant Richard Matheson to write a screenplay which became a made-for-television film entitled *Bram Stoker's Dracula*. (Matheson's craft as an author and screenwriter will merit mention a few times in the present book.) This film starred the veteran actor Jack Palance (= Volodymyr Palahniuk [1919–2006]). Matheson made use of the recently substantiated link between the literary character Dracula and the fifteenth-century Wallachian prince, Vlad the Impaler, and he also brought in a reincarnation theme that he apparently borrowed from the Universal Mummy films and which is cleverly employed. This whole theme, as well as the very title of the Curtis/Matheson film was taken over by Francis Ford Coppola for his film of the same title made in 1992. I will discuss the reincarnation theme in greater detail in my essay on the mummy films. Of course, writers such as Whitley Strieber and Anne Rice would take the vampire genre to a different level, but one fully informed by their own knowledge of the obscure dimensions. Then the genre would be turned in a more teen-idol direction with "Buffy," the Twilight series, and beyond.

The Mysteries of Dracula

The hidden dimensions of Stoker's novel—and hence of its subsequent literary and film adaptations—run the gamut from the occult and Satanism to the psychological and erotic, to the political and ethnic, and to the by now well-known links to medieval Romanian history. The McNally-Florescu book *In Search of Dracula*, as subsequent research has shown, significantly overstated the link between the character of Dracula in the novel and the historical figure of Vlad Țepeș. As we see from the extensive quote from the novel below, wherein the Count lays out an extensive genealogy and background story, this does not link him with Vlad at all. Apparently, the novel was already virtually complete when at the last minute Stoker discovered the *name* "Dracula" and substituted it for the name he had used throughout the final draft: "Vampyre"! Another interesting fact is that McNally and Florescu were not the first to make this connection. In my research for my high school paper I cited the book *The Supernatural* (1965) by Douglas Hill and Pat Williams, which already identified the "Drakula" of Stoker's novel with the Romanian nobleman, Vlad.

Satanism

The connection between Dracula and the practice of Satanism is close. Although the normal manner of creating a vampire is through the "kiss" of another vampire, that is, through its feeding off of a person causing that person's death, after which he or she too rises from the grave to feed on the living, the novel *Dracula* reports that Count Dracula did not become a vampire in that manner. Rather it is said that he became a vampire through involvement with the so-called Scholomance, and that he had apparently made a pact with "ordog." Mina Murray's [Harker's] Journal records Dr. Van Helsing as saying:

> The Draculas were, says Arminius, a great and noble race, though now and again were scions who were held by their coevals to have had dealings with the Evil One. They learned his secrets in the Scholomance, amongst the mountains over Lake Hermanstadt [sic], where the devil claims the tenth scholar as his due. In the records are such words as 'stregoica'—witch, 'ordog,' and pokol'—Satan and hell; and in one manuscript this very Dracula is spoken of as 'wampyr,' which we all understand too well. (Stoker 1897, 224)

Hermannstadt is now called Sibiu and was the center of German culture in Transylvania beginning in the twelfth century. The word *stregoica* refers to the Romanian *strigoi*, which are noxious spirits of the dead, but also living persons with special magical powers such as the ability to transform into animals, invisibility, and the gaining of vitality from drinking the blood of the living. So, these are the direct source of Romanian vampirism. The word is related to the Italian *strega*, "witch." The word "ordog" should be properly spelled *ördög* and is the Hungarian term for the Evil God opposed to the Good God. In Christian times this figure is equated with Satan. *Pokol* is also a Hungarian form of a Slavic word for "hell." The manuscript Stoker refers to here is the German pamphlet discovered by McNally and Florescu which depicts Vlad the Impaler as a cruel tyrant, and calls him not a vampyr, but a *wütrich*, or "berserk." This does seem, however, to be the only documentary link between the character of Dracula and Vlad.

Stoker obviously had access to an article from 1885 by Emily Gerard entitled "Transylvanian Superstitions" that mentioned the Scholomance, which was said to be a "school supposed to exist somewhere in the heart of the mountains, and where all of the secrets of nature, the language of animals, and all imaginable magic spells and charms are taught by the devil in person." It is furthermore stated that: "Only ten scholars are admitted at a time and when the course of learning has expired and nine of them are released to return to their homes, the tenth scholar is detained by the devil as payment." It may well be that Dracula was the tenth scholar in some term of study at the Scholomance. As the Scholomance was said to be near the German town of Hermannstadt, this is strongly reminiscent of the legends of the Black School recounted in Icelandic folklore, also said to be somewhere in Germany, where all sorts of dark arts are taught and where the devil is said to take the last student to leave at the end of the appointed term of study.

Occult Powers

The connection with the devil and with witches just mentioned opens the door to the realm of occult powers of all sorts. Victorian England was a place in which there was great interest in the occult, and Stoker exploits this interest to a high degree in *Dracula*. We see that to Dracula are ascribed the powers of a *strigoi*, the ability to control animals and take on their shapes, and the gaining of strength through the taking of blood. We hear that Dracula has the power to become larger or smaller, to become "elemental dust" and travel on moon beams and pass through solid objects. He also has superhuman physical strength. Some of Dracula's powers seem more drawn from the world of

Mesmerism, which still commanded fascination in Victorian England. Dracula could mesmerize other people and cause them to do his will, he could also meld his mind with theirs, seeing what they see, hearing what they hear. This faculty proves problematic when Van Helsing discovers that anyone in such a state can also be a window back into the environment of Dracula as well. For the most part the occult powers of Dracula can be seen as mechanisms of gaining special knowledge (telepathy), control of others (humans or animals), and actual ability to transform from one sort of being to another. This last ability may be connected to Dracula's initiation into some sort of *alchemy*. At one moment, it is mentioned that Dracula was an alchemist, and some think that the masses of gold in his castle is somehow linked to this fact (or it could be the loot he had gathered over the centuries).

The Psychological World of Vampires

The world of *Dracula* is deeply connected to the idea of psychology as understood in 1897. In this pre-Freudian age, psychology was still much more linked with more esoteric ideas—such as hypnotism, Mesmerism, and even spiritualism—than it would be in the twentieth century. The erotic side of the vampiric mythology was being developed many years before Stoker wrote his novel. This is a powerful aspect of Joseph Sheridan Le Fanu's novella *Carmilla*, which exudes a definite sensuality despite its solidly Victorian sensibilities. It tells the story of a young girl who is seduced by another young woman in a lonely Styrian castle. One passage from the text forms a template of vampiric seduction:

> The amphibious existence of the vampire is sustained by daily renewed slumber in the grave. Its horrible lust for living blood supplies the vigor of its waking existence. The vampire is prone to be fascinated with engrossing vehemence, resembling the passion of love, by particular persons. In pursuit of these it will exercise inexhaustible patience and

An illustration from Sheridan Le Fanu's *Carmilla* (1872).

stratagem, for access to a particular object may be obstructed in a hundred ways. It will never desist until it has satiated its passion, and drained the very life of its coveted victim. But it will, in these cases, husband and protract its murderous enjoyment with the refinement of an epicure, and heighten it by the gradual approaches of an artful courtship. In these cases it seems to yearn for something like sympathy or consent. In ordinary ones it goes direct to its object, overpowers with violence, and strangles and exhausts often at a single feast. (Sheridan Le Fanu 2013, 94)

Carmilla was adapted to film in Hammer's *The Vampire Lovers* (1970). This and two subsequent films, *Lust for a Vampire* (1971) and *Twins of Evil* (1971), form what is known as the "Karstein Trilogy." The expression of this sexual component in the vampiric literature would grow over the years as authors became more liberated to write about such themes, until it finally completely subsumed the archetype making it more much attractive than repulsive.

Blood and Sex

By the end of the nineteenth century, the connection of blood with eroticism was becoming well established in the literature of the earliest sexologists of Germany and beyond. In his famous work *Psychopathia Sexualis* (1886), Richard von Krafft-Ebing writes regarding a twenty-six-year-old subject, "J. H.," that he found pleasure in experiencing the bleeding of females:

> He had had real desire for this unknown pleasure, but he accidentally learned what it was when one of his mother's maids cut her hand severely on a pane of glass, which she had broken while washing windows. While helping to stop the bleeding he could not keep from sucking up the blood that flowed from the wound, and that in this act he experienced extreme erotic excitement, with complete orgasm and ejaculation.
>
> From that time on, he sought, in every possible way to see and, where practicable, to taste the fresh blood of females. That of young girls was preferred by him. He spared no pains or expense to obtain this pleasure. (Krafft-Ebing 1965, 73)

In one famous book produced by the Victorian thinker Havelock Ellis, *Studies in the Psychology of Sex* (1905), we find the following case of a married woman identified as "R. D.":

> She has practised masturbation from an early age—ever since she can remember—by the method of external friction and pressure. . . . Ugly men (if not deformed), as well as men with a reputation of being *roués*, greatly excite her sexually, more especially if of good social position. . . .
>
> Clean cuts and wounds greatly attract her, whether on herself or a man. She has frequently slightly cut or scratched herself "to see the blood,"

and likes to suck the wound, thinking the taste "delicious." This produces strong sexual feelings and often orgasm, especially if at the time she thinks of some attractive man and imagines that she is sucking his blood. . . .

So far as practicable she has sought to carry out these ideas in her relations with her husband. She has several times bitten him till the blood came and sucked the bite during coitus. . . . the pleasure is greatly heightened by thinking of various tortures, chiefly by cutting. She likes to have her husband talk to her, and she to him, of all the tortures they could inflict on each other. (Ellis 1942, I:2, 122–23)

Psychic Vampires

The concept of the "psychic vampire" was already beginning to be developed in Stoker's day. The concepts were closely linked to the increasingly popular ideas of occultism and psychic transfers of not only information, but also energy, or "life-force," between individuals—either willingly or unwillingly, consciously or unconsciously. These concepts have come to the forefront in the so-called vampire community of our own contemporary world. This theme was actually the dominant idea in the little-known and underappreciated "other" vampire novel of 1897: *The Blood of the Vampire* by Florence Marryat. The vampire in that novel is a psychic vampire, who draws people to her with sexual magnetism and depletes their energies, causing their destruction. The vampire's name is Harriet Brandt and she is the daughter of a Haitian mother and a Swiss father. She is known in the racial terminology of the day as a quadroon, who can actually pass as a Caucasian. This is somehow seen as part of Harriet's "curse" and is linked to her vampiric nature. Harriet just wants to love and be loved, but she causes the destruction of those who come into her circle. Eventually she destroys herself.

Theda Bara—the Vamp

The now almost forgotten female archetype of the late nineteenth and early twentieth century known as the "vamp," and epitomized by the silent screen actress Theda Bara (= Theodosia Burr Goodman), was indeed seen as a vampiric entity at the time. She was perhaps the first great sex-symbol of the movies. Her image was set by her starring role in the film *A Fool There Was* (1915). From then on, she was called "the Vamp." This was a shortened form of "vampire," and is based on the image of the super-sexual woman who depletes men's energies. The term "vamp" was derived from a Rudyard Kipling poem "The Vampire" (1897). This was in turn inspired by a painting of the same title by Kipling's cousin Philip Burne-Jones, also from 1897.

Again, that such ideas are not limited to the world of art, literature, and the occult is substantiated by the words of William J. Robinson in his book *Married Life and Happiness* (1922):

> the name of vampire can be applied to the hypersensual woman in its literal sense. Just as the vampire sucks the blood of its victims in their sleep while they are alive, so does the woman vampire suck the life and exhaust the vitality of her male partner—or victim. And some of them— the pronounced type—are utterly without pity or consideration. (Robinson 1922, 90)

In the golden age of the vampire—the decades following the publication of *Dracula*—the concept of the vampire was truly part of more widespread popular culture in a more serious way than perhaps it is today.

The current position of the vampire archetype as a romantic figure, a man who exudes animal magnetism and irresistible sex appeal, owes something to Stoker's characterization, but only a small portion. Stoker actually spends a good deal of time making Dracula appear repulsive. The "matinee idol" image of the vampire is almost entirely the result of Bela Lugosi's portrayal and his own personality. It is widely reported that Bela Lugosi got many

Theda Bara in vampire pose, 1918.

more written letters from women proposing marriage as fan mail than did Rudolph Valentino. An objective survey of the image of the vampire shows that it was Lugosi who introduced this element, and it was not universally adopted: Christopher Lee, who played more roles as Dracula than any other actor, did not use it. Frank Langella's work in the 1979 remake maximized it, and in recent years sexuality has taken a central position in the whole vampiric mythology, chiefly fueled by the work of Anne Rice and extended by the "Twilight" and "True Blood" phenomena. But it perhaps has remained somewhat of a hidden truth that it is really to the unique personality of Lugosi and his own characterization of Dracula that this trend can be traced.

Politics and History

Although the link had been made previously, the book *In Search of Dracula* by Raymond McNally and Radu Florescu in 1972 much popularized the idea that the literary character of Dracula was based on the historical personality of Vlad the Impaler. As we have already noted, this link is not a strong one in the actual text of Stoker's novel, with virtually only the byname Dracula, "son of the dragon/devil," being the connection. However, Stoker does give a fairly rich and deep backstory to the character in certain passages. The most contiguous of these comes when one night in Dracula's castle the Count reveals to Jonathan Harker something of his history and background in a long diatribe quoted here in full:

> *Midnight.*—I have had a long talk with the Count. I asked him a few questions on Transylvania history, and he warmed up to the subject wonderfully. In his speaking of things and people, and especially of battles, he spoke as if he had been present at them all. This he afterwards explained by saying that to a *boyar* the pride of his house and name is his own pride, that their glory is his glory, that their fate is his fate. Whenever he spoke of his house he always said "we," and spoke almost in the plural like a king speaking. I wish I could put down all he said exactly as he said it, for to me it was most fascinating. It seemed to have in it a whole history of the country. He grew excited as he spoke, and walked about the room

pulling his great white moustache and grasping anything on which he laid his hands as though he would crush it by main strength. One thing he said which I shall put down as nearly as I can, for it tells in its way the story of his race:—

"We Szekelys have a right to be proud, for in our veins flows the blood of many brave races who fought as the lion fights, for lordship. Here in the whirlpool of European races, the Ugric tribe bore down from Iceland the fighting spirit which Thor and Wodin gave them, which their Berserkers displayed to such fell intent on the seaboards of Europe, ay, and of Asia and Africa too, till the peoples thought that the were wolves themselves had come. Here, too, when they came, they found the Huns, whose warlike fury had swept the earth like a living flame, till the dying peoples held that in their veins ran the blood of those old witches, who, expelled from Scythia had mated with the devils in the desert. Fools, fools! What devil or what witch was ever so great as Atilla, whose blood is in these veins?" He held up his arms. "Is it a wonder that we were a conquering race; that we were proud; that when the Magyar, the Lombard, the Avar, the Bulgar, or the Turk poured his thousands on our frontiers, we drove them back? Is it strange that when Arpad and his legions swept through the Hungarian fatherland he found us here when he reached the frontier; that the Honfoglalas was completed there? And when the Hungarian flood swept eastward, the Szekleys were claimed as kindred of the victorious Magyars, and to us for centuries was trusted the guarding of the frontier of Turkey-land, ay, and more than that, endless duty of the frontier guard, for, as the Turks say, 'water sleeps, and enemy is sleepless.' Who more gladly than we throughout the Four Nations received the 'bloody sword,' or at its warlike call flocked quicker to the standard of the King? When was redeemed that great shame of my nation, the shame of Cassova, when the flags of the Wallach and the Magyar went down beneath the Crescent? Who was it but one of my own race who as Voivode crossed the Danube and beat the Turk on his own ground? This was a Dracula indeed! Woe was it that his own unworthy brother, when he had fallen, sold his people to the Turk and brought the shame of slavery on them! Was it not this Dracula, indeed, who inspired that other of his race who in a later age again and again brought his forces over the great river into Turkey-land; who, when he was beaten back, came again, and again, and again, though he had to come alone from the bloody field where his troops were being slaughtered, since he knew that he alone could ultimately triumph! They said that he thought only of himself. Bah! what good are peasants without a leader? Where ends the war without a brain and heart to conduct it? Again, when, after the battle of Mohács, we threw off the Hungarian yoke, we of the Dracula blood were amongst their leaders, for our spirit would not brook that we were not free. Ah, young sir, the Szekelys—and the Dracula as their heart's blood, their brains, and their swords—can boast a record that mushroom growths like the Hapsburgs and the Romanoffs can never reach. The warlike days are over. Blood is too precious a thing in these days of dishonourable peace; and the glories of the great races are as a tale that is told." (Stoker 1897, 27–28)

As can be seen here, Stoker ascribes a Hungarian background to the Count, and there is no overt mention of any connection with

Hidden Dimensions of Dracula

Vlad the Impaler. The general gist of the passage is that Dracula comes from a fierce and barbaric people, with the implication that just as they were bent on conquest and domination, so he remains today. This clearly sets up the idea that Dracula is somehow motivated to invade and conquer England in the name of his vampiric cult.

One of the clear paradigms present in the book *Dracula* is the conflict between the East and the West. The East represents a threat to the West, in the form of dangerous ideas (e.g., communism, superstition, occultism) as well as immigration from the lands that made up the East. (To the average Englishman of the day, this was probably anyone from east of the Rhine River.) In the late nineteenth century, Britain was receiving an influx of such foreign immigration, which was small as compared to what would happen in the late twentieth century, but nevertheless noticeable. Foreigners were acquiring property in Britain for the first time, and there is clear reference to this in Dracula where the Count is shown to be buying property (Carfax abbey). This real estate deal is the whole reason why Jonathan Harker travels to Transylvania. (In the book, it is Harker who visits the castle, whereas in the stage play and film it is Mr. Renfield.)

Another key set of regional or national symbols comes in the form of the characters of Jonathan Harker, Abraham Van Helsing, and Quincey Morris. These exemplify the vital virtues of the West—the gentleman, the scientist, and the cowboy. Two of these character-symbols, two men and their knives, are key to the interpretation of *Dracula* in political and historical terms. The expedition of protagonists chasing Dracula back to his home in Transylvania at the end of Stoker's novel, and the scene of the vampire's final demise are fraught with symbolic imagery of an unusual sort. Jonathan Harker represents the persevering British Empire, armed with the kukri knife (symbolically acquired from colonial lands); while Quincey Morris, the Texan, represents the heroic American West armed with the bowie knife.

The final moments of Count Dracula are recorded in the words of Mina Harker:

> for as Jonathan, with desperate energy, attacked one end of the chest, attempting to prize off the lid with his great Kukri knife, [Morris] attacked the other frantically with his bowie....
>
> But, on the instant, came the sweep and flash of Jonathan's great knife. I shrieked as I saw it shear through the throat; whilst at the same moment Mr. Morris's bowie knife plunged into the heart.
>
> ... the whole body crumbled into dust and passed from our sight. (Stoker 1897, 351–52)

The peril from the East has been vanquished by an alliance between the British Empire and the American West. In 1897 there was hardly a historical record of such an alliance. Was this a prophecy contained in the pages of *Dracula*? Perhaps it was something of a political manifesto of what Stoker believed would be necessary to stave off the coming encroachment of evil forces making their way westward from that sinister "whirlpool of European races" in the East.

Some people have tried to make Stoker's tale one of anti-Semitism. This might seem farfetched, as it probably in fact is. Clearly Dracula is not Jewish on any level or in any version, so the "evidence" for anti-Semitism appears entirely circumstantial and quite weak: that Britain was at the time (in the 1890s) undergoing a significant amount of Jewish immigration from Europe, including eastern Europe. So, the theory goes, the audience would "naturally" (if unconsciously) connect the vampiric invader with the Jews! Based on the background story that he does give to Dracula and his people, it seems more obvious that Stoker sees the invader as being from an "uncivilized," savage and barbaric population from the East, who come from a confused "whirlpool of nations." But Stoker cannot be charged with being simply anti-foreigner, as two heroes in the story, Mr. Morris and Van Helsing, are non-English: a Texan and a Dutchman, respectively.

The symbol of Van Helsing is also important. He is the spirit of science and rationalism in the West—a spirit of rationalism that can be arrayed against the superstition and occultism of the East, but which must delve into the Unknown and the mysterious in order to combat these irrational forces. Van Helsing also constitutes an organizing function who forges the other characters into a virtual order of vampire hunters. He does this by first educating them in the fact that such outlandish things exist, and then training them in the ways to fight them.

Vlad and the Order of the Dragon

Another key historical concept that is rarely discussed is the actual origin of the name "Dracula." Ultimately the name is derived from a connection to a chivalric order founded in 1408 by the Sigismund von Luxembourg, the King of Hungary, who also eventually became the Holy Roman Emperor. In Latin, the name of the order was *Societatis draconistarum*, "Order of the Dragon," or more precisely, "Society of the Dragonists." This order was founded to protect the person of Sigismund, as well as to organize the Christian resistance to the invasion of eastern Europe by the Islamic armies of the Ottoman Turks. Sigismund initiated Vlad II of Romania in Nuremberg around February 8, 1431. After that he became known in his own land as Dracul, "the Dragon." Vlad II's son, Vlad III, known by his moniker "the Impaler," was also a member and was known also by the nickname Dracula, "the little dragon" or "son of the dragon." Interestingly, the Romanian word *dracu* can mean either "dragon" or "devil." Vlad Dracula was for the most part viewed historically and in contemporary circles among the Christians of Romania as a hero, with few overtones of a sinister nature. He did have a reputation as a cruel tyrant among the Germans of Transylvania due to his anti-German policies. In general, the reference to the "dragon" is one connected with this militant, anti-Islamic order. Many other families were associated with the order in the region, including the Báthory family to which the infamous Elizabeth Báthory, of course, belonged.

The mention of the name Dracula and the personality of Elizabeth Báthory both cause us to issue a note of historical

Vlad III, "the Impaler" (16th-century painting).

caution for the sake of the truth here. As mentioned earlier, it does not appear that in fact Bram Stoker knew much more than the name "Dracula" to which he attached his lead character and nowhere in his surviving research notes does a connection with Elizabeth Báthory appear. The imaginative scholarly writings of McNally and Florescu from the 1970s, however, have made a lasting impression on literary and film history. Raymond McNally wrote a book as a sort of follow-up to their landmark

In Search of Dracula called *Dracula Was a Woman* (1983), which is both a biography of Elizabeth Báthory and an argument for Stoker basing the Dracula character at least in part on her story. None of this appears to have been the case actually. The lengthy quote from the novel printed above shows what Stoker had to say about the backstory of the character Dracula.

Dracula is an archetype of magical male power—the ultimate exponent of what has perhaps come to be called "toxic masculinity." Except this archetype has even mastered all efforts to demonize him and has emerged in popular imagination as an ideal role model and an object of feminine desire—no matter how "toxic" he is. A more "realistic" view of Dracula, and the vampire generally, was probably put forward in the image created by Albin Grau for *Nosferatu*. It is my supposition that Grau's vision was part corpse and part extraterrestrial being.

Conclusion and Aftershocks
Modern Vampires and the Cult of the Vampire

One dimension of the horror film that is often overlooked is its role as an inspiration for people to form actual cults—systems of belief and/or magic based upon them. The contemporary vampiric cult would be unthinkable without the narratives, imagery, and aesthetic provided by the vampiric horror film. This cult is perhaps best explored in works such as Norine Dresser's *American Vampires* or the *Psychic Vampire Codex* by Michael A. Belanger, as well as many websites devoted to the current "vampire community" or the "vampire lifestyle." Such cults run the gamut from the exclusive and highly philosophical Order of the Vampyre within the Temple of Set to groups of teenagers slinking around at night drinking each other's blood and enacting other rites as part of a sexual underground community. Some believe they can transfer vital energy from one person to another and all of this is usually charged with a high degree of erotic focus. One of the most thoughtful and generally insightful treatments of the current "Vampyre phenomenon" is found in Don Webb's book *Energy Magick of the Vampyre* (Inner Traditions, 2021).

A typology of the modern vampire practitioner might appear as follows:

—**Type A**: *Sanguinarians.* They believe that they must consume actual human blood in order to maintain their physical and mental vitality. They often consider themselves to be the only "real" or "true" vampires.

—**Type B**: *Psychic Vampires.* These believe that they can obtain nourishment of a mental and physical sort from drawing on the "aura" or psychic (sometimes called pranic) energy of other people. This is done to address what is felt to be an imbalance or deficiency in their own systems. They too consider themselves to be the authentic type of vampire.

—**Type O**: *Living Vampires.* They neither draw blood nor take psychic energy, but maintain a strict code of ethics and organize themselves into "clans" and maintain a vampiric lifestyle and aesthetic.

—**Type AB**: *Transcendental Vampires.* Some of these consume blood, others draw psychic energy, but in all cases they believe themselves to have an immortal soul which is transferred to younger vampires upon death in order to continue their existences.

Clearly, the origins of the contemporary vampire cult can be traced to the influence of horror films (especially those produced after about 1970); the vampire novels of Anne Rice, beginning with *Interview with the Vampire* (1976); and the popularity of the Romantic "Victorian" aesthetic. It is probably driven in many cases by a sexual paraphilia connected to blood—seeing it, tasting it, and so on. As we have seen, this particular paraphilia has been well documented from the nineteenth century. Such paraphilias can, of course, be acquired through exposure to the aesthetics of the scene in connection with other sexual impulses and desires. In any event, this whole subculture has attained the level of a true subcultural cult following.

Other examples of this film-to-cult phenomenon would be the documented link between the 1971 film *The Dunwich Horror* and the growth of Lovecraft-based cultic activity, and the multilayered links between horror films and the Church of Satan created by Anton Szandor LaVey in 1966. Beyond this there is also the phenomenon of whole religions being based on literary works of science fiction or works which appear to be science fiction, for example L. Ron Hubbard's Scientology or the Church of All Worlds, a Wiccan-based sect that drew upon ideas contained in Robert Heinlein's *Stranger in a Strange Land* (1961). A whole book could be written on the topic of the fictional origins of actual religions or magical orders. As time has gone on, this phenomenon has reached absurd proportions with religions based on the Big Lebowski, Edward D. Wood, Jr., and a spreading celebration of Festivus. This last modern "cult" has an interesting pedigree, as it was invented by the scholar Daniel O'Keefe who began celebrating it with his family in the 1960s. His son, Dan O'Keefe, was a writer for the *Seinfeld* sitcom, and wrote a script based on the idea in an episode entitled "The Strike." The elder O'Keefe also wrote a scholarly book on magic entitled *Stolen Lightning* (1983).

Ultimately, on an esoteric level, the cult and myths of the Vampire clearly demonstrate one of the major themes in the present book, that of the Outsider. The creators of the modern Vampire myth were to one degree or another sexual outsiders: Polidori, who was likely gay; Stoker, a bisexual; and Le Fanu, who was obsessed with lesbianism. On some level the modern myth of the Vampire reflects the idea of an archetypal subculture, an underground of those Others with forbidden tastes and appetites, who find themselves oppressed (and their desires frequently repressed) such that the myth of a powerful cult composed of such individuals (often governed by a charismatic leader) acts as a liberating idea and as a pattern upon which to actualize their desires in the world. Like all Outsiders, they want to get on the Inside—or, failing that, to escape from the limitations of history and enter into the realm of myth.

II

The Mythology of the Mummy
Ananke̊ and Kharis

The mythology and grandeur of ancient Egypt has fascinated the world since ancient times. Even then it was a land upon which all sorts of mysterious ideas could be projected. Its culture invites the observer to let his imagination run wild about what is possible. Ancient Greeks, Romans, and Hebrews all wove their stories into the world of the Nile and its magical secrets. It is no wonder, then, that in the wake of a new wave of Western "Egyptomania" following the discovery of the intact tomb of the Pharaoh Tutankhamun in 1922, filmmakers would be inspired to weave some myths of their own.

In delving into the secrets hidden in the cinematic mythology of the "living mummy," we will be disappointed if we expect to find any ancient Egyptian mysteries there. Egyptian lore knows of no living mummies and no reincarnation. The secrets hidden in these films are, like so much else as regards ancient Egypt, largely a projection of Western esoteric lore onto the Egyptian aesthetic and images. This is a process already being practiced by the ancient Greeks and Romans. Loopy academics have even had the audacity to criticize mummy movies as examples of "cultural appropriation"! In point of fact, when we—whether as individuals or as cultures—look at something strange and exotic that is somehow unintelligible to our conscious minds, we usually interpret phenomena related to it as a reflection of ourselves. For centuries Egypt was a fantastic mirror of the imagination—little to nothing was known about it really, as the understanding of its hieroglyphic writing had been lost for centuries. Only recently has Egypt begun to give up her secrets. Therefore, the cinematic mythology of the mummy, like the sparse literature upon which it was based, seems to be a thoroughly "Western" construct.

As opposed to *Frankenstein* or *Dracula*, the Mummy films do not at first seem to have much of a clear literary heritage. This is not to say, however, that there are no literary antecedents. Several popular pieces of literature probably fed into the imagination of the creators of the Universal "mummy mythology."

The genesis of this whole project of the *Gothick Meditations at Midnight* began after I saw Francis Ford Coppola's film called *Bram Stoker's Dracula* in 1992. I was immediately struck by what I recognized as his use of the mummy mythology from the Universal Pictures Mummy franchise of the 1930s and 1940s. What later came to light was that this was actually taken from Richard Matheson's screenplay for the Dan Curtis made-for-television *Dracula* version of 1974. In any event, this mythology of the eternal lover and the eternally reincarnated object of that love has proven to be an effective, meaningful, and powerful myth that has been adapted one way or another in several films.

The widely read and very influential novel *She* (1886/87) by H. Rider Haggard (1856–1925) contains an early narrative antecedent to the mummy mythology of the Universal series. There the sexual roles are, however, reversed, and there is no living mummy involved in it. At one point in the tale Ayesha (She-Who-Must-be-Obeyed), a queen and immortal living goddess in a magical central African realm (Kôr), meets a man named Leo, whom she sees as the reincarnation of her ancient lover, Kallikrates. She has kept the perfectly preserved body of Kallikrates, but she destroys it after she comes to believe that Leo is his reincarnation. It is interesting to note that Leo is actually seen as a *descendant* of Kallikrates, not some willy-nilly reincarnation. In the end Ayesha tries to get Leo to enter a pillar of fire through which she had originally gained immortality. He is reluctant to do so, so she enters it—but on this entry the effect is reversed and Ayesha is thereby destroyed.

The stories most often cited as the original "living mummy" tales are by Sir Arthur Conan Doyle (1859–1930): "The Ring of Thoth" (1890) and "Lot No. 249" (1892). We will explore the themes of these stories momentarily. Another connection comes from Bram Stoker's lesser-known novel *The Jewel of Seven Stars* (1903). A nod must also be given to the original genius of Edgar Allan Poe. He wrote a living mummy story long before Doyle in the form of a somewhat humorous short tale published in 1845 entitled "Some Words with a Mummy." Poe, however, might have drawn from the first instance of a living mummy tale, which was the futuristic science-fiction novel by Jane Webb (= Jane Wells Webb Loudon, 1807–1858) entitled *The Mummy! A Tale of the Twenty-Second Century* (1827). This was written when the author was a teenager. The novel tells of how the mummy of Cheops is reanimated by science (but with the favor of God) in the year 2126, in a world in which the author predicts many scientific and societal advances. Webb's novel was a reaction to the content of another young woman's novel, Mary Shelley's *Frankenstein*, seen as a Romantic criticism of modern science, whereas Webb holds out optimism for a better future. Her Cheops is not a monster, but a wise and timeless entity.

It does appear, however, that the Arthur Conan Doyle tales form a direct link to the screenplay of *The Mummy* (1932). The creative force behind the original screenplay of the 1932 film was John Balderston (1889–1954). He had been a journalist in Egypt at the time of the discovery of Tutankhamun's tomb, but he was a master scriptwriter, as well. He had revised the theatrical play of *Dracula* done by Hamilton Deane for the American stage and had written the script for the 1931 film for Universal starring Bela Lugosi. Universal then set him to work on a new project for Karloff called "Cagliostro: King of the Dead." The story was one of an ancient Egyptian magician who is jilted by a lover and so he makes plans to hunt her through eternity. He makes himself

Photograph of Arthur Conan Doyle, ca. 1920, with spirit image he identified as his son Kingsley, who had died from influenza in 1918. (ACD Collection, Toronto Public Library)

immortal by injecting himself with "nitrates," and seeks and kills women though time that remind him of his ancient lover. It is this magician who was identical with the Italian magician and charlatan Alessandro di Cagliostro (= Giuseppe Balsamo) in the eighteenth century. The contemporary scene finds "Cagliostro" living in San Francisco with his Nubian slave. There he focuses on a woman named Helen Dorrington and causes a crime wave using a radio-wave death-ray device until he is ultimately foiled by the usual heroes. This film was never made. The script evolved into *The Mummy*. John Balderston fixed the script by changing it almost totally. A fairly bad idea was made into a great classic. Hate and revenge were replaced by love.

The Arthur Conan Doyle work "The Ring of Thoth" tells the story of an Egyptologist, John Vansittart Smith, who goes to the Louvre Egyptological department to study some papyri. There he sees and meets an unusual looking man with odd skin and eyes. Mr. Smith falls asleep and awakens in the middle of the night. In the darkness he sees the unusual man perform some sort of rite over a mummy, unwrapping it to look at the face—that of a beautiful girl—and to examine various rings in a display case. Smith confronts the man and learns his story: he is actually an ancient Egyptian named Sosra, a priest from "Abaris," who discovered "a substance which, when injected into the blood, would endow the body with strength to resist the effects of time, of violence, or of disease." Sosra also injected a fellow priest named Parmes with the same substance. Subsequently, both of them fall in love with the daughter of the regional governor. Her name is Atma. Sosra wanted to make Atma immortal with him, but she hesitated, and died of disease before he could administer the substance. Both Sosra and Parmes wish to die and be with Atma. Parmes discovers an antidote to the life-giving elixir, but refuses to give it to Sosra, telling him that it is hidden in the ring of Thoth. Parmes dies, leaving Sosra to live forever. Through the centuries Sosra lives in many places and in modern times starts to keep up with Egyptological research. He reads of the discovery of the tomb of the governor of Abaris' daughter, whose mummy has been taken to the Louvre. Sosra goes there and takes a job as an attendant and on that fateful night he discovered the correct ring and plans to transition to the other side. Having learned this story, Mr. Smith is escorted out of the building. Later he reads a newspaper account of the strange discovery of a disturbance in the Louvre Museum and the scene of a dead man of indeterminate age embracing a mummy.

Another tale by Doyle written just two years later is "Lot No. 249," which is set in 1884 on the campus of Oxford University in England. The characters are mostly students at the university, the majority of whom are robust and athletic scholars, but one pudgy misfit, Edward Bellingham, is "a demon for languages" and has mastered many Eastern tongues. Bellingham is generally disliked, and so he develops a number of grudges in life. One of the dapper students of medicine, Abercrombie Smith, befriends Bellingham, and notices a few odd quirks about him. The misfit has his room filled with Egyptian artifacts, including a mummy case complete with a mummified body of a large man. The case has a tag on it "Lot No. 249," which is the designation given by the dealer who sold him the mummy. (In those days such things were quite common.) One day Smith hears Bellingham scream out and investigates. He discovers the scholar apparently working over the mummy with some strange leaves (identified as "balsamic resin") and reading from a scroll of papyrus. The mummy is partially out of its box on the table, but apparently quite lifeless. One day Bellingham tells Smith: "It is a wonderful thing to feel that one can command powers of good and evil—a ministering angel or a demon of vengeance." This and other strange events cause Smith to wonder. So it turns out that those who have any sort of friction with Bellingham are mysteriously assaulted by a shadowy dark figure. Smith finally determines that Bellingham has discovered some "Egyptian trick" whereby he can reanimate his mummy can cause it to do his bidding by inflicting violence on his enemies. In the end, Smith forces Bellingham at gunpoint to destroy his mummy with an embalming knife and to burn the mysterious leaves, the mummy's body parts, and the papyrus Bellingham so treasures. Clearly, the power to reanimate the dead and command them resides in the contents of this papyrus. After this act, Bellingham departs from the university and is last heard of in the Sudan. Doyle concludes with the words: "But the wisdom of men is small, and the ways of nature are strange, and who shall put a bound to the dark things which may be found by those who seek for them." Here we have a living mummy who does violence to the living and who is reanimated by a combination of a mysterious leaf and by magical words spoken from a scroll.

Immortal Mummies on the Screen

The living mummy has been a mainstay of the horror genre for as long as horror films have been made. In 1911 a one-reel film entitled *The Mummy* told of a female mummy brought to life by an electrical shock. But she retained all her beauty of thousands of years ago, and she has an undiminished libido as well, so she ends up marrying a man, despite the thousands of years' difference in their ages! This film is unfortunately now lost.

Kharis and Ananké

But what lies even deeper, behind the world of images? As we sit in the artificial caves, the shining light flickers from behind us onto the wall of the cave, there it casts shadows and light interpreted by those who dwell in the World of Horrors as reality itself—where do we, the Children of the Night, find our reality? Look behind the images to find the forms, inquire behind the words, there to discover the hidden Words.

Mummy films have three distinct phases. The first consists of one film, the 1932 classic *The Mummy*. It provides the basic mythology for all subsequent versions. In it we learn of the monstrous deed of an ancient Egyptian priest and magicians named Imhotep, who, overcome with grief at the death of his beloved princess Ankh-es-an-amon, tries to revive her lifeless form by means of the reading of a magical scroll—the Scroll of Thoth. He is caught in the midst of this process and sentenced to be mummified alive and buried with the scroll. In the early twentieth century his tomb is discovered and he himself is revived when one of the archeologists reads the magical incantation from the Scroll of Thoth. The scene—shot in virtual silence by Karl Freund—in which the assistant archeologist Norton reads from the scroll reanimating the mummy is one of the greatest in the history of horror films. In modern Cairo the reanimated Imhotep, now going by the name Ardath Bey, discovers, through the use of magic, the soul of his beloved princess, now incarnated in the body of a modern-day woman. It then becomes his mission to cause her to remember her past existence, and eventually to

The Mummy (1932)

perform a magical rite in which the soul and form of the princess are once again linked—and both united with him for eternity. Of course, he is foiled in his evil plan by a combination of the "good guys" and the goddess Isis, who causes him to crumble to dust at the end of the film.

The general ideas of a "monster" who is immortal while maintaining his ego consciousness and a "beauty" whose soul is immortal through a series of reincarnations through time was suggested by, and derived from, the literary works of Bram Stoker and others. Dracula is an immortal monster, while the theme of a reincarnated Egyptian is found in his less well-known novel *The Jewel of the Seven Stars* (1903). These themes were first combined by John L. Balderston in the original 1932 film *The Mummy* and revived in the rather obscure *The Curse of the Faceless Man* (1958) and then in Dan Curtis's *Bram Stoker's Dracula*, which was in turn used again in Francis Ford Coppola's film which took the same name. So Balderston created the dynamic of the immortal lover and his reincarnated beloved as it related to the Mummy films and Richard Matheson applied it to the Dracula mythology. The whole theme had also been explored by H. Rider Haggard in his tale of *She*.

The Mummy *series* as such was inaugurated by Universal in the 1940s with a film entitled *The Mummy's Hand* (1940). In this version, and the subsequent ones (*The Mummy's Tomb* [1942], *The Mummy's Curse* [1944], and *The Mummy's Ghost* [1944]) the priest-magician's name has been changed to Kharis, and that of his princess to Ananka. Whoever was responsible for these name changes seems to have been aware of an *arcanum*, on some level. This was made apparent to me when, while exploring the texts of Greek Magical Papyri, I discovered the name of an abstract goddess form: Anangh—transliterated Anankê [pron. ahn-AHNK-ay]. This was too close to Ananka for it to slip by me. I immediately also thought of Kharis, and at once realized his name was nothing other than the Greek word CariV—transliterated alternatively as Kharis or Charis [pron. KHAR-iss]. Both are key terms in the Hermetic system of Helleno-Egyptian magic as practiced in the very late centuries BCE and

The Mummy's Hand (1940)

the earliest centuries CE.

Ananke may be translated as "force," "necessity," "compulsion," or even "fate." As a personified goddess-form she is called upon in the magical papyri to compel events, to cause them to come about as a matter of preordained fate after the magician has exerted his personal will through her.

Charis is generally translated as a "gift" (or "grace"), a "favor"—such as might be bestowed by a god or *daimôn* in order that the recipient be able to undertake great tasks. From this word is derived the related term *charisma*—a "bestowal of favor or grace." In Hermetic operative theory, *charis* (grace) is the opposite way from *ananke* (force) for obtaining magical results.

In this cinematic myth we are confronted with the idea that the (male) "monster," due to some unspeakable crime in the past involving his love for a perfectly formed woman ("princess"), has been *gifted* (or cursed) with physical immortality; and that meanwhile the essence or "spirit" of his ladylove has been *compelled* to undergo a series of metempsychosis perpetually until they meet again at this point in time. As we will see, this may have some unconscious (?) link to the much-misunderstood concept of Platonic Love.

A word should also be added as to the interpretation of the name of the female role in the original *Mummy* film in 1931. There the name of the woman is Ankh-es-en-amon, also the name of a historical personage of the XVIII Dynasty and the royal wife of Tutankhamun himself. Ankh-es-en-amon lived between 1348 and 1322 BCE. But what is important from an esoteric point of view is that her name means literally "her life is in Amun (= "the Hidden One")" or "living for Amun." This could be interpreted as meaning her life is hidden, her true life being concealed from the mundane world.

The Mummy films of the 1940s also added the element of a whole secret cult that supports Kharis in his endeavor to protect the tomb of the princess and to aid him in the recovery of her soul. In the earlier films there is reference to the "Priests of Karnak" as the caretakers of Kharis; in *The Mummy's Ghost*, this is changed to the "Priests of Arkam." The chief work of the cult is to keep Kharis alive by dosing him with "tana-leaf" juice, and to avenge the tomb-robbing of the European "infidels." Karnak is

The Mummy's Ghost (1944)

a well-known temple site in Egypt, but the word "Arkam" would appear to be a tribute to the works of H. P. Lovecraft, whose fictional town of Arkham, Massachusetts figured in many of his stories. Lovecraft died in 1937 and his work soon developed a "cult following."

An important note to be added here is that the idea of the Priesthood of Karnak/Arkam introduces another kind of immortality into the picture: that of Tradition. The priesthood, in order to keep Kharis alive, had to develop and maintain a continuous chain of initiation whereby new priests were groomed to take over the duties of tending to Kharis, generation after generation. This immortal "Gift" was maintained at the price of constant and unwavering dedication to the continuation of the rites of the priesthood. This is akin to the Mazdan priests of Ahura Mazda who have kept certain ritual fires burning continuously for thousands of years. The power is not only present in the eternal flame, but in the *necessity* of the maintenance of an unbroken tradition, which is *needed* to keep the flame alive.

There is a mystery as to how the names of Kharis and Ananka came to be the names of the characters in this series. Some writer or story-developer in the studio must have had some fairly serious knowledge of the beliefs of late antiquity to have even arrived at these concepts. As they were introduced in *The Mummy's Hand* and continued throughout the series, the point of entry for the ideas must have been in the first film in the series in 1940. One of the authors of the screenplay is listed as Maxwell Shane. He was an educated man, having studied law at both USC and UCLA. As a note, he was also later a writer and producer for the Boris Karloff–hosted television anthology series *Thriller* in the early 1960s.

A fascinating dimension of these magical concepts is that they can be seen to be reflected in the runic tradition of the ancient Germanic peoples as well. The Greek word *charis* perfectly translates the rune-name *gebō*, "gift," while *ananke* equally well translates the rune-name *naudiz*, "necessity."

From the metagrammatical perspective, both *kharis* and *ananke* are feminine nouns—so at the most radical level of meaning we may be dealing with a somewhat "Carmilla-esque" theme.

It should also not go unnoted that it is said to be the single word:

ANANKE

inscribed into a stone inside the cathedral of Notre-Dame in Paris, that inspired Victor Hugo to write the Gothic masterpiece *Notre-Dame de Paris* (1831)—later retitled by the first English translator in 1833 as *The Hunchback of Notre Dame* to appeal to a more "Gothic" readership. The author noted that years later the inscription appears to have been scraped away and whitewashed. The word caused Hugo to speculate as to what suffering and anguish led the individual who carved the word to do so—and from that meditation his great book arose.

Oddly, the theme of the princess being reincarnated in a living modern woman whom the mummified ancient Egyptian recognizes and attempts to re-possess, is missing in the first two films of the renewed series: *The Mummy's Hand* and *The Mummy's Tomb*. In *The Mummy's Hand*, the High Priest of Karnak, Professor Andoheb (impeccably played by George Zucco), attempts to immortalize himself and Marta by means of the application of the tana-leaf potion. In this film Ananka is little more than a name and a relic to be protected by Kharis and the Karnak Priesthood. The original theme of the princess being reincarnated in a contemporary woman is only taken up again in the third and fourth installments of the 1940s series. The whole unity of narration in the 1940s series of films is one of the most ragged in film history. This is likely due to the great number of writers who worked on the scripts and directors who executed them. It is not just the relationship of Kharis to Ananka that is problematic; the chronology is bizarre: time periods are stretched, and times in which the story is set are indicated as being many years later than seems plausible. Also, inexplicably, the location of the action is shifted from New England to Louisiana for the last film. That is made all the stranger because in the third film Kharis had disappeared into a marsh while carrying Amina/Ananka—so in the fourth film it is as if their bodies had mysteriously re-emerged thirteen hundred miles away in the swamps of Louisiana, although it is said that they were "buried" there. In the end, without intending to do so, and therefore all the more true to the principle of the classic horror film being the equivalent of a cultural Rorschach test, the 1940s Mummy series hit upon the idea of the multidimensional, parallel universe modality of narration.

The mythology of the 1940s Mummy series really hinges on the ideas of the secret priesthood and the miraculous power of the tana-leaf elixir. Certain ritual formulas are repeated in all four films, almost verbatim.

For example, there is the oath of the priest who assumes the role of the High Priest of Karnak:

> *I swear by the mighty power of Amon Ra, whose anger can shatter the world, and by the dread power of Set, that I will never betray my trust as the High Priest of Karnak.*

There is also a revelation about the correct formula for the use of the tana-leaves to animate and motivate Kharis. These are the instructions for the tana-leaf ritual given to Professor Andoheb in *The Mummy's Hand*:

> *Three of the leaves will make enough of the fluid to keep Kharis's heart beating. Once each night during the cycle of the full moon, you will dissolve three of the leaves and feed the fluid to Kharis. You will use nine leaves each night to give Kharis movement and life. Should unbelievers seek to desecrate the tomb of Ananka you will use nine leaves each night to give life and movement to Kharis. Thus you will enable him to bring vengeance on the heads of those who try to enter.*

When I first saw these films as a kid, there was a certain

The Mythology of the Mummy

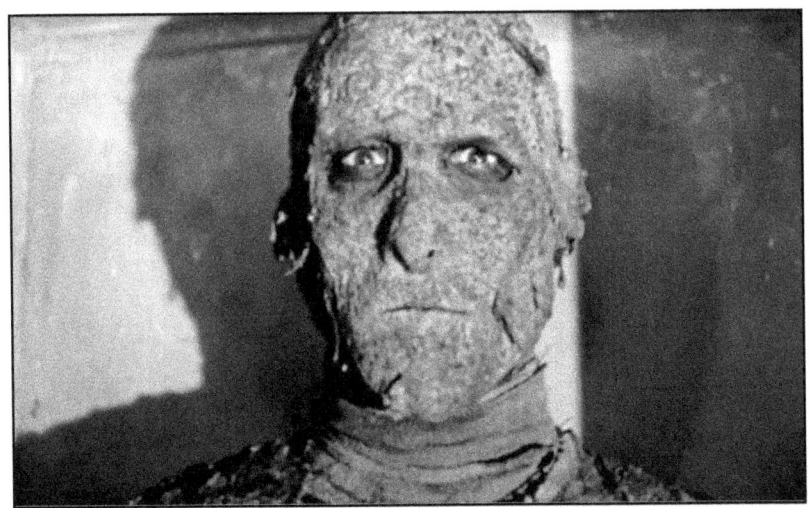

Christopher Lee in *The Mummy* (1959).

prominent element that I was hardly consciously aware of. This was the recurring theme of the disaster brought on by the priest of Karnak/Arkam being tempted by lust for a sexually attractive female, a lust that may not come over him until he has her in *bondage*. At that final moment, it occurs to him to try to make both her and himself immortal by means of the tana-leaf elixir. At that moment, the spell is somehow broken and catastrophe ensues. In one way or another, this ritualistic theme is reiterated in all four films.

A new symbolic twist was added in *The Mummy's Curse* whereby the long and well-established link between Kharis and the moon (he is supposedly only reanimated with the cycles of the full moon) is contrasted with a solar theme linked with the Princess Ananka. In a very effective scene where she rises from the swamp, the sun can be seen to be giving her vitality, and at one point she even remarks that the sun gives her life.

In 1959 the English film company Hammer resurrected Kharis and the whole mummy mythology in the film aptly named *The Mummy* and starring the new master of horror, Christopher Lee. The Hammer production uses many of the tropes of the Universal films (e.g., a magic incantation to revive the mummy, the reincarnated princess, and it even includes a foray into a swamp). All in all, this film can be seen as a Technicolor update of the myth.

Platonic Love

Platonic Love is often thought of only as "spiritual love," with no erotic or physical component. This is false. Platonic love is the recognition of the spiritual force of attraction and affinity between two souls that can be traced back to the common or similar origin of the two. Plato explores the idea of Love (Greek: *Eros*) in his dialogue entitled *The Symposium*. It is there that we read of the doctrine of the origin of human souls as being originally of three types: masculine, feminine, and a mixture of the two in the Hermaphrodite, half masculine and half feminine. Zeus split these entities apart in a primordial age. This resulted in there being a pair of souls ever in search of their "other half" in order to find true love (really a sort of self-completion). This doctrine is, by the way, the ultimate origin of the "New Age" idea of the "soul mate." A direct quote from the ancient text brings this home:

> For Love [Eros] must never be withstood—as we do, if we incur the displeasure of the gods. But if we cling to him in friendship and reconciliation, we shall be among the happy few to whom it is given in these latter days to meet their other halves. . . . [W]hat I am trying to say is this—that the happiness of the whole human race, women no less than men, is to be found in the consummation of our love, and in the healing of our dissevered nature by finding each his proper mate. And if this be a counsel of perfection, then we must do what, in our present circumstances, is next best, and bestow our love upon the natures most congenial to our own. (Plato 1963, 545–46)

In cases of Platonic Love, the difficulties lie in the inability to recognize the primordial link between the souls and the problems brought about by the two types of inner approaches: the ancient and obsessive Imhotep / Ardath Bey and the modern and dreamy Ankh-es-an-Amon / Helen Grosvenor—the fixed and mutable, the static and dynamic, the archetypal male and female.

So, in the final analysis, the original "Mummy Mythology" is an expression of the Mystery of Love, the unchanging, determined and steadfast power of the Lover and the ever changing, fickle, and perplexing nature of the Beloved. Love, described by the lives of its subject (lover) and object (beloved) is often an inherently tragic tale. The story of Imhotep and Ankh-es-an-amon, or Kharis and Ananka, is mirrored in many a romantic relationship in our everyday lives—each lover enters the relationship hoping that the beloved will never change, or, conversely, that the beloved will change to fit more the ideal the lover has for the object of the lover's ardor. With all of its fantastic elements, and all of its tana leaves and magical incantations, the stories of the mummy films are really archetypal romances.

Only by the gift (*kharis*) of the gods is the sorrow caused by need (*ananké*) overcome at that moment when both subject and object are able to express and receive love mutually in its true, steadfast, and immortal form.

The horror of the unfortunate eternal lover, Kharis, is that the Gift of his love can never be bestowed on his beloved—not in this world. He is never changing, while she is eternally changing forms. By the same token, the unfortunate beloved, having changed her form, is no longer able to recognize her true lover and can only recoil at his approach.

III
Phantom of the Opera
The Ghost in the Machine

As a Monster Kid reading the pages of *Famous Monsters of Filmland*, there was one figure that seemed to stand above all the others as if in some sort of holy aura: Lon Chaney in *Phantom of the Opera* (1925). This aura stemmed from several sources, but mainly because the film was next to impossible for us Monster Kids to see. Later I learned there was much more to the story. Other remakes of the classic lacked something essential; this was true of both the Claude Rains 1943 version made on the same set as the original, or the Hammer version of 1962 that I saw on one of my Saturday morning pilgrimages to the Casa Linda Theater. I even bought a short little 8mm reel which contained only the six minutes or so of the unmasking scene from the 1925 film. You could send away for such things using the marvelous ads in the back of *Famous Monsters*—you could get other wonders like a Venus Flytrap or some great Halloween masks. (We were all happy to wait six weeks to get our goodies.) Much later, when I was a senior in high school, I actually read the novel by Gaston Leroux—and the last mysterious veil was lifted. The whole mythology of the Phantom was fundamentally different in the novel and in the 1925 version than it was in any

of the remakes. A more mature view would also reveal that the characterization of Chaney was a great masterpiece of acting. He truly *embodied* Erik de Rouen. He inhabited the role like no other actor ever would or could. The main reason for this is that Chaney, a complex man, had a soul in some regards akin to that of the character (or actual man?) who was Erik de Rouen. Investigations into the origins of the story and the film first made about it reveal many mysteries, but leave many questions unanswered.

In recent years, a whole new group of Phantom fans (or "phans" as they call themselves) have been generated based upon the Andrew Lloyd Webber musical version of the story. The musical became extremely popular on the stage and was filmed in a lavish production in 2004. All of this has even inspired a body of "fan fiction." Perhaps the contents of this essay will provide some new ideas for them.

The central theme that one must deal with when thinking about *The Phantom of the Opera* is that the writer Gaston Leroux clearly claimed that the events recounted in the book are not fiction, but rather that they are based on facts.

First let us review the events of the life story of Erik (not his real name, but apparently a "stage name.") He was born in a village near Rouen, France. The year of his birth can be estimated to be around 1830, if he was fifty years old or so at the time of the events the book reports on, which is said to be 1880–1881. He is born with a horrible facial deformity that made his face appear skull-like. He was apparently rejected by his mother and never knew his father, who was a master mason. At a very young age he ran away from home and joined a traveling "Gypsy" caravan in which he made his living as a freak-show attraction billed as "the living dead man." While in this group he becomes a magician, learning the skills of illusion and ventriloquism. In connection with the latter skill he develops an extraordinary singing voice. The fame of this individual spreads in the East as he travels about the world. His familiarity with the Far East is mentioned in the book. It is there among the "Tonkin pirates" he learns how to breathe underwater using a hollow reed. Erik gains the attention of the Shah of Persia when a fur trader from Samarkand mentions Erik to the Shah. This Shah could have been none other than Naser al-Dîn Shah Qajar, who ruled Persia from 1848 to 1896. The Shah-en-shah (emperor) sends a *dâroga*, or "inspector," to fetch Erik and bring him to Persia. Erik goes to the court of the Shah and makes his various services available to the monarch. This includes his architectural skill and his abilities as a political assassin. Of Erik, it is said: "He committed a number of horrors because he seemed not to know the difference between good and evil" (Leroux 1996, 327). Erik is an expert in what is called the Punjab Lasso, a noose used for strangulation. It was during his time of service to the Persian Emperor that he was happiest, a time which is referred to as the *rosy hours of Mazendaran*, and here there is an allusion to a romantic relationship with a woman referred to as "the sultana." One of the main things Erik does in Persia is assist with the construction of an elaborate palace with secret passages and trap doors. This could be none other than the reconstruction of the enormous Golestân Palace in Tehran, which was completed in 1865. It is built on the site of the citadel (Persian *arg*) of Tehran. One feature of the palace was conspicuous to the eyes of Westerners: it had an enormous virtual lake of water underneath it. This was a cistern for the collection and storage of water—essential in the climate of Iran. The structural similarities with the Palais Garnier are, however, remarkable. Today this space is dry and houses a museum.

Astoundingly, I also discovered that the Shah Naser al-Dîn had a dungeon built immediately adjacent to the Golestân Palace, to its southeast. This dungeon was called the *Siyâh-Châl* (Black Pit). It was infamously used in the 1850s where the leaders of the Baha'i religion were imprisoned and tortured. Was this the dungeon in which the historical Erik (should he have actually existed), plied his skills in the service of the Shah? If this is not suggestive enough to the imagination of the reader, that Leroux was correct in telling us that the *Phantom of the Opera* reported on actual events and people, research furthermore revealed that the Black Pit was demolished only a few years after its construction—once it had apparently fulfilled its nefarious purpose. And what was built on its exact location? An opera house! This was built on the site in 1868 and called the Tikyih Dowlat. These coincidences may be too much for most people to believe that they were merely random events. Such circumstantial evidence makes us believe that Leroux may indeed have been telling at least some truth when he insisted that the events recounted in his novel actually happened. After the completion of the sinister aspects of the palace, the Shah is said to have ordered Erik to be blinded, so that he could never build another structure like it—but then decides to have him executed as an even better form of insurance policy. Thereupon the *dároga* helps Erik escape the empire and make his way to Constantinople. In that city, the capital of the Ottoman Empire, Erik performs services for the Sultan just as he had done for the Shah in Persia, but eventually he has to flee for similar reasons. He then makes his way to Paris and participates in the construction of the Palais Garnier. There he constructs passageways and secret spaces as he had done in the palaces he had designed in the East. The *dároga* is usually referred to as "the Persian" in the novel. He appears to be both Erik's protector and someone who keeps him under surveillance—for the Shah?

Through the various retellings of the story in a variety of films, the character of Erik is progressively made to be more and more sympathetic. Clearly, the character of Leroux's novel is a sociopath who did not know the difference between good and evil. His ugliness is what the Germans call an *Existenzfehler*, a defect which is innate, inflicted by nature. (This can be extreme deformity, or extreme beauty, as well.) The 1925 Universal production is the most faithful to the book, although as we will see its production was haphazard. The remakes of 1943 (Universal) and 1962 (Hammer) changed the reason for the Phantom's facial deformity entirely to be the result of acid being thrown in his face. In both of these storylines he is a betrayed genius, whose musical work is being stolen from him. This makes him a more sympathetic character automatically. The Andrew Lloyd Webber musical version reverts to the congenital deformity—but especially in the film adaptation of the musical the actor Gerard Butler appears to have merely forgotten to turn over the in his tanning booth and his "deformity" is not anything anyone would find shocking in real life. In this last case the Phantom has been turned into a full-blown *romantic* figure, successfully redesigned to be the arduous object of female fantasy.

Literary Background

The personality behind the creation of the story of *The Phantom of the Opera* is the French author and journalist Gaston Leroux (1868–1927). He was more known for his journalistic work than his fiction early on. As a younger man, he inherited millions of francs and lived an extravagant lifestyle. He was a gambler and a womanizer. After he had almost spent his entire fortune he began to work in greater earnest as a writer. He was a court reporter and theater critic—both venues were useful in writing his masterpiece later in life. He covered the second Dreyfus Trial, for example. He also traveled the world as a newspaper correspondent and covered the Russo-Japanese War as well

Gaston Leroux at his desk, circa 1919.
(Bibliotèque nationale de France)

as the 1905 Russian Revolution. But in 1907 he abruptly left the profession of journalism and began to write novels. He specialized in the mystery and detective novel and was a pioneer in the early production of films from his works. *The Phantom of the Opera*, the novel which has made him immortal, was serialized between 1909 and 1910 when it was turned into book form and immediately translated into English. During his career as a writer of fiction, Leroux published thirty-three novels and was extremely popular in France. Leroux died suddenly at the zenith of his fame in 1927 at the age of 58.

An overriding fact that many people regularly overlook is that in the book *The Phantom of the Opera* the author claims up front, and in an insistent manner, that the basic facts of the book actually happened and that the phantom was a real man who really lived—and died—in the opera house known as the Palais Garnier. Most critics would simply chalk this claim up to a typical Romantic literary device of inventing "actual sources" or basing the narrative on discovered letters, documents, or other artifacts to lend an air of believability to the most outrageous narratives.

The novel tells the tale of the Palais Garnier in Paris, which is reported to be haunted by an "Opera Ghost." A stage hand is found hanged, but the rope that hung him disappears. A performance is held to celebrate the retirement of the managers of the opera house, and a Swedish understudy from the chorus named Christine Daaé is asked to sing in place of the leading singer, Carlotta. A nobleman named Raoul de Chagny recognizes Christine as a childhood sweetheart. When he attempts to visit her in her dressing room, he hears a man's voice praising her, but when he enters, Christine departs and no one else is there. Later when Raoul asks Christine about the voice, she tells him that she is being tutored by the "Angel of Music," whom her now deceased father used to tell her about. She visits her father's grave, followed by Raoul. There a hidden figure plays the violin and when Raoul approaches the he is attacked and knocked unconscious. At the Palais Garnier the new managers receive a letter demanding that Christine should sing the role of Marguerite in *Faust* instead of Carlotta and that box five be reserved for him. These demands are ignored. When Carlotta attempts to sing she croaks like a frog and the great chandelier comes crashing down into the audience, killing a person. The Phantom kidnaps Christine from her dressing room and reveals his identity as Erik. He plans to keep her prisoner for a few days, but his plans change when she unmasks him, revealing his face. Christine later describes the face at some length to Raoul: "you have seen skulls that have dried over the centuries ... the mask of Death with four black holes that are its eyes and nose ... his lipless teeth" (Leroux 1996, 180). She describes the face in terms of her reaction to it as terrifying and hideous, and something she cannot stop seeing in her imagination. After she has revealed his hideous face, Erik determines to take possession of her permanently, but Christine asks him to let her to return to the world for two weeks; he allows this but with the stipulation that she wear his ring and be faithful to him. She meets Raoul on the rooftop, and they plan to run away together. The Phantom hears this and enters a jealous rage. Christine determines to sing one more time as a way of saying farewell to Erik. During her performance of Marguerite in *Faust*, Erik abducts her and demands that she marry him. Raoul is helped to enter the depths of the opera house by that mysterious patron known only as "the Persian." They are at once trapped in an elaborate mirrored room, and Erik adds a threat to kill Raoul in his attempt to coerce her. She offers herself to him as a "living bride." This moves Erik to release the men. When Erik is alone with Christine, he lifts up his mask and kisses her on the forehead, she returns the kiss, and he reveals that he has never given or received a kiss in his life, not even from his own mother. He then secures a promise from Christine that she will visit him on his death day and return the ring he gave her; she agrees and Erik allows Raoul and the Persian to escape. Erik has the Persian promise to report his death, as he plans to die "of love." His death is reported in the newspaper with the words: "Erik is dead." Later Christine returns to the lair and with the ring he gave her she buries Erik's body where it will never be found. She and Raoul leave together and disappear.

The World of Film

The Phantom of the Opera material has undergone as many as fifteen adaptations over the years in several languages, including a Chinese version. The Universal Pictures 1925 production was beset by production problems, poor direction and a faulty script that led to different versions being produced, rejected, and re-edited with different elements being added and deleted. The double DVD package by Milestone provides great deal of insight into this whole process. The final release can be summarized as follows:

> A new season of the opera is beginning with Gounod's *Faust*. Raoul de Chagny attends in hopes of hearing his girlfriend, Christine, sing. She is the understudy of the prima donna of the opera, named Carlotta. Raoul goes to Christine's dressing room and proposes to her, but asks her to give up singing. She refuses to give up her career. Later we learn that the managers of the opera are resigning, in part because of the dictates of the "opera ghost" who writes them demanding notes, such as one

La Place de l'Opéra, Paris (photo postcard, ca. 1916).

requiring that box number five is to be reserved for him. Backstage the ballerinas are frightened by a man wearing a fez, a stagehand named Joseph tells them he is not the phantom, that he has seen the phantom's face, which is like a skull. Carlotta receives a note demanding that Christine sing her role of Marguerite in the next performance of *Faust*. Terrible consequences are threatened if his demand is not met. Just then Christine is in her dressing room talking to the hidden phantom who tells her to take Carlotta's place and think only of her career and her master. The next day she tells Raoul that she is being tutored by the "Spirit of Music," Raoul scoffs and she angrily leaves. For the next performance, Carlotta is ill and Christine steps into the role, the managers try to see who is in box five but can only discern a shadow. The following performance sees Christine reach a high level and she receives a standing ovation from the audience. The stagehand, Joseph, is found hanging by a noose backstage. His brother swears vengeance.

Raoul waits outside Christine's dressing room and hears the voice declare: "Soon, Christine, this spirit will take form and will demand your love!" The Phantom sends more notes demanding that Christine continue to sing and that if she is not allowed, there will be a curse on the house. For the next performance Carlotta takes the stage, and the Phantom enacts the curse as the chandelier over the audience falls down on them. Christine runs to her dressing room and is lured by the voice to enter a secret door behind a mirror where she is led down a spiral stair on horseback into the lower region of the building. She is then transported by gondola over an underground lake into the secret lair of the Phantom. There the Phantom identifies himself and confesses his love for her. She faints. When she awakens in a special chamber he has built for her, she finds a note that says she is free to go about in the lair, but she must never look behind his mask. She then sneaks up on him from behind while he is at the organ playing music from his Don Juan Triumphant composition. She removes his mask revealing his deformed face. In a rage, he informs her of his plan to hold her prisoner, he does allow her to go back to the surface one more time, but tells her that it is forbidden to see Raoul. At a masked ball that night, the Phantom makes an appearance as the Red Death from Poe's story. Christine and Raoul meet on the rooftop of the opera, overseen by the Phantom from above them. She tells Raoul her story and they plan to flee to London. The man in the fez tells them which exit to use to avoid Erik. The next night Raoul visits Christine in her dressing room and she tells him the Phantom knows their plans. Raoul assures her that they will escape later in a carriage waiting outside. But during that evening's performance

Erik abducts Christine. Raoul goes to her dressing room and find the man in the fez. He reveals himself as Inspector Ledoux, who has been studying the Phantom since his escape from Devil's Island. They go below through a secret passage, but are caught in the Phantom's torture chamber room. Erik discovers them and applies extreme heat in the space, but they escape though a trap door, but this leads to another chamber where they are locked in by the Phantom. He gives Christine a choice, using two levers—one will save Raoul, but she will have to marry him; while the other will blow up the building and kill everyone. She picks the one to save Raoul, but by doing so the chamber he and Ledoux are in is flooded with water, threatening to drown them. Christine begs the Phantom to save them, promising to marry him, whereupon they are released. Just then, a mob led by the brother of the hanged stagehand storms the Phantom's lair. Erik escapes taking Christine with him to the waiting carriage. Raoul recovers Christine, and the Phantom takes off in the carriage. He is eventually caught by the mob and thrown into the Seine to drown. Raoul and Christine are shown on their honeymoon.

Lon Chaney

The one thing that makes the 1925 production of this story great is the acting and influence of the star, Lon Chaney (1883–1930). Direction on the set was weak, so Chaney often had to fill in to make the production more effective as well. Chaney was an American cultural phenomenon and was known as the "Man of a Thousand Faces" due to his abilities in the art of makeup and special bodily modifications. In the 1920s it was a common saying when one saw a spider or some other creepy creature: "Don't step on that spider! It might be Lon Chaney!" Stories spread about the horrific pain and mutilations he underwent in

Lon Chaney as the Phantom (1925).

the creation of his makeup: fish hooks in his nose, disks under his cheek bones, tremendous weight added to his body, and so on. Many of these stories were just that. People could not believe that his effects could have been achieved without extreme measures. His appearance as the Phantom remains one of the great iconic creations of the art of cinematic makeup. He did all of his own work, of course. This is something that would have been brought to an end had Chaney lived longer, as the advent of union contracts would have prevented him from doing his own makeup later. Chaney only appeared in one talking picture, a remake of *The Unholy Three* (1930) in which he demonstrated is mastery of acting in the new medium as well. His characterization of Erik was a masterpiece of silent screen acting. He was able to horrify audiences at one moment and move them to sympathy just moments later.

Only the 1925 silent version of the story with Lon Chaney ever approaches the core of the literary or historical tale. Generally, the original core myths of the book have been replaced by the "betrayed genius" myth, which was first introduced in the 1943 Claude Raines version. This myth shows a genius of the arts or science having his work or ideas stolen and used by an unscrupulous thief while the true creator is rejected and scorned. This myth no doubt very much appealed to the filmmakers of Hollywood who constantly had to battle the process of having their ideas stolen and used by others for great profit. I can remember how my friend Bill Wittliff, when he was writing some of his first original screenplays for films such as *Raggedy Man* and *Barbarossa*, would take measures to ensure that no one entered his writing space to see his works in progress until they were wrapped up. In Hollywood, one guy gets the idea of a man in a kid's body, and pretty soon two movies come out with the same basic idea. Stolen ideas and robbery of one's creativity is a serious concern. It is, however, not a part of the *original* Phantom myth.

Underlying Structures

As in Victor Hugo's *Notre-Dame de Paris* (*The Hunchback of Notre Dame*) it is the *building* that is really the main character of the story. The Paris Opera House—actually the Palais Garnier located at 18 Rue Scribe—is not merely inhabited by the phantom (ghost), but it is said that he had a decisive hand in actually *designing* the building—or at least the secret parts of it *down below*. If, however, we view this remarkable building in its component parts we can see that it can be viewed as a microcosm of the world and of the human condition.

Let us analyze the Palais Garnier in its particulars as both a multidimensional stage for the action as well as a complex character in the story as well. When we look at the structure, we see these things: a front part which is for social gatherings and social interaction. It is a series of galleries where people mix, mingle, converse, and see and be seen. Then there is the auditorium where the audience sits to experience the performance. Within this section, high above is the famous chandelier. In the nineteenth century, of course, it had to be lowered and the candles lit, and then hoisted up again to illuminate the space of the auditorium. (It would not be until the innovation of the German artist Richard Wagner that houses would be darkened for performances.) The next section is the complex and elaborate staging machinery. This is the location of the stage, but also of the mechanisms used to change the sets and raise and lower pieces of the scenery. At the rear of the building are offices and rehearsal halls and rooms. Below the building are cells and spaces, including what is sometimes referred to as a "lake." This is a watery cistern that holds water which drained into the substructure of the building during the construction of the opera house. When we take in the image of this whole structure, we see the picture of a subconscious mind in the watery abyss below, balanced by the illumination of the light above. There are also four different kinds of consciousness or human activities illustrated and exemplified by the structure: (1) an outer (extrovert) image and instrument of social interaction; (2) a collective space, over which the light of illumination shines and in which the minds of individuals are enlightened by the performance; (3) the inner mechanism of imagery, the inner workings of the mind as it endeavors to communicate and influence the minds of others; and finally (4) the hidden creative and administrative parts of the brain responsible for organizing and generating the thoughts, feelings, and elements of performance which will later be projected onto the stage of the house. This structure is a three-dimensional map of the mind of the showman and black magician. Does it all

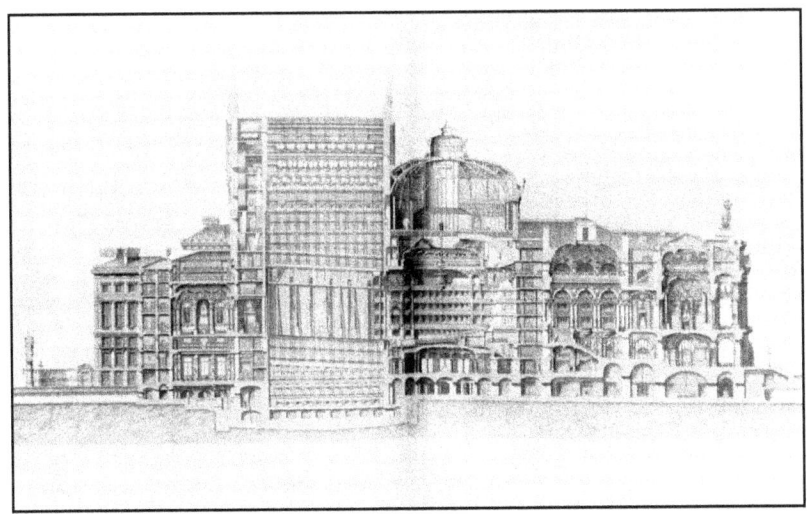

Cross-section of the Palais Garnier (Steinhauser 1969, plate 7).

betray the guiding hand of Erik de Rouen?

This building is a great machine, an inert structure only capable of life once it has been endowed with a *spirit*—the phantom—who actually constitutes the ghost in the machine. Another way of understanding the title of the work is "the spirit of the machine," or "the spirit within the work." The Latin word *opus*, from which "opera" is derived, can mean a structure, building, or "works" in general.

Within this superstructure there are certain principles or forms that inhabit and animate it. In the case of the narrative of *The Phantom of the Opera*, we see a certain constellation of characters who appear to represent archetypes or psychic constructs within the context of the "machine":

Erik
Carlotta : Christine
Raoul : the Persian
the Old Managers : the New Managers

An Internet search of the psychological interpretations of the Phantom of the Opera will yield many interesting results. Each have something insightful to say. For a novel of the kind

Leroux was supposedly writing, it is clear that the archetypal power inherent in the story is palpable. Clearly, the story can be seen as one of a depressive psychopath. Christine obviously has her Electra complex (believing that the Phantom is the Angel of Music her departed father had told her about) which leads her to trust and have affection for the Phantom despite his crimes. Most such interpretations, however meaningful they might be, tend to look at the Phantom as an object of the study. But what about looking at the elements from the Phantom's own perspective? The phantom is the ego or self within the system, he is wounded and disfigured, scared by the very facts of his life to such an extent that no one would love him. This he believes, and the events of his life have affirmed this view through experience. His only way out, his only way to find love, is to do so by means of the gifts that life has given him and the talents that he has developed, to some extent as a result of his isolation and exile from normal humanity. He has to condition his environment so that his fragile ego can survive; to do this he has constructed hidden chambers in which to live, wears a mask, and manipulates the management of the structure. The old managers are driven away, and have been replaced by new ones, providing new challenges to his plans. Christine is the object of his love and desire, but she is also his project, his own Galatea, which he shapes into the ever more perfect object of his love. Ultimately, he wants to lay aside his mask and be loved for who he really is—and who he really is can only be glimpsed only through his work. To fulfill his plans for her, he must eliminate her rival, Carlotta. Similarly, in order to make his dreams come true, he must overcome his own rival, Raoul. The key factor in the whole system is the Persian who is the repository of knowledge. The Phantom embodies Mystery, but the Persian knows the secrets. Because the Persian both protects and surveils the Phantom—as well as shields others from the Phantom when need arises—he acts as a sort of moral agent to balance the boundless excess of the Phantom's obsessive genius. In the end the moral compass is asserted, and even the Phantom succumbs to the dictates of fate, which he must accept.

There is no more perfect illustration of the theme of the

Outsider than Erik in the annals of horror film and literature. He fits almost all of the criteria laid out by Colin Wilson in his description of what the Outsider is. The most potent aspect of the theme is that he wants to cease being an Outsider by means of the exercise of his soul and his ingenious talent.

The Mythic Elements

The novel is replete with references to certain mythologies. Many have seen in the story an allusion to the myth of Orpheus and Eurydice, and more explicitly there are overt links to the myth of Faust and Don Juan. The Faust myth is referred to from within the context of the opera being performed in the Palais Garnier during the time of the narrative, while Don Juan is the subject of Erik's own masterpiece of the operatic art upon which he is working. Clearly, from within the motivation of the character of Erik, the Don Juan myth is an element which brings meaning to his desperate life.

Over seventy operas were written and performed between 1600 and 2015 based upon the myth of Orpheus and Eurydice, so the idea of an Orphic dimension to the story may have occurred to Leroux, an opera aficionado. Certainly it has occurred to more than one subsequent interpreter of the story. But it does not really fit with the story, as the Phantom cannot be seen as Orpheus except insofar as both are dedicated to *music*. And with respect to the abduction of a female figure and imprisoning her bellow the earth, the Phantom is far more of a Hades figure than an Orphic one. Raoul makes a pathetic Orpheus. The myth of Orpheus and Eurydice is a late addition to the Orphic corpus of lore; the original of this myth is actually that of Persephone, who is abducted by Hades and retrieved by a more neutral Hermes under the guidance of Zeus. Hades tricks Persephone into eating pomegranate seeds in the Underworld, and having tasted the fruit of Tartarus, must periodically return there.

But it seems that Leroux is leaving greater clues as to the mythic meaning of his story by means of the references made to two other myths: that of Don Juan and Faust. The opera being performed during the plot of the story is *Faust* (1859) by Charles

A scene from *Phantom of the Opera* (1925).

Gounod (1818–1893). The libretto for Gounod's opera was based on Goethe's version of the legend of the German scholar who sold his soul to the Devil for knowledge, power, and pleasure. Gounod's opera ends with a scene in a dungeon where Marguerite is awaiting execution for the murder of her child, for which she was unjustly convicted. Faust, who had brought her to this state, has just been at a Walpurgisnacht orgy with Mephistopheles, where he was promised the love of exotic beautiful women. Faust and Mephistopheles enter her cell and Faust wants to save her, but she trusts in God and the angels. Marguerite is saved as Faust looks on helplessly and Mephistopheles curses impotently. Christine, like Marguerite, is surrounded by evil and useless men (except the Persian).

Another myth, of somewhat more modern origin, must have also influenced Leroux's view of the story. He has Erik actually working on an opera of his own entitled *Don Juan Triumphant*. So perhaps the story and myth of Don Juan contains some clues as to the underlying meaning of the narrative. The oldest known representation of Don Juan (Italian: Don Giovanni) is in Spain in the early 1600s. The story is of a wealthy libertine who seduces women using all sorts of wiles and trickery, believing he always has time to repent of his sins—in the many versions of the story that have been told, sometimes he is condemned to hell, in others he is forgiven by God. Clearly, Erik is no "Don Juan" in the usual or colloquial sense. However, at the time Christine unmasks him, he says to her: "When a woman has seen me—as you have—she becomes mine. She loves me forever. I'm a real Don Juan. Look at me! I'm *Don Juan Triumphant*." Erik sees his hideous secret as a mystery which, once revealed, becomes a bond between him and the one that has beheld it. In general, "Don Juan" is a metaphor for a sadistic, cruel man who performs damnable acts throughout his life. From Leroux's presentation of the operatic work by Erik, it seems clear that what is intended by this feature is that Erik, although he is a psychopathic and sadistic killer, is to be spiritually redeemed by his work of pure genius and beauty. This ideology shows the morality of artists, in which their lives are justified by their greatness and creativity, not by their goodness and conventional morality.

Psychologically, the story of *The Phantom of the Opera* is a tale of a genius and a great soul imprisoned in a hideous form, rejected and loathed by the world, who must flee that world and take refuge in a citadel of his own making, to protect and shield that soul from the damaging effects of a society which has rejected him. Unfortunately, the genius is far too damaged ever to be able to hope for love or happiness, so he feels forced to abduct the object of his desire, but not before, in the manner of Pygmalion, transforming that object into the ideal recipient of his love.

One of the hidden meanings of the mythic elements surrounding the Phantom of the Opera is that many of us have twisted, ugly parts of ourselves which we inevitably must mask as our fellow human beings would, we feel, find them all too ugly to accept. The only way out, for many who are possessed of these sorts of feelings, is to achieve a work of great inspiration and genius which will be our salvation. It can be found in the history of the world that many times some of the greatest and most beautiful achievements have been motivated by the darkest of desires. Only the lucky ones will ever find a Christine who will actually love them, even if only a little bit and only temporarily, despite all of their ugliness.

Aftershocks

In less than a hundred years the material connected to the idea of the Phantom of the Opera created an enormous amount of interest. The book was a sensation, the 1925 film a phenomenon, and one that spawned over a dozen remakes and other films inspired by the original (e.g., *Phantom of the Paradise*). The musical version by Andrew Lloyd Webber took the material to an entirely new level of popularity, and catapulted it out of the horror realm and into a more romantic genre. It has been determined that Webber's theatrical creation has become the most popular production of its kind in history. There is a whole cottage industry surrounding "fan fiction" inspired by this version in a way similar to the fan fiction surrounding other franchises such as "Twilight."

During the years when I was intensely meditating on the archetypes discussed in this book, the tragic life of the American pop star Michael Jackson reached its final stages. As this was happening, I thought to myself: this fellow is much like Erik, a reclusive and twisted romantic musical genius headed toward a disastrous crescendo. Only now, in the final phase of composing this essay, did I research the possible connection between

Jackson and the Phantom and discovered that he was obsessed with the imagery of the myth and approached Webber in the desire to play the Phantom in the film! Those familiar with the story of Mr. Jackson can recall how—unconsciously, I am sure—he actually transformed his face, initially in an attempt to make himself more "beautiful," but the attempt ended in his face coming to look more and more like that of Erik as described in the original material.

IV
The Wolf Man and the Rites of Passage

The werewolf or wolf-man is one of the major icons of the horror film genre. Like so many of the others, it lacks a clear literary source. But what the theme lacks in the field of the *belles lettres*, it more than makes up for in the area of folklore and myth. However, the direction that myth takes us can be rather unexpected for most people.

The werewolf was one of the earliest monsters I was exposed to as a kid. The first two horror movies I have clear remembrances of on television are *The Werewolf of London* and *Frankenstein Meets the Wolf Man*. From the beginning, I always thought that the werewolf portrayed some sort of super power rather than a pathetic disease. Later I was to discover that my first impressions were correct. Despite the cinematic emphasis that werewolfery was somehow a horrible curse, the deepest roots of the phenomenon will be found to be in ancient and ancestral rites of sorcery and initiation into manhood. As I write about in the essay (XI) on William Castle, the horror film itself has a role as a rite of passage in American society. A rite of passage is an initiatory process through which an individual passes from one state of being to another—from boyhood to manhood, for example. Such rites typically follow a three-phase pattern:

1. Rites of Separation
2. Rites of Transformation
3. Rites of Reinclusion (or return)

One day in the late summer of 1961, my mother and I were going to visit a family who were longtime close friends of ours. The kids all called my mother "Aunt Betty." She had promised to take me to the movies afterward, to see *The Curse of the Werewolf*. She told me not to tell the kids in the family that we were going,

The Curse of the Werewolf (1961)

because they would make a big ruckus and would want to come with us, and she knew that their father only wanted them to see "Disney pictures." Well, of course, I spilled the beans and we all went to the movies. The boy in the family was my good friend, Tommy. He was not used to seeing such films, so he hid his eyes every time Oliver Reed made his transformation. But eventually he actually watched the werewolf undertake his gory sport—immediately after which Tommy exclaimed so loudly that the whole theater could hear: "I had the guts to watch it that time, Aunt Betty!" The audience burst out laughing. Tommy was becoming a man. Later he would follow in his father's footsteps and become a United States Marine. (As a footnote, to me the Disney movies were the real horrors: I still haven't recovered from *Old Yeller*.)

The werewolf is about transformation—sometimes to our advantage, sometimes to our horror. This transformation wells up from the depths of our organic beings, back to levels of existence beyond our present level of consciousness. Those who are able to control these primordial urges and powers can live with them happily. But those who cannot control such urges will themselves be consumed by them.

Myth and Folklore

The idea of a man being able to assume a wolf or wolf-like shape or aspect in order to hunt or fight in battle in a more effective way is an ancient and widespread one. In a classic study, *The Werewolf* (1933), Montague Summers recounts examples from all parts of Europe, from Greece to Britain and from Italy to Russia. But nowhere is the phenomenon better attested than in the Scandinavian realm. this is because in Old Norse literature we often get a perspective from within the werewolf world itself. Usually accounts of werewolves come from the point of view of those who fear them. They are seen as an evil "Other." But in the Norse literature we often get a more sympathetic view.

Norse literature abounds with depictions of men who were able to transform themselves into bears or wolves. Originally those who became bears and fought in battles in their bear-shapes, filled with a special battle-rage were called *berserkar*. A *berserkr* literally means "bear-shirt," and this was due to the fact that they put on a bearskin instead of armor in which to do battle. The process of transformation was called *berserksgangr*, from which our "going berserk" is derived. The berserk-warriors had a special close relationship to the ancient Germanic god Odin or Wodan. Of equal importance and prominence were the *úlfheðnar*, "wolf-coats," who wore "wolf-shirts" (*úlfstakkar*) as they were transformed. Norwegian witchcraft trials often mention the use of a wolf-skin belt to help effect the transformation. One who had the power to shift his shape is said to be *hamrammr*, "shape-strong," and to be a *hamhleypa*, "shape-leaper/shifter."

As far as the examples of the bear and wolf as metaphors for warriors is concerned, it is noteworthy that these two animals attack and hunt in two distinct manners: the bear alone and the wolf in an organized pack. These are the two main heroic fighting styles of the ancient Germanic peoples as well: the lone champion and organized band. But we also have the cultural reference embodied in the term "the lone wolf." There is a tragic and super-heroic dimension in this formula. The wolf *should* hunt in an organized pack, the wolf that hunts alone must be more powerful, cunning, and courageous than those that hunt in packs. But he is also seen as a metaphor for the tragic outlaw. The Germanic outlaw was a man who had committed some crime for which he was judged to be "outside the law," to be a sort of non-person, for a set period of time. During this time those whom he had offended could kill him without legal repercussions. The tribe or "state" did not take responsibility for "capital punishment," the family of the victim took that responsibility. Such a man was referred to in Old Norse as a *vargr í véum*, a "wolf in the (pagan) sanctuary"—someone excluded from the company of his fellow tribesmen.

It is likely that the transformation into an animal was an important part of ancient Germanic rites of passage or warrior initiations, as well as battle tactics. One of the most famous depictions of this process is found in the famous *Völsunga Saga* (chapter 8) where we read about how Sigmundr and his son

The Wolf Man and the Rites of Passage

Helmet-plate ornament depicting a wolfskin-clad warrior (right) from Torslunda, Sweden, 6th–7th century.

Sinfjötli come across a house where two men are sleeping with gold rings around their necks, they are sleeping as if in a trance. Two wolf skins hang over them, and it is said that a spell has been cast on them so that they can only come out of their wolf-shapes every ten days. Our two heroes don the skins and transform into wolves. Then they set out to ravage the countryside. Eventually the two get into a fight and the father gravely wounds the son with his fangs, but a raven (Odin) comes with a magic leaf to draw across the wound and thus heal Sinfjötli.

It seems clear from this and other evidence that the symbolic transformation of men into wolves was a part of ancient rituals of initiation of boys into the men's societies, or *Männerbünde*, as they are called in German. It is equally clear that his sort of thing is the deep background of the phenomenon of lycanthropy. The ability to transform one's self into the shape of a ferocious beast was akin to a super-power, not a curse or an infectious disease of the body or a disorder of the mind. But as the story of Sigmundr and Sinfjötli shows, the whole process is realistically fraught with dangers and pitfalls.

Films and Literature

In the development of the werewolf in popular culture, film has played a much larger role than literature. The one piece of fictional literature that helped boost interest in the werewolf phenomenon in a contemporary setting was Guy Endore's *Werewolf of Paris* (1933). I will discuss this novel a bit later.

Universal Pictures began its lycanthropic venture in 1935 with the *Werewolf of London*, the title of which was probably a play on that of Endore's book. (Actually, they had already started thinking about a movie entitled "The Wolf Man" a full ten years before the film with that title was eventually made.) The project was given to Robert Florey and the title character was supposed to be played by Boris Karloff. The script went through many rewrites: in one version, the werewolf was created as a result of being a child reared by wolves in the Tyrolian woods; in another, it was the result of a witch's curse. This is the project that eventually evolved into the *Werewolf of London*. Universal went back to the drawing board in 1941.

To understand the phenomenon of the werewolf in cinema one must understand the life of its main creator, Curt Siodmak (1902–2000), and the central historical event of the twentieth century, the rise and defeat of National Socialism in Germany and the effects of that phenomenon in the lives of human beings. Siodmak had been an innovative leading light of German cinema in the Weimar era, who was the main writer on *Menschen am Sonntag* (1929), a landmark film about contemporary middle-class life among young people in Weimar Berlin. (Also working on this film were Curt's brother, Richard Siodmak, Billy Wilder, and Edgar Ulmer!) This whole world came crashing down in 1933 when Hitler assumed power. The wolf had been unleashed in Germany—"Wolf" was Hitler's code name—and the "disease" of Nazism had infected many an average Hans or Fritz. They

Werewolf of London (1935)

seemed to have fallen under the spell of some unseen force. By some weird synchronicity it was on the precise date of the release of *The Wolf Man*, December 12, 1941, that the "Wolf" held a secret meeting in the Reich Chancellery in which he ordained the imminent annihilation of the Jews. This coincidence speaks to some of the thought Siodmak had put into the werewolf mythology.

For *The Wolf Man*, Siodmak composed the poem that became the leitmotif for the Universal "Wolf Man" films:

> *Even a man who is pure of heart,*
> *And says his prayers by night*
> *May become a wolf when the wolfbane blooms*
> *And the autumn moon is bright.*

(In the sequels to *The Wolf Man*, the last line was changed to "And the moon is full and bright.")

Siodmak created or codified much of the modern cinematic werewolf mythology for his screenplays *The Wolf Man*, *Frakenstein Meets the Wolf Man*, and *The House of Frankenstein*. He did so out of elements of various bits of folklore and imagination. From the vampire lore he borrowed the trope of an infectious disease: if one is bitten (infected) by a werewolf, one becomes one himself. The transformation takes place under the influence of the full moon and the werewolf can only be killed by silver (bullet, knife, or other instrument). As we have seen in folklore and older traditions, the process was seen more as a magical power than a curse or "disease." But Siodmak's mythology was so powerful and skillfully wrought that it persists today.

The Universal werewolf mythology culminated with *The House of Dracula* (1945), in which Larry Talbot is finally "cured." In the original *Wolf Man* the moon is mentioned, but never shown, and the transformations seem to take place independent of its influence. The concept that the transformation was forced by the effects of the full moon was first introduced in the 1935 film the *Werewolf of London*.

The werewolf phenomenon is rooted in the individual human being's relative lack of instincts and the weakness that results from this. Man is a "cultural animal," and a spiritual being. Our bodies are poor excuses for natural vehicles for surviving and thriving in the natural world. We lack the strength, protection (fur, tough paw-pads), offensive weapons (fangs, claws), heightened sense of smell, and fixed social order to be effective. Humans had to overcome these shortcomings through artificial extensions:

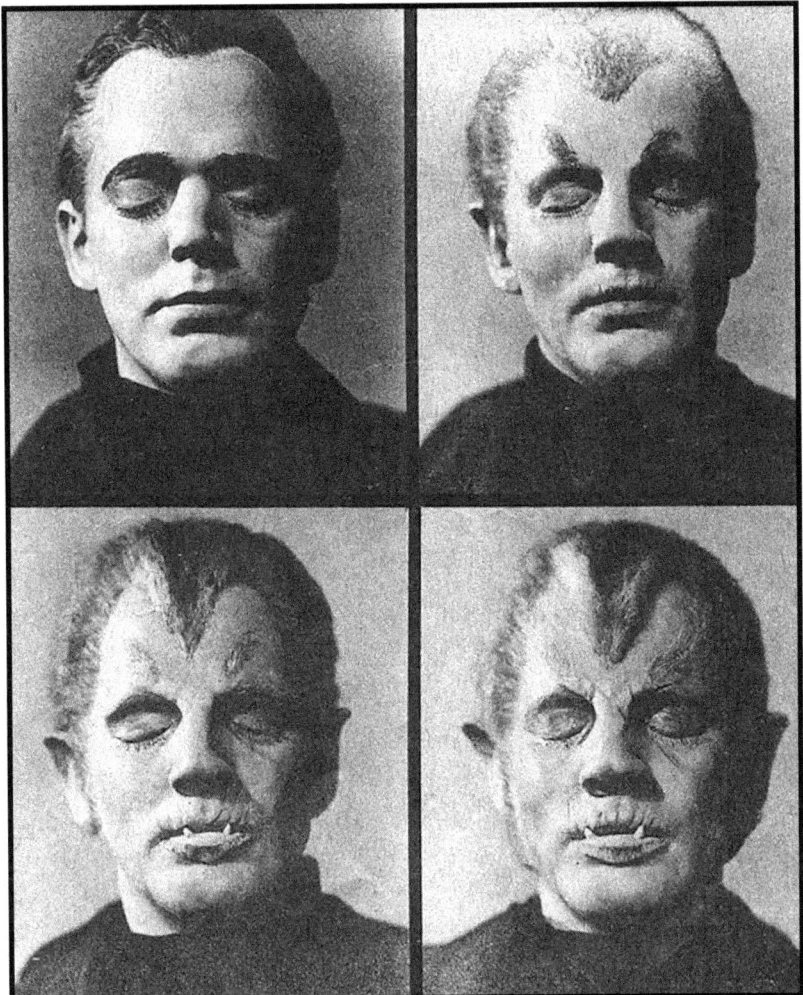

Transformation in *Werewolf of London* (1935).

clothing, armor and weapons, and through situational and motivational psychology by which humans are led to organize into effective groups (politics). Our instincts, as weak as they are, have to be supplemented with progressive *learning* from one generation to the next. Tradition and culture have to be developed in order for man to survive. Our only innate advantage is our intelligence. One of the ways this intelligence is used is through the development of skilled *observation* of models that work. We can learn from other humans who have learned their lessons and

Woodcut illustration of a werewolf, 18th century.

are willing to pass them on, but many lessons were also learned by observing more successful animals. The best example of this is the wolf. The wolf is a social creature. It hunts cooperatively in packs and has strategies for stalking and taking its prey. These characteristics were modeled by early humans. The successful hunter had to become more wolf-like. The wolf is endowed by nature with these gifts; man had to learn them and teach them to others. Man's special gifts are three: intelligence, oral organs of articulation, and the opposable thumb. These provide man with the capacity to reason and understand, to communicate by words in a complex language to others what he knows, and to be able to build or craft refined objects which his mind has imagined or conceived. It should also be noted that man's best friend, his dog, was bred from now-extinct subspecies of wolf. All dog breeds of today represent man's artistic creativity.

For early traditional man, the virtual transformation into a wolf may have been seen as an important stage in the development of skills and abilities he needed to survive and thrive in his often-harsh environment. It should be remembered that physically, man is an incomplete and weak creature—we lack physical attributes such as the fur, claws, and fangs that are necessary to thrive in a biologically competitive environment. But man has something no other (known) creature has: consciousness, self-awareness, and other non-natural gifts. These are used to learn to compensate for whatever is lacking in nature.

The wolf is also a powerful symbol of initiatory transformation in northern European mythic culture. We have seen how the ritualized transformation of man or boy into wolf was an initiatory experience for males, but one story we all know also uses the symbolism of the wolf as an illustration of feminine initiation: girl into woman. That story is "Little Red Riding Hood" (German *Rotkäppchen*), as recorded in the collection of tales made by the Brothers Grimm. In the story, which hardly needs to be repeated here, the little girl is pursued by the wolf and eventually swallowed. A woodsman comes along and splits the wolf open, and there is a great amount of blood, the little girl emerges unharmed—yet now a woman, not a girl. This is symbolic of her first bleeding from a menstrual cycle. On the screen this was made more obvious in the 1984 film *The Company of Wolves*, based on Angela Carter's story of the same title, first published in her book *The Bloody Chamber* (1979). Carter is also the author of the book *The Sadeian Woman* (1978) and she demonstrated a deep understanding of the sexual implications of the topic.

The hidden dimension of the werewolf tradition is indeed its pronounced *sexual* aspect. This spans a gamut between stories about the idea of boys becoming men, girls becoming women, as well as the satisfaction of "animalistic" appetites. The wolf in Germanic lore is known for being a symbol of the appetites and the desire to satisfy those appetites. Odin's mythic wolves are named Geri and Freki, which mean "Greedy" and "Ravenous," respectively. As later lore makes clear, these appetites are not necessarily just for "food," but rather for sexual desires as well. Because the wolf is also symbolically known for his cunning and reputed cruelty, these aspects would also have naturally accrued to the werewolf (if not for the Hays Commission!). One of the first studies to delve into this generally was Robert Eisler's *Man into Wolf: An Anthropological Interpretation of Sadism, Masochism and Lycanthropy* (1948)—a strange book that could have only been written by a German. The text is thirty-four pages with over two hundred pages of notes and appendices—there are even footnotes in the footnotes! Of course, most of our human projections onto the wolf are incorrect from a zoological perspective. The werewolf and the myth of the werewolf has its archetypal roots more in the all-too-human spirit than in actual wolf behavior.

The Curse of the Werewolf (1961) was Hammer Films foray into the genre and remains much beloved by me. No sequels were made—it stands as a "lone wolf" in the genre. It is *loosely* based on a 1933 novel by Guy Endore (= Samuel Goldstein, 1901–1970) entitled *The Werewolf of Paris*. Endore was a novelist, translator, and screenwriter blacklisted in the 1950s for his affiliation with the Communist Party. He wrote a historical novel on the life of the Marquis de Sade called *Satan's Saint* (1965) and translated Hanns Heinz Ewers's classic *Alraune* for Stein & Day in 1929. Endore's book does not shy away from the aforementioned sexual element of actual werewolf mythology. This element would generally be missing from the cinematic world of the werewolf in the classic era, for obvious reasons. But the wolf as a symbol of lustful, aggressive, and even perverse male sexuality is deeply embedded in our Anglo-American culture. In earlier times sexually aggressive men were often called "wolves," and the "wolf whistle" was part of popular culture.

Endore's *The Werewolf of Paris* tells the story of a man named Bertrand, born on Christmas Eve in a rural part of France to a peasant girl who had been raped by a priest. The child is brought up by the kindly family of his step-uncle, but the boy grows up with sadistic sexual desires expressed in dreams. He also begins to transform into a wolf during the night to carry out his desires. He tries to hire prostitutes to satiate limited versions of his lust, but ends up going on a murderous rampage and fleeing to Paris. His uncle pursues him and tries to track him down by studying patterns in local crimes. Bertrand joins the military during the Franco-Prussian War (ca. 1871) where he meets and seduces a beautiful and wealthy volunteer at the canteen: Sophie de Blumenberg. She is a masochist obsessed with death, and out of love helps Bertrand stop his criminal activity by allowing him to erotically cut her and consume her blood. (Ah, romance!) For a time, love seems to have cured Bertrand. Bertrand's fear of killing Sophie drives him to go elsewhere to express his desires, and in the process he is caught killing another soldier, arrested, and sentenced to treatment in the La Sante prison. Bertrand eventually commits suicide, as had Sophie, unable to cope with her separation from Bertrand. There follows an appendix that describes the exhumation of Bertrand's grave eight years later. In the grave was found no human body but rather that of a "dog" which was not yet fully decomposed.

Set in Spain, the film version departs from the book in many respects. To fully translate Endore's book into a film, it would have to be X-rated. *The Curse of the Werewolf* does have some interesting ideas, however. The opening scenes depict the story of a man imprisoned in a dungeon for years, such that he has regressed to an animalistic state. He rapes a mute peasant girl who gives birth to a boy on Christmas, but she dies in childbirth. The boy, named Leon, is raised by the people (Alfredo and Teresa) who found the girl wandering in the woods. After a hunter smears blood on Leon's face from his kill, the boy begins changing into a wolf as a child and hunting local livestock. He is shot and wounded by a shepherd, and his foster father discovers the truth. A priest tells him that only though love can the boy be saved. The boy grows into a man (played by Oliver Reed) and has been free of werewolfery for years, with the help of the love of his foster parents. The time comes for him to leave home and find work, his foster parents reluctantly allow him to leave. He goes to a nearby village and apprentices at a winery. He falls in love with Cristina, the daughter of the vineyard's owner. It is a forbidden love, however, and so Leon's friend convinces him to go to a brothel with him. There Leon's lusts are stimulated and he transforms into the werewolf, killing a number of people. He runs back to Alfredo's house with plans to run away with Cristina, whose love prevents his transformations. But he is arrested on suspicion of the murders. In jail he once more transforms into the werewolf and breaks out of the bars. He is cornered by Alfredo in the church bell tower and shot with a silver bullet made from a crucifix.

Clearly, *The Curse of the Werewolf* is tinged with idea of Lamarckian evolution. Jean-Baptiste Pierre Antoine de Monet, Chevalier de Lamarck (1744–1829) was a French proponent of biological evolution before Darwin. Lamarck's theory is one of *acquired characteristics*: the giraffe's neck is long because previous generations of giraffes stretched their necks and passed the longer neck on to their offspring. (This is counter to Darwin's now-established theory of *natural selection*: the giraffe has a long neck because only long-necked ones were able to eat food and thus fit to *survive* and reproduce.) In *The Curse of the Werewolf*, the explanation seems to be that the degenerate conditions to which Leon's natural father was subjected caused a sort of animalistic aspect to be transferred to his offspring.

Conclusion and Aftershocks

In later years some of the idea of the power to change one's self into a wolf-like creature came to return to the most archaic idea that such a transformation was a magical power or a special ability desired by warriors and warlocks. It seems that an underlying, yet usually unspoken, dimension of the classic werewolf trope is just that—it is a secret power, but one that soon becomes a frightening burden to bear.

Within the general genre of humans transforming themselves into fierce creatures, we must also say a word about the *Cat People* (1942) made by RKO Studios produced by Val Lewton (= Vladimir Leventon, 1904–1951) and directed by Jacques Tourneur (1904–1977). Here, as well as in Endore's *Werewolf of Paris* and the subsequent *Curse of the Werewolf* based on Endore's ideas, the essential and original element of sexual desire plays a central role. In *The Cat People*, sexual desire causes the ancient curse to rise up and allow the transformation to take place. This aspect is softened in films before a certain time, but it returns to the forefront in the 1981 remake titled *Cat People*.

Although it plays out in a modern setting, *The Howling* (1982) renews an aspect of ancient lore that there is something *cultic* about the craft of lycanthropy. In this sense, the werewolf films are stories within stories on a hidden level: the horror film and its viewing is a sort of modern (especially American) *rite of passage*, and the whole idea of transformation of man into wolf is in itself a sign of such a transformation. It is for this reason that the modern myth of the werewolf has had such durability and flexibility in the contemporary mind and in modern culture.

The werewolf paradigm was a significant part of initiatory life throughout the ancient Indo-European world, from Rome to Scythia and from Scandinavia to Greece. Because of the obvious elements of danger bound up with the idea of the werewolf and the practice of transformations from a human to a wolfish nature this process in practical sorcery has been marked by extreme secrecy. For those who might want to experience some of the "romance" of the werewolf, you might want to consult a book such as Denny Sargent's *Werewolf Magick* (Llewellyn, 2020), or for a more "down-to-earth" and perhaps authentic approach take a look at Anton LaVey's article "How to Become a Werewolf" from 1978.

Clearly, the whole werewolf mythology—that belonging to archaic folklore and that belonging to modern literature and film—is a complex and profound thing. Its esoteric aspects span from the realm of rites of transformation and superhuman power to the curse of atavistic criminal and anti-social characteristics rising up in individuals who cannot control them. I spent several years as a fairly well-controlled werewolf, but I'm better now.

V
Frankenstein
A Man-made Creation

Because even from my early childhood I was, inexplicably, a Germanophile, I was drawn to "Frankenstein" as my favorite monster because his story felt so rooted in German culture, with its mad scientist, ruined castles, the Bürgermeister and his villagers. The whole aesthetic and ambience seemed German, as well it should have. The films of Universal most especially were consciously patterned after the German Expressionist masterpieces of the silent screen. As we dig deeper into the literature, the Germanic qualities seem to fade somewhat, but they are still prominent, as we shall see.

It was a copy of the Classics Illustrated version of *Frankenstein* that gave me what I remember as my first jolt of interest in the whole topic of monsters. I was not very literate at the time, so it was probably from the series of images that I got my first impressions of the world of monsters. Shortly thereafter I saw *Frankenstein Meets the Wolf Man* on television. The cosmos of monsters, hidden knowledge, and the secrets of life and death all burst forth for me in my child's brain—not yet grasping the meaning of the symbols I was viewing.

The book *Frankenstein* continues to conceal mysteries and call forth questions and controversies, as all great works of literature ought to do. The early film versions produced by Universal have become part of American iconography together with the image of Dracula. Both the literature and the films deserve our repeated examinations. Each examination reveals another level of meaning.

Literature and Film

As was the case with *Dracula*, *The Hunchback of Notre Dame*, and the *Phantom of the Opera* before it, *Frankenstein* had a "monster" based on a great—or at least well-known—work of literature. This was one of the hallmarks of early Universal horror films. Nowhere else, however, is the disharmony of the cinematic and literary art forms more obvious. All who have seen the *Frankenstein* horror films are always really surprised when they read the book. The films and literature are only similar in the broadest thematic outline: a scientist creates a living monster out of the parts of dead men and animates it through artificial means and the creature ends up harming the creator. Whereas the films are constrained by the conventions of Hollywood narratives, the book is far more nuanced and complex, all of which is to be expected. The great artistic achievement of the two best Frankenstein films: *Frankenstein* (1931) and *The Bride of Frankenstein* (1935)—which together really form one coherent story, since the second film begins at the exact moment the first one ends—lies in the cinematographic art design and the brilliant characterization of the monster by Boris Karloff (William Henry Pratt).

In looking at the esoteric dimensions of the cultural myth of Frankenstein, I will have to examine the two worlds of literature and film, and the themes which bind the two realms together. In this case these two media, the written word and film, present two different stories, or their emphasis is laid on two different things. In the world of literature, Victor Frankenstein is portrayed as a brilliant but irresponsible student who creates a being which he cannot or will not take care of, and it ends up becoming his better and destroying everything the scientist loves—and, ultimately,

Boris Karloff as Frankenstein (1931).

the scientist himself. In the films, the *doctor* (he got a promotion when he went to Hollywood) is misguided, full of hubris, and in way over his head with his new creation. It destroys many lives, but does so in an entirely innocent manner—it cannot be made wholly responsible, as it is the equivalent of a child or mentally disabled person. The maker must bear the responsibility, but in the end, it is the monster that is destroyed (?) and not the maker. The monster does become a godlike judge at the end of *The Bride of Frankenstein*, when he allows Henry and Elizabeth to go free, before condemning his new "bride," the decadent Dr. Pretorius, and himself to death with those words: "We belong dead!"

Mary Shelley's Frankenstein

When Mary Shelley (1797–1851) published her novel *Frankenstein*, she was only twenty-one years of age, and she had conceived of the story when she was still a teenager. She was born Mary Wollstonecraft Godwin. Her father was William Godwin (1756–1836) a leading English radical libertarian and anarchist philosopher who was a well-known proponent of the idea of free love. His major work was *Enquiry concerning Political Justice* (1793). Mary's mother was the feminist philosopher Mary Wollstonecraft (1759–1797). Her major work was *A Vindication of the Rights of Woman* (1792). She died from complications of bearing her daughter only a month after the child's birth. Young Mary was seduced by one of her father's followers, the great English poet Percy Bysshe Shelley, whom she met beside her mother's grave. It is said they consummated their love in that graveyard. Shelley was also a close confidant of the older Lord Byron, with whom he and Mary spent the summer of 1816 when the story of *Frankenstein* was conceived. More about this famously haunted summer in a bit. The members of the Byron party are all determined to "write a ghost story." Mary claims to have had the basic idea occur to her in a dream—or nightmare. The book was at first published in a way so that Mary could not be identified as the author.

The novel tells a story narrated from three different perspectives: that of the captain of a ship, that of Victor Frankenstein, and that of his creation—or the Creature itself. The narrated events take place in the 1700s, some decades before the book was written.

Victor Frankenstein is a young student living with his family near Geneva, Switzerland. He departs to Ingolstadt, Germany to study at the university there. (This university was later moved to Munich.) He is a student of chemistry and obsessed with old theories about imparting life to dead matter. He creates a

Miniature portrait of Mary Shelley by Reginald Easton, allegedly drawn from her death mask (ca. 1857).

humanoid of large size (because it was easier to work with) and brings it to life. The Creature is hideous to look at. Victor runs away and when he returns to his quarters finds that the Creature has escaped. Victor falls ill from the strain and only after four months is he able to return home. When he does so he discovers that his little brother, William, has been murdered. Victor sees the Creature lurking in the area and realizes it is responsible for his brother's death. Despite this, William's nanny is convicted of killing the boy and is hanged. When Victor retreats to the mountains, the Creature confronts him and relates his story to Victor.

The Creature tells of wandering in the forest and learning that those he met feared and hated him due to his appearance. By seeing himself reflected in water he discovered his own ugliness and why people loathed him. He tried to hide from people but found a house in the woods where a family lived. From secretly watching them he learned to speak and to read from a satchel of books he found in the woods. He befriends the patriarch of the family, who is blind. But when the others see him, they all abandon the house. So, the Creature departs as well. He is now articulate and literate. By reading in Victor's journal, which he had taken, the Creature traced his way to Victor's home. There he murdered his little brother and framed the nanny for the crime.

The chief demand the Creature makes at their meeting is that Victor create a *female* version of the Creature to act as his companion. If Victor fails in this, the Creature threatens to destroy Victor and his whole family. Victor agrees, and the Creature keeps up with the progress of the scientist's work. Victor heads to the Orkney Islands to work on the female creature, but has grave doubts about the wisdom of creating such an entity. He fears the female will be more evil than the male and that they might breed a new race that would plague all of mankind. When Victor finally destroys his work in progress, the Creature confronts him and says: "I will be with you on your wedding night." Upon Victor's return, he is charged with the murder of his friend whom the Creature has killed, framing Victor for the crime. Victor is acquitted. Back in Geneva he plans to marry his longtime sweetheart, Elizabeth. On their wedding night the Creature strangles Elizabeth. Victor tries to avenge himself, but the Creature escapes. Victor pursues the Creature northward toward the North Pole. In the pursuit, Victor collapses and is picked up by the sea captain, who brings him on the ship. This vessel becomes trapped in the ice and the ensuing hardship causes many to die, including Victor. The captain finds the Creature mourning over Victor's body. He tells the captain that Victor's death has not brought him any satisfaction and that he has resolved to kill himself. The Creature drifts away toward the North on a small iceberg into an eternal darkness and cold, never to appear again.

This is a story of how science is able to create things for which the creators do not have the wisdom to manage, and how these creations, innovations, and inventions can have disastrous unintended consequences. One of the most intriguing aspects of the story is how the creation is shown to become in many ways the superior of the creator. The creature is motivated by its sense of moral outrage at the way it has been treated by its creator and has the courage to demand justice and act on these demands to the very end.

The Frankenstein of Whale and Balderston

From an artistic perspective, it is most interesting to analyze the legacy of the Frankenstein material by looking at the two films *Frankenstein* and *The Bride of Frankenstein* as a single narrative. The subsequent sequels *The Son of Frankenstein*, *The Ghost of Frankenstein*, and *Frankenstein Meets the Wolf Man* (1943) each have their moments of greatness, and an effort is made to tie the narratives all together, but the later films lose the coherence of the message of the original story created by James Balderston and several others under the direction of James Whale.

The first two Frankenstein films tell the story of Dr. Henry Frankenstein who collects newly dead bodies in order to try to piece together a man. He and his assistant, Fritz, rob graves to do this. Frankenstein sends Fritz to steal a brain from a lab. Fritz breaks the container holding a normal brain and takes one of a criminal instead. Henry's fiancée, Elizabeth, is worried about him, sequestered as he is in his fortress-like laboratory. She enlists the help of colleagues to try to get him away from his experiments, but they arrive just at the time he is about to apply his electrical equipment to animate the dead body composition with the "ray" that brought life to earth. When Henry sees the first signs of life in his creation, he becomes hysterically enthusiastic. Enthusiasm soon turns to depression as he discovers that the monster is a simpleton. Fritz constantly torments the creature, until the monster kills him. Now Henry and his colleagues agree that the monster must be destroyed. It is injected with a powerful drug that renders it unconscious. Henry collapses from the strain and is taken home to prepare for his wedding. Dr. Waldman proceeds to try to take the creature apart on the operating

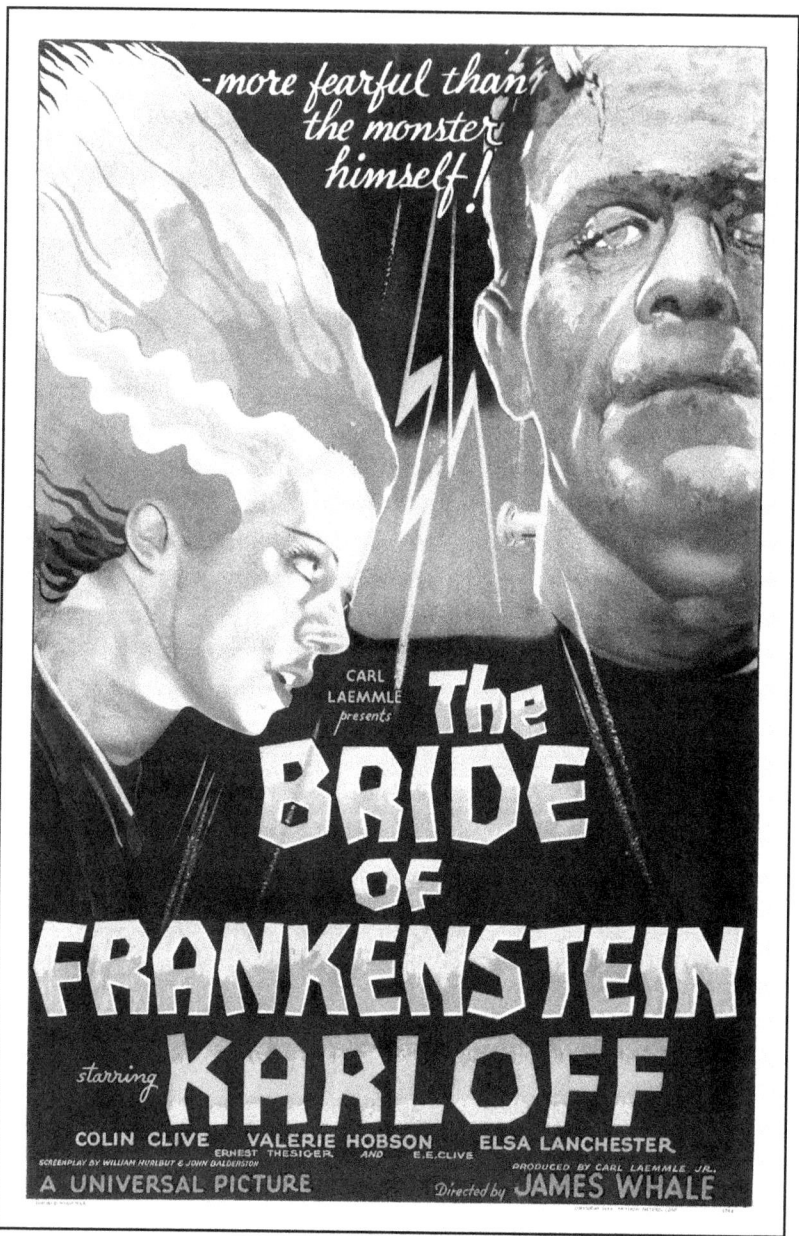

The Bride of Frankenstein (1935)

table, but it awakens and kills him, making its escape into the countryside. There it meets with a little girl, Maria, and joins her, childlike, in throwing flowers into a lake. When the flowers are gone, the monster innocently throws the little girl in the water and she drowns, which the monster finds disappointing. Back at Frankenstein's home, Henry is happy, but then gets news that Waldman has been killed. The creature enters Elizabeth's room causing her to faint, but it departs, leaving her unharmed. In the meanwhile Maria's father enters the village with the little girl's body. The villagers, with the participation of Henry, form a search party to capture or kill the creature. During the search Henry is separated from the rest and is seized by the creature, who drags him off to an old mill. The villagers hear Henry's cries and find the creature has dragged the scientist high up in the mill. As the structure is surrounded the monster hurls Henry down and then the mob sets fire to the mill, apparently killing the creature inside. Thus ends the film *Frankenstein*.

 The narrative of *The Bride of Frankenstein*, despite being made four years later, takes up at the exact moment where *Frankenstein* left off. As the villagers are gathered around the smoldering mill, Maria's father wants to see the monster's bones for himself and goes into the ruins of the structure. There he falls into a watery pit down below and is confronted by the still living monster. The creature strangles him and drowns the man's wife as she comes down searching for him. Meanwhile at Castle Frankenstein, Henry has recovered consciousness and still expresses his interest in unlocking the secrets of life and immortality. Shortly thereafter Henry is visited by one of his old mentors, Dr. Septimus Pretorius, who shows Henry his specimens of homunculi—small living beings created artificially by an alchemical process. At this point, Pretorius suggests they should create a female version of the monster and they agree. Pretorius then offers a toast: "To a new world of gods and monsters!" They set out to gather the parts for their new creation. In the meantime, the monster is wandering the forest, comes upon a drowning shepherdess and saves her, but hunters see this and shoot at the creature, setting off a mob, which hunts the creature down. They capture it and tie the monster to a pole, in a scene reminiscent of a crucifixion. It is put in a dungeon but breaks its chains and escapes again. The monster then makes its way to the hut of a pious blind hermit, who befriends the monster, feeds it, and begins to teach it to speak. This idyllic situation does not last long as two hunters pass by, see the monster, and in the ensuing conflict the hermit's cottage is burned and the monster escapes. He finds his way to a crypt and meets Dr. Pretorius there and learns of the plan to create a woman. Dr. Pretorius visits Henry and Elizabeth, now happily married, and tells Henry that it is time to begin their collaboration. Henry refuses, but then Pretorius calls in the monster who speaks, demanding Henry's help. Elizabeth is kidnapped by the monster and held hostage. Henry returns to his tower-laboratory and once more begins to become enthused about creating life. As a storm breaks outside, the lightning is harnessed to animate the Bride, who is brought to confused life. She is introduced to the Monster, but she rejects him with a powerful scream. The Monster reacts bitterly: "She hate me! Like others." In a rage, he begins to destroy the laboratory while Henry and Elizabeth make their way to the exit. The Monster grasps the lever to an explosive charge and tells the newlyweds to leave. But he demands that Pretorius and the Bride remain behind. "We belong dead!" he declares. With a tear running down his cheek, the Monster pulls the lever and the tower explodes.

Although the character of the Frankenstein's Monster would inspire dozens of re-envisionings and remakes, no cinematic effort would rival the power of the narrative presented in the first two films of the Universal *Frankenstein* series. Just as Lugosi had redefined the character of Dracula for all time in the public's imagination, Karloff did the same for the Monster.

The Genesis of Frankenstein

The novel *Frankenstein* cannot be fully understood apart from the times and ideological context out of which it arose: English Romanticism of the late eighteenth and early nineteenth centuries. Romanticism was an international movement, especially strong in England and Germany. Its intellectual roots

Percy Bysshe Shelley

can be traced to the French writer Jean-Jacques Rousseau, who said "I felt before I thought." Here it is meant that emotion is a more basic and fundamental part of human life than the pure logic and reason extolled by the Enlightenment thinkers.

Romanticism was a generational rebellion against what was seen to be the excessive rationalistic optimism of the Enlightenment and the sterile aesthetics of Classicism. Romantics turned inward—to the nightside of nature and to the world of dreams for inspiration. Visionary Romantics could already see the looming destructive force of science and technology unleashed upon the human race. Mary Shelley was among these. Her father and mother were far more aligned with the Enlightenment thought process, against which the Romantic mindset was a rebellion. Mary's lover, Percy Shelley, was a deeply Romantic soul. He was obsessed with ideas of the occult, immortality, spirits, and dreams. Mary and Shelley "eloped" to Europe in the summer of 1814. They traveled around in various places on the Continent, including along the River Rhine. In May of 1816, Shelley and Mary met up with Lord Byron, Dr. Polidori, and Claire Clairmont near Geneva, Switzerland and they spent the summer in the Villa Diodati, which Byron had rented on the shores of Lake Geneva. The events of that haunted summer are Romantically treated in the Ken Russell film *Gothic*. The company read from a book entitled *Fantasmagoriana, ou Recueil d'histoires d'apparitions, de spectres, revenans, fantômes, etc.* (1812), which was a French translation of German stories published in the *Gespensterbuch* (1811–1815). The atmosphere was charged with electricity, erotic tensions, speculations about life being restored to dead tissue (through Galvanism, etc.), and ghostly portents all around. Byron proposed that they each undertake to write a "ghost" story of his or her own. In the introduction to the 1831 edition of *Frankenstein*, Mary tells us that she conceived of her book in a sort of dream: half waking, half sleeping. The Germanic atmosphere of the stories in the *Fantasmagoriana*, coupled with the journeys made along the Rhine, fueled Mary's imagination. The events of the summer are sometimes confabulated in the journals of the people who were there, and in some cases sections of these documents are entirely missing. It makes one wonder what really happened there. In any event, Mary successfully completed her story, as did Dr. Polidori (whose tale "The Vampyre" is discussed in Essay I).

One of the hidden dimensions surrounding the Frankenstein material lies in the controversy as to the actual authorship of the book. Of course, it is credited to Mary Shelley and one of the joys in reading the story and teaching about it is when you and others realize that the book was conceived and written by a "girl" of a mere eighteen or nineteen years of age! When the book first appeared, her authorship was hidden, as woman authors in general were controversial in the very early nineteenth century. As time went on, however, she did become known as the book's author. Especially in the twentieth century Mary Shelley became a celebrity in the world of feminist theory and literary history. One book dedicated to showing that Percy Shelley and not Mary was the primary author is John Lauritsen's *The Man Who Wrote Frankenstein* (2007). He seems to have his own axe to grind, making the novel a study in gay literature! The best way to show who wrote the book is to submit its text to computer analysis. I am not aware of this having been done. Comparisons between the style of *Frankenstein* and that of Mary's later works, such as *The Last Man* (1826) have been used to argue that she was not the primary author of the book. What appears to be the consensus middle ground on the question—and which probably makes the most sense—is that Mary conceived of the story and wrote the book, or a version of it, and that Shelley, acting more as an editor than author, greatly revised the style and perhaps certain elements of its content. Many of the great writers of recent literary history were really only as great as they seemed to be due to skillful editors. In the final analysis, the book *Frankenstein* appears to be the work of Mary Shelley, with considerable input from her husband in matters of composition.

Did Frankenstein Exist?

The thesis of the book *In Search of Frankenstein* by Radu Florescu is that the character of Frankenstein is based on a German alchemist named Johann Conrad Dippel (1673–1734) who was associated with a castle near Darmstadt, Germany known as Castle Frankenstein. It is said that Dippel was able to engender life in dead matter using alchemical principles. In Dippel's dissertation entitled *Maladies and Remedies of the Life of the Flesh*, he explains how, by using a special funnel, the animating principle could be transferred from one corpse to another. So—as Florescu's theory goes—Shelley and Mary learned of this story on their travels and this was the origin of the name Frankenstein in her book. In fact, it may have been no more than the name itself which was evocative to her. This would be similar to the way that Bram Stoker, in the last phase of his research for his vampire novel came across the name "Dracula" and made it a

Johann Conrad Dippel (1673–1734)

part of his book almost as an afterthought. In both instances the discovery of these *names* was essential to the power of their legacies.

Tourists can still visit the Castle Frankenstein in Germany, which has exploited its connection to the story of Frankenstein to some extent, but has as yet to become overly commercialized. There is an annual Halloween celebration there—a sort of artificially imported custom in Germany.

An interesting key to a deeper interpretation of the book *Frankenstein* is offered by the use of certain words in the text. Several times Victor is referred to as the "author" of the monster and as being himself an "artist." While both of these terms can be seen as merely alternative terms for "creator," their association with artistic creativity as usually understood should not go unnoticed. The book itself can be seen as a sort of "monster," or creation of the author. Such creations can sometimes be seen

**Ruins of the inner part of Castle Frankenstein.
(Photo by Pascal Rehfeldt)**

to have a deleterious effect on the lives of their creators, and oftentimes the book can (through the ways in which it informs, inspires, and transforms its readers) seem to become wiser and more noble than the creator. Beyond this it also becomes a sort of immortal being, and by association brings immortality to the creator. These things can also be said of the monster as described in the narrative of *Frankenstein*. This would also be a key to the subtitle: "The Modern Prometheus." Prometheus is a figure of Greek mythology. He is a titan who challenges the authority of Zeus by stealing the divine fire from the gods and giving it to mankind. Humanity had up to that point been a disappointment to Zeus, who contemplated destroying the species. But by providing mankind with the fire of the gods, Prometheus helps to author the grandeur of mankind, which can actually be seen to eclipse the wisdom and greatness of the Olympians themselves.

Although in most of the films dealing with the Frankenstein Monster the creature is a hapless automaton, the characterization provided by Karloff in the original film, and especially in *The*

Bride of Frankenstein, clearly portray the creature as an example of the Outsider. Nowhere is this kinship more profoundly illustrated than in the *Bride* scene wherein the monster sees his own reflection in the water, which mirrors the experience of the Outsider in the story by H. P. Lovecraft described in the introduction. He has seen himself and thereby knows why he is being rejected by the Insiders. In the end, the Monster is only looking for love, friendship, and acceptance. This he cannot find, and so tries to bring himself to an end.

One aspect of the film that usually goes unnoticed is the fact that the Monster is endowed with the brain of a criminal. Fritz accidentally ruins the normal brain he was sent to steal from a laboratory. In many ways, we can assume that the character traits, defects, and qualities expressed by the Monster have their origins in organic makeup and in the previous life and experiences of the anonymous criminal whose brain has given shape to his life.

The Golem Legend

The relationship between the story of *Frankenstein* and the Jewish legend of the golem cannot go unremarked. In 1808 the Germanist Jacob Grimm, who is also one of the fathers of modern folklore studies, reported on the Jewish legend of the *golem*:

> The Polish Jews, after certain spoken prayers and observing fasting days, made an image of a man out of clay or earth, and when they spoke the miraculous *Schemhamphoras* over him, he had to become alive. He cannot speak at all, but he understands more or less what is said or commanded; they named him *Golem* and used him as a servant to take care of all sorts of housework, only he is never allowed to go outside the house. On his forehead is written the word *aemaeth* ("truth," or God), but every day he increases in size and becomes a bit bigger and stronger than everyone else in the house, no matter how small

he was in the beginning. Therefore, out of fear of him, they erase the first letter, so that nothing remains except *maeth* ("he is dead"), whereupon he collapses and turns back to clay.

But once for one man his *golem* became extremely tall, and out of carelessness he allowed him to keep growing, such that he could no longer reach up to his forehead. So then, out of fear, he ordered the (*golem*) servant to bend down and take off his boots, having the thought that when he bent down he could reach his forehead. This happened too, and the first letter was luckily obliterated, only the whole weight of the clay fell down upon the Jew and crushed him. (Quoted in Völker 1971, 7; my translation)

This narrative of the *golem* and how he is created is obviously based on ideas taken from Jewish magic and mythology. The ideology of the magic of Hebrew letters expounded in works such as the *Sepher Yetzirah* ("Book of Creation") is in play here. This Kabbalistic lore is the key to much of Jewish sorcery stemming from the Middle Ages.

Here magic, not science, is used to animate inanimate matter in imitation of the creation of man out of clay by the God of the Old Testament. In the originally censored portions of the 1931 film *Frankenstein*, Henry Frankenstein seems to make reference to this when he utters the words "Now I know what it feels like to be God!" in this dialogue exchange when the Monster first stirs with life after it has been animated by the electricity:

> **Henry Frankenstein**: Look! It's moving. It's alive. It's alive. It's moving, it's alive, it's alive, it's alive, it's alive, IT'S ALIVE!
> **Victor Moritz**: Henry—In the name of God!
> **Henry Frankenstein**: Oh, in the name of God! Now I know what it feels like to be God!

Illustration by Hugo Steiner for Gustav Meyrink's *The Golem* (1915).

In the original release the "blasphemous words" were obliterated with the sounds of electrical discharges from the special-effects machines provided by Kenneth Strickfaden, but have been recovered and restored. They can be heard in the Universal Legacy Collection version of the film.

The moral of the story in both the case of Mary Shelley's tale and the *golem* legend is the same: meddling in magic, or science, without foreknowledge and wisdom will lead to one's own destruction. This was an often-repeated message in many horror and science-fiction films of the twentieth century.

Other Themes

The theme of the *Doppelgänger* has sometimes been ascribed to the story of Frankenstein. At first glance this seems rather far-fetched, as Victor and his creation do not look similar. However, when we realize that Victor is the creator or author of the creature, and we also understand that any artist can only create in his art object a replica of himself, we can understand the creature being a double of Victor on a different level, perhaps on a higher octave of creation. But again, in order to make positive use of this kind of creation, the artist must be prepared to care for that creation, shepherd it into the world, and take responsibility for how it behaves in the wider cosmos. On these counts, Victor fails—and bears the horrifying consequences.

The apparent story is one of a scientist, a creator, an author of a creation who shapes a being with human characteristics, thoughts, and feelings and then abandons it, behaves irresponsibly toward it, and it takes its vengeance upon him and destroys the life of the creator and all that he loves. But beyond or behind this superficial narrative there is another one, which tells the story of a creator who, like Zeus, created a species of being which actually became his superior. In Mary Shelley's novel, the creature is clearly a being superior to Victor, yet who evolved with none of the advantages possessed by the creator. In this regard, *Frankenstein* continues to be a Romantic Manifesto which postulates that a simple being with simple desires and wishes is (in potential) a happier and better being than one driven by complex desires and schemes. Frankenstein's creature, like the Phantom of the Opera, is an outcast—an Outsider—who is rejected and scorned by the other beings in his environment, all of which drives him to his criminal behavior.

To a certain extent at every iteration of the Frankenstein saga there is the implicit Romantic criticism of the Myth of Progress. From the period of the Enlightenment onward, Western civilization has based itself on the idea of Progress. This is the concept that if mankind rationally dedicates itself to the solving of larger problems—in science, technology, and in the human social order—the human species can be *perfected*. In many ways, this was the secularization of the Christian Myth of Salvation. The Myth of Progress simply replaces faith with rational thought as the method or principle by which salvation or perfection can be achieved. The Romantic critique of the Myth of Progress hinged on the idea that emotion and matters of the heart must come before concerns of the intellect in order for the system to work. In so many ways our society is still carrying on these philosophical debates, but most often those engaging in the discussion are woefully ignorant of its history and development. What could be a crisp and focused discussion becomes a muddled mess of half-baked notions and unreflective reactions. Even philosophical constructs, as well-intentioned as they may have come into being, take on a life of their own and, like the Monster of Frankenstein, can come back to destroy those who created them. Think of the political constructs of the nineteenth century, such as Socialism, which begins as a hopeful desire to ensure freedom, prosperity, and justice for all and ends in oppression, poverty, and violence for most and in the gulags and concentration camps of the real monsters of history. *Frankenstein* remains a warning against the threat of the law of unintended consequences. Serious students of the history of the myth are forearmed against its effects.

The Universal Pictures series of *Frankenstein* films constitutes a tetralogy: *Frankenstein* (1931), *The Bride of Frankenstein* (1935), *Son of Frankenstein* (1939), and *The Ghost of Frankenstein* (1942), with a marvelous addendum: *Frankenstein Meets the Wolf Man* (1943). This last film is the first of the "monster mash-ups" that were to follow (*House of Frankenstein*, *House of Dracula*). But the 1943 film was more poignant than those other more commercially

The Bride of Frankenstein (1935)

desperate efforts. *Frankenstein Meets the Wolf Man* should really be seen as the second film in the "Larry Talbot Saga," as it is his drive to rid himself of the "curse" of his lycanthropy that sends him searching for the medical or scientific solutions that a Dr. Frankenstein could perhaps provide. This narrative thread is also strongly present in the later "*House of*" films and really serves as an element to propel their plots.

In each of the Universal *Frankenstein* films, the monster survives his supposed destruction at the end of the previous film in the series, because the monster appears indestructible. Although it was probably not "planned" or deliberately written up in a way to provide continuity from film to film, there does seem to be an unconscious theme about the logistics of how the monster survives. At the end of *Frankenstein*, the monster falls down through the floors of the burning windmill and lands in a pool of *water* below, out of which he rises up having survived the fire. At the end of *The Bride of Frankenstein*, the body of the monster must have fallen down into the *stone/earthen* rubble of the tower laboratory which was blown up by explosives. In *Son of Frankenstein*, Igor claims to have "found" the body of the monster, still alive, but weakened. At the end of that film, the monster is pushed into a subterranean lake of boiling sulphur, only to be recovered out of the solidified mineral by Igor at the beginning of *The Ghost of Frankenstein*. Again, at the end of that film, the monster supposedly succumbs to fire, but in *Frankenstein Meets the Wolf Man* we see that once more the monster has fallen into a subterranean body of *water*, which has been frozen into *ice*, such that Larry Talbot discovers him in this condition.

Perhaps on an esoteric and unconscious level, this sequence of forms of physical media in which the Monster is preserved expresses a certain meaningful, almost *alchemical*, progression. Water leads to rebirth and after he has been submerged in water below the mill, the Monster emerges to enter upon his most humanizing phase of life. At the conclusion of *The Bride of Frankenstein*, he is buried in stone rubble and the progress he had made is lost. After being submerged in boiling sulphur, he emerges in a weakened state until the lightning rejuvenates him. In alchemy, Sulphur is said to possess the quality of change, associated with the hot and dry qualities of fire—at the end of *The Ghost of Frankenstein*, the Monster is subjected to a fiery end, but apparently drops once more into a watery abyss below the castle, for it is in ice that Larry Talbot finds him in *Frankenstein Meets the Wolf Man*. Ice is a restrictive, entropic force. Now the

Frankenstein

Frankenstein Meets the Wolf Man (1943)

Monster has been reduced to a blind killing automaton. This state of blindness is written into the script, but it is never fully explained in the film. The Monster now has Igor's brain, and it is supposed to have been the incompatibility of blood types that has rendered the Monster blind.

But it must be admitted that the most enduring and deepest mystery of all the Frankenstein films is why, in the *Son of Frankenstein*, does Peter, the son of the elegant and distinguished Wolf and Else von Frankenstein, speak as if he were a cedar chopper's son from South Texas?

On the Mad Scientist or Magician

Certainly, one of the most persistent features of horror films over the years has been that of the "mad scientist." This topic really deserves an extensive essay of its own, but for now we will have to be satisfied with a brief excursion. Sometimes, when supernatural forces—rather than apparently natural ones—are

Les Yeux sans visage (1960)

in play, it appears that we could better speak of a "mad magician." In the case of magicians, however, it is more usually the case that we are dealing with the paradigm of a person who has invoked powers greater than he himself has the power to control. On the other hand, the mad scientist appears to be more classically insane because he is after all supposed to be a scientist, a rational man, whereas his experimental pursuits are usually highly irrational and even self-destructive, and hence "mad." But the archetypal "mad scientist" is not evil, at least not to begin with. He may be unwise, irresponsible, and even misguided, but the best of them always have some higher or more noble purpose in mind. The Rebbe Löw wants to save his people from oppression; Frankenstein is curious about the origin and nature of life; Dr.

Genessier wants to restore his daughter's beauty; and so on.

The mad scientist or doctor is often driven by love to do his questionable work. Two of the greatest examples of this are *Mad Love* (1935) and *Eyes without a Face* (1960). In the former, we find Dr. Gogol who is obsessed with an actress in the Theatre des Horreurs (based on the Grand Guignol, which existed in Paris from 1894 to 1962). This is a theater specializing in the presentations of tableaus of cruelty. *Mad Love* is based on a novel by the French master of science fiction, Maurice Renard, entitled *Les Mains d'Orlac*, which gave rise to several films over the years. *Mad Love* had the advantage of starring Peter Lorre at the apex of his talent. (Lorre is often misrepresented as a "Hungarian"; he was actually a German-speaking Jew from Austria who strongly identified with German culture). The screenplay was written by John Balderston and Guy Endore, and was directed by Karl Freund. Here we see the expected obsession of erotic love which drives the doctor to perform his insane experiments. Quite contrary to this, in the 1960 film *Eyes without a Face* (*Les Yeux sans visage*), we see Dr. Genessier, who is driven by his love for his disfigured daughter to engage in experiments in attempting to transplant a new face onto his daughter. (This type of medical procedure has recently passed out of the realm of the horror film and science fiction into medical fact.) But in the case of Dr. Genessier, he has to find some beautiful, yet unwilling, "donors" for his experiments. This necessitates the murder and mutilation of his victims. The mad doctor also apparently conducts experiments on animals, as he has a menagerie of laboratory animals in his secret clinic. But stereotypically, the mad scientist seems to be driven by a desire to dominate the world, to make the world respect and acknowledge his genius—often a genius that had been previously spurned or rejected by his scientific community.

Certainly the "mad scientist" has his most ancient corollary in the archetype of the visionary, mantic magician of more archaic times. The French theoretician of magic, Marcel Mauss, pointed out the essentially *antisocial* nature of magic and the magician. The technologies of what can be called religion and magic are virtually identical, or can be. The difference is that in religion, operations and rituals are dedicated to the correct and beneficial functioning of nature and culture for the general benefit of society as a whole. In the case of magic—or more precisely, *sorcery*—the benefit can be for an isolated individual separate from, and often contrary to, that of society as a whole. Thus, we see many tales of folklore that refer to the use of sorcery or magic in ways which are in fact dangerous to society or even to the individual who does not have the wisdom to guide the forces that are being summoned. This is the story of Frankenstein as well as most "mad scientists" of the horror genre.

VI
H. P. Lovecraft
and the
Shadows
Out of Time

Howard Phillips Lovecraft impresses himself more and more onto the popular culture of the world as each year goes by. Almost entirely ignored in his lifetime, he now commands attention from a wide variety of people, although recently he has also excited controversy among the politically correct. Still he, and his works, and those of his students and followers, excite people from social groups as diverse as occultists and magicians, role-playing gamers, science-fiction or horror writers, and professors and political activists. Literary critics have always widely denigrated Lovecraft for his style and for just about every other reason. But even there he may have been cleverer than he appears at first glance.

As a kid, the last movie to scare me was *Die, Monster, Die!* (1965), starring Boris Karloff and Nick Adams, which was released in 1965. The screenplay for this film was based on H. P. Lovecraft's story "The Colour Out of Space" (1927). I remember it played on a double bill with Mario Bava's *Planet of the Vampires*. Another film that had been especially creepy to me was *The Haunted Palace* (1963). This movie was billed as being based on E. A. Poe (from his poem of that name), but actually it was based on the Lovecraft novella entitled *The Case of Charles Dexter Ward* (1927). Looking back on my reactions to these films now, I see that the reason these movies were disturbing to me as a kid was not that they were done all that differently from the other American International releases of the day, but because of the deep, almost *atavistic*, quality of the source material. No matter how badly the source was mangled, the lurking power of the Great Old Ones would still shine through, as if carried on the *colour* out of space, right into the darkness of the Casa Linda movie theater. As we will witness, even Lovecraft's literary output was similarly colored by later writers who used his frame material (which came to be called the Cthulhu Mythos) to expand on their own imaginations.

In the cases of these films, each of them has a significant literary background that may not have been used to construct the narrative of the stories in detail, but nevertheless served to shape—even if almost unconsciously—an underlying mythic substrate which would shine through in veiled ways. This hidden otherworldly glow is what is most responsible for the unsettling feeling one gets while watching these movies. There just seems to be *something* more, or *other*, going on than what is found in the normal horror picture—even if the filmmakers did their best to make them appear to be like any other horror film.

H. P. Lovecraft

Despite the fact that Howard Phillips Lovecraft lived a short and externally uneventful life, major biographies have been written about him, and his thoughts, words, and works have earned him devotion both during his own lifetime and thereafter. His popularity has only grown over the years, although his actual philosophy, once understood, has also earned him a newfound disdain in certain circles.

He was born on August 20, 1890, in Providence, Rhode Island, and died at the age of 46 in that same city on March 15, 1937. Howard was a child prodigy: he was reciting poetry by age two, reading by three, and writing stories by six. Yet, due to emotional disorders, he was unable to finish high school. He

Howard Phillips Lovecraft, photographed in June 1934.

became a recluse, sleeping by day and reading by night. After about five years he began to find meaning in writing and began publishing around 1913. From early on he was a prolific letter writer and it is estimated that he wrote around 100,000 letters in his lifetime, especially to many fellow writers and fans such as Forrest J Ackerman, Fritz Leiber, Frank Belknap Long, A. Merritt, E. Hoffmann Price, Clark Ashton Smith, Julius Schwartz, August Derleth, Robert E. Howard, and a young Robert Bloch.

Lovecraft's productive years were between 1917 and 1935. He lived almost his whole life in Providence, leaving only during the time of his short-lived marriage to Sonia Greene (1924–1926) when he lived in Brooklyn, New York. His stories were only published in pulp magazines, such as *Weird Tales*, during his lifetime, and always for very low pay. Lovecraft spent much of his life in poverty, sometimes going without food in order to be able to pay the postage for letters to his correspondents. During the last two or three years of his life, he had even ceased to try to sell his stories to the pulps. His fiction output covers what would later be published in book form as three volumes of prose and one of prose which he either ghostwrote or massively revised for other writers (often inserting elements from his "Cthulhu Mythos" into them). After Lovecraft's death, his friend August Derleth became his *de facto* literary executor, also publishing many stories based on fragments, notes, and ideas suggested by Lovecraft.

Lovecraftian Literature and Films

From 1965 to 1973, four major motion pictures were made from ideas suggested by four works by H. P. Lovecraft. These were the aforementioned *The Haunted Palace* and *Die, Monster, Die!*, plus two more in the 1970s: *The Dunwich Horror* (1970) and *The Shuttered Room* (1967). The first three of these were supposedly based on works written entirely by Lovecraft, while *The Shuttered Room* goes back to a story written by August Derleth based on Lovecraft's ideas. These pictures force the narrative structure into a more conventional, "Gothicized" framework: there is usually the obligatory romance and involvement of the themes of innocent young women being drawn into dangerous and horrifying circumstances. None of these elements are ever found in the Lovecraft tales themselves.

The Haunted Palace

The Haunted Palace is based on the Lovecraft novella *The Case of Charles Dexter Ward*. Originally, Roger Corman simply wanted to make a film based on the Lovecraft story, but the studio insisted on making it part of the lucrative Edgar Allan Poe series of films and so retitled it after a poem by Poe and connected it to his name. The Lovecraft story concerns the investigation of Doctor Marinus Bicknell Willett into the case of one of his patients, Charles Dexter Ward, who had been committed to a mental institution due to insanity and physiological changes, but who was now reported missing from his cell. Dr. Willett discovers that Ward had earlier spent years trying to find the grave of one of his notorious ancestors, a certain Joseph Curwen, an eighteenth-century shipping magnate reputed to be an alchemist—but also a necromancer and murderer. A secret report about a raid conducted on Curwen's farm included incantations, weird lights, explosions, and the fact that the raiders shot a number of inhuman entities.

Willett's investigations show that Ward had recovered Curwen's ashes and, using magical formulas concealed in Curwen's home in Providence, he resurrected his dead ancestor from his "essential saltes." It turns out that Curwen, who greatly resembles his descendant, murders Ward and assumes his identity—whereupon he resumes his malevolent activities. But since Curwen behaves and speaks so differently, he is assumed to be Ward gone insane. He is then locked up in the asylum. Willett's investigation brings him to a house in Pawtuxet Village built on the site of Curwen's old farmstead. He discovers a catacomb under the house and during a terrifying journey through it discovers a malformed monster in a pit and also finds out about the intergenerational conspiracy Curwen was involved in to resurrect powerful men from the past and obtain their

The Haunted Palace (1963)

secrets to control the future of the world. In the course of this investigation, Willett calls up an entity hostile to Curwen, but passes out during the experience. He wakes up in the house, with the entrance to the underworld sealed, but in possession of a document written in Latin which instructs him how to destroy Curwen. Willett goes to Curwen in the asylum and reverses the spell of resurrection and Curwen falls to dust.

The film Roger Corman produced based on this story begins in the year 1765 when the town of Arkham is suspicious of the strange goings on in the large palace-like estate that overlooks the town. They think the owner, Joseph Curwen (Vincent Price) is a warlock. There is a scene in which a young girl wanders up to the house as if in a trance, enters and is led to a subterranean dungeon, where she is bound and made a part of a bizarre ritual in which an invisible creature rises up from a covered pit. The girl is seen leaving the palace, still in a trance. The townspeople storm the palace and drag Curwen out, tie him to a tree and burn him as a warlock. Before he dies, he pronounces a curse that he will rise from the dead and take his vengeance.

The scene shifts to 110 years later as Curwen's great-great-grandson, Charles Dexter Ward and his wife, Anne, arrive in Arkham to claim Ward's inheritance of the mansion. He notices the great number of deformed individuals wandering around the town. Examining the house, Ward sees a painting of Curwen, and notices the strong resemblance between them. He becomes increasingly obsessed with Curwen and his demeanor seems to change.

A local doctor named Marinus Willet explains the story of Curwen's death to Ward and indicates to him that the curse is blamed for many of the children of the townsfolk being deformed. Dr. Willet recounts that Curwen owned the *Necronomicon* and could invoke the Elder Gods, such as Cthulhu and Yog-Sothoth, and that it was Curwen's plan to mate mortal women with these entities to breed a new superhuman race. This is what led to the inherited deformities among the people of the town.

Eventually, Ward is fully possessed by the spirit of the dead Curwen, as are the descendants of others still living there. Curwen/Ward begins to take his revenge on the descendants of those who burned him on that tree. Panic spreads in the town and the people make plans to storm the mansion. Dr. Willet and Anne try to rescue "Charles," but they are ambushed, and Anne is prepared to be the new "mate" of the thing down below. The townspeople breech the house and begin to burn it, the portrait of Curwen is destroyed, and Charles is at least partially restored to his current identity. Anne is released and they all escape the destruction. In the end, it is hinted that the spirit of Curwen is not entirely absent from Ward's body.

The Colour Out of Space

"The Colour Out of Space" is story told from the point of view of a nameless surveyor sent to a site near Arkham called the "blasted heath," to find out what happened there to cause the calamity. This is traced back to a meteorite that fell onto the land of a farmer named Nahum Gardner. The surveyor learns the story from a man named Ammi Pierce who lived through "the horror." After the meteorite fell scientists from Miskatonic University try to study it, but the specimens are destroyed. The area, especially around the farm's well, emits a strange colour—something other than what is normal for our visible terrestrial spectrum. The crops that come in the next year are large, but foul tasting and inedible. Animals in the area are altered in strange, but undescribed ways. Members of the Gardner family slowly go mad and have to be locked in the attic. The whole area has a strange *glow* in the dark. The well on the farm seems to be the center of the strange phenomenon. The Gardner family isolates itself from the rest of the community, with only Ammi as an informant.

Two of Nahum's sons disappear, and one dies. Ammi visits the farmstead and discovers the horrors being exerted by the colour out of space, which destroys the whole Gardner family. Ammi flees and returns with six other men from Arkham to examine the ruins of the farm. They discover the skeletal remains of Nahum's sons along with several other creatures in the bottom of the well. Whatever this thing is, it has been feeding on the living beings in its vicinity, drawing them to it and holding them in a mysterious grip. While they are there the colour begins to emit from the well and spread all over the area. Later Ammi returns to the farm with six other men and they discover the remains of Nahum's sons at the bottom of the well along with the skeletons of several other creatures. Soon after that the colour starts to rise out of the well and then something shoots up out of the well and into the sky. A small part of it remains behind and returns to the well. The surveyor reports that Ammi's mind is not right, as he fears that remaining part of the "colour." It is hoped that the whole area will soon be covered by a reservoir.

This fairly simple story—weird meteor falls, emits deadly force, and is apparently the extraterrestrial (or extra-dimensional) vehicle for a sentient being which devours living things and lives in the well, only to (mostly) return whence it came—is remodeled

Die, Monster, Die! (1965)

into a standard Gothic narrative by the AIP filmmakers. We meet Stephen Reinhart (Nick Adams) as an American scientist who visits the estate of his fiancée's family, the Witleys, in England. There he finds a devastated landscape around the house and a nearby meteor crater. The local inhabitants would not help him find the place or talk to him about the family. His fiancée's father, Nahum Witley (Boris Karloff), is keeping the radioactive meteorite in his basement and using it in experiments to mutate plant and animal life. These experiments cause mutation and madness in their subjects. Latetia, Nahum's wife, is mutated and driven insane—she dies in an attack on Steve and Susan. Then the maid, Helga, who has been mutated and driven mad by the radiation attacks Nahum, falls on the meteorite and causes Nahum to mutate himself. Now the mutated Nahum comes after Steve and Susan, falls from a balcony, and hits the floor in a burst of fire—which predictably burns the whole mansion down. Steve and Susan escape and live happily ever after. On the face of it, this all seems absurd. Perhaps it was the whole radiation theme just three years after the Cuban Missile Crisis and while we were still regularly doing duck-and-cover drills in school that creeped me out so much. But even more likely is that the Colour Out of Space simply glowed through the ludicrous plot of *Die, Monster, Die!*

The Dunwich Horror

In the story written by Lovecraft entitled "The Dunwich Horror" we read of the remote and decaying village of Dunwich, the home of the Whateley family. There a son, named Wilbur, is born to a deformed albino woman named Lavinia Whateley. The patriarch of the family, a sorcerer known as Old Zebulon Whateley brings the boy up on his isolated farm. The landscape is dotted with hills adorned with standing stones and apparent sacrificial stone tables. Wilbur grows at an unnatural rate and has a strange appearance and odor. Zebulon indicates that Wilbur's father is someone, or something, known as Yog-Sothoth. The old man also teaches his grandson things from his library of fragmentary and decayed tomes. Among the volumes is a fragment of the *Necronomicon*. But this most important text is missing certain sections. Much time is spent enlarging the farmhouse over the years to contain *something* that is large and growing in the building. Cattle are bought from local farmers, which either disappear into the house or are later seen with oozing wounds on them. In due course old Zebulon dies, and Lavinia also disappears. Wilbur has to move the contents of the house out into outbuildings, as the entity in the house has grown to occupy the entire space of the building.

It is Wilbur's intention to open the gates to allow the Great Old Ones entry back into this world which they once ruled and will rule again, with his help. To do this he needs the pages missing from his copy of the *Necronomicon*. Dr. Henry Armitage, the librarian of the university refuses him access to the book. To get this material he breaks into the library of the Miskatonic University, but he is killed by a guard dog—witnesses observe the monstrously grotesque features of his anatomy before his body disintegrates.

Without Wilbur to tend to the entity in the Whateley house, it grows and breaks out and during nightly forays into the countryside and begins to lay waste to farms, killing people and livestock. The thing is invisible, but leaves prints the size of barrels wherever it goes. Dr. Armitage, using a powder to render the creature momentarily visible, also employs spells from the *Necronomicon* to destroy the entity. In the end, Dr. Armitage explains:

> But to this thing we've just sent back—the Whateleys raised it for a terrible part in the doings that were to come. It grew fast and big from the same reason that Wilbur grew fast and big—but it beat him because it had a greater share of the *outsidedness* in it. You needn't ask how Wilbur called it out of the air. He didn't call it out. *It was his twin brother, but it looked more like the father than he did.* (Lovecraft 1963, 202)

The film version of *The Dunwich Horror* (1970) is an AIP production of Roger Corman with a screenplay written in part by the Academy Award–winning writer (for *L.A. Confidential*) Curtis Hanson in his first major effort. The story is very much in line with other post–*Rosemary's Baby* horror films. Departing from the Lovecraftian ambiance by making Wilbur a suave playboy, full of virile and seductive charm, while the extra-dimensional cult that he seems to be involved with (seen mostly in the dreams of the girl he is trying to seduce into the cult) is a quasi-hippy, free-love, pagan, orgiastic sort of thing. It could easily be taken that Wilbur is just trying to loosen up an uptight world, man.

The Dunwich Horror (1970)

I very much suspect that this film had a great deal to do with the growth in interest in Lovecraft by actual practicing magicians and occultists. The two most widely published accounts of actual occult ideas in Lovecraft (Kenneth Grant's *The Magical Revival* and Anton LaVey's *The Satanic Rituals*) appeared just two years after this film's debut very early in the year 1970.

At the beginning of the film we see a woman give birth to what are apparently twins. Then we jump forward in time twenty years to see Dr. Henry Armitage of Miskatonic University finishing a lecture and handing his assistant, the lovely Nancy Wagner (Sandra Dee), the rare *Necronomicon* to return to the library. She is followed by a handsome stranger who introduced himself as Wilbur Whateley (Dean Stockwell). He asks to look at the book

H. P. Lovecraft and the Shadows Out of Time

and under his hypnotic charm she allows it. Armitage interrupts and takes the book away. The professor warns Nancy as he is aware of the Whateley family's reputation for sorcery. Wilbur manipulates Nancy into taking him home in her car, invites her into his strange house in Dunwich out the country. There he invites her in, drugs her with a potion (which causes strange visions and dreams of pagan orgies). Wilbur's grandfather old Zebulon Whateley (Sam Jaffe) warns Wilbur to send her away. Her car is disabled by Wilbur and she decides to spend the weekend with him. Armitage and Nancy's classmate, Elizabeth, come looking for her and Nancy refuse to leave. Armitage and Elizabeth investigate and discover that Wilbur's mother, Lavinia is still alive, living in an insane asylum. She had given birth to twins, but one was stillborn. The process was so traumatic, she lost her mind and almost died. Elizabeth enters the Whateley home to investigate further and opens a locked door—releasing what is apparently Wilbur's hideous twin, which kills Elizabeth and escapes into the countryside. When Wilbur and Nancy return, Zebulon confronts them and is accidentally killed in a fall down the stairs. Wilbur tires to conduct a "nameless rite" funeral in the town cemetery but is run off by a mob of New England redneck Christians. Meanwhile Wilbur's twin is invisibly running wild in the countryside, the Whateley estate burns down and Wilbur has mounted a seaside ritual altar to open the gate to his father—Yog-Sothoth. Nancy is offered to the father for mating purposes (Wilbur seems intent on sloppy seconds!). But Armitage, armed with the *Necronomicon*, hurls counter-spells at Wilbur causing him to be struck by lightning and killed. In the end Nancy is led away, apparently unharmed, but it is indicated that she is pregnant with the child of her extra-dimensional suitor.

The Shuttered Room

"The Shuttered Room," a story that is actually a posthumous "collaboration" between Lovecraft and August Derleth, tells the story of Abner Whateley who has received a sophisticated scientific education while away from his ancestral home at Dunwich. His grandfather, Luther Whateley, has died and left him his estate and written instructions on how to deal with it. Abner remembers that his grandfather had shuttered up his daughter, Sarah in a room attached to the old mill. The document tells him to kill anything he finds alive in that room, no matter how small or *humaniform* it might appear. Sarah had been locked away by her father after she had visited their relatives, the Marsh family, from the coastal town of Innsmouth and cavorted with them in a lascivious manner. Abner remembers seeing his grandfather take food—raw meat—to his aunt's room. Sarah lived out her whole life in that room.

When Abner goes to explore the forbidden shuttered room, he finds only scattered bedclothes a few pieces of furniture and a horrible fishy smell. Abner breaks the shutters and also a bit of the glass pane in an attempt to get fresh air into the squalid den. He does see a small, apparently toadlike creature scamper under a bureau, but pays it little heed.

The next day Abner meets various relatives who express a concern that he has not returned "to start things up again." As Abner examines the mill for anything of value, he notices tiny batrachian webbed foot- or handprints on the millwheel leaning to and from Sarah's old chamber. Luther finds papers describing the unusual activities of the Marshes who mixed with South Sea islanders, how they acquired a degenerate appearance and their worship of strange gods such as Dagon and Cthulhu. The story goes that these "islanders" were actually Deep Ones, an amphibian race that dwells in an underwater city offshore near Devil's Reef. These brings grow large the more they are fed and become smaller with less food. It is reported that Sarah was seen cavorting naked with a man named Ralsa Marsh and a whole swarm of other Innsmouthers. The document further reveals that Luther had locked Sarah up in the room, and at one point mentions that "R. is out again." Then there is a list of various sorts of killings that took place in the vicinity, first it is small animals, then large ones, and finally people. An entry follows: "R. back at last." Abner then reads that it was then that Luther nailed the shutters on Sarah's windows closed. After this Abner discovers that the window he had broken in the room is now completely pushed out from the inside. And the area party-line phone is buzzing with news about mutilated cows and homes are being threatened by some large thing that shuffles and hops about. Much anxiety is expressed as to whether "it's come back." Furthermore, Abner learns that the locals are starting to blame *him* for the renewed troubles. So he makes preparations to escape the area, but as he is leaving a noise comes from the blighted room, which causes him to investigate. When he enters the room with an oil lamp for illumination he finds a huge and hideous half-human, half-amphibian creature squatting in the middle of the room—it lunges at Abner and he throws the oil lamp in self-defense, setting the thing on fire. It screams out in agony: "Mama–mama–ma-aa-ma-ma-aaah!" The whole of the mill and house go up in flames and Abner makes his getaway. Sarah had borne an amphibian child from her unholy union with her cousin Ralsa Marsh, and they lived together in the shuttered room until her death and Abner's accidental release of the little monster, who again grew large on the things it ate in the countryside.

The film made bearing the title "The Shuttered Room" appears to have been only vaguely suggested by the short story. It tells of a young woman returning to her childhood home which she has inherited. She had been sent away when she was very young to protect her from some horrible thing. It turns out the horrible thing is her twin sister who lives in a shuttered room, a twin that is apparently mentally and emotionally disturbed—and homicidal. In the end the whole building is destroyed by fire, with the "evil twin" inside. In England the film was released under the title *Blood Island*. The most Lovecraftian thing about it is the gang of degenerate and violent New England rednecks who harass people.

The Unspeakable Truth

H. P. Lovecraft is well known for having little to no reference to sexuality or romance in his stories. Any hint of "romance" is entirely absent and female characters almost totally lacking. Lovecraft's world is virtually male-only. Attempts to "psychoanalyze" Lovecraft through his writings seem misguided—especially those of a Freudian bent which view the tentacles and gaping mouths of the entities he describes with the all-too-obvious interpretation. The usual effort to decode the inner mysteries of Lovecraft's universe through these means focus on his supposedly repressed sexuality. His "monsters" (or Elder Gods) are symbolic of the repressed contents of his own psyche. He feared sexuality, so he projected it onto his monstrous atavistic entities of eldritch horror. These interpretations might seem plausible due to the details of the author's biography coupled with the popularity of such interpretations of literature and life during the mid-twentieth century. This form of literary criticism is called *positivism*. Such interpretations are also convincing to some because the hold a *grain of truth* in them—but they do not reveal any *hidden truth*, which is what interests us here.

The truth of Lovecraft is that a large part of his mythos is in fact *sexual*, but not erotic. When the post-Freudian person hears the word "sex," images of eroticism and physical beauty most typically spring to mind. But Lovecraftian sex strips the topic bare of all aesthetics and romance. It becomes what it was originally—a means for the production and reproduction of organic entities—physical bodies. Viewed from his cosmicist perspective, this process is enormous and involves unfathomable expanses of time and space. H. P. Lovecraft, referred to his own philosophy as "Cosmicist." Cosmicism is an atheistic philosophy which holds that the cosmos is entirely *indifferent* even to the very existence of humanity.

Repeatedly, Lovecraft refers to this process of sexual reproduction in the context of organic degeneration. In the post-Darwinian intellectual culture of the West hope was held out for the perfection of humanity by means of selective breeding, or *eugenics*. On the one hand Mr. Lovecraft must have sympathized with these ideas—so his view of horror and the "weird" was tinged with, if not defined by, the possibilities of *dysgenics*. This means that society as well as individuals could actually regress, devolve, from a civilized state back into a primordial condition bordering on the amphibian level. In eons past, when protohumans were in this state, they worshipped entities called the Old Ones. As a part of their devolution they desired to call these old Ones back to rule the world again, as they had in those epochs of abysmal time.

Today Lovecraft is sometimes attacked for his politically incorrect attitudes, although these attitudes appear to have been no more radical than many an average man of his time period and locality. He is derided for being a racist, but he only occasionally even mentioned people of other races in his stories. Far and away, he saved his most horrified sensibilities for his own "white trash" New Englanders. A large part of his whole mythology and storytelling methods are tied up with the deplorable dysgenic conditions he thought were to be found in the New England countryside—his mythic Miskatonic valley. In "The Dunwich Horror" he describes conditions there:

> the natives are now repellently decadent, having gone far along that path of regression so common in many New England backwaters. They have come to form a race by themselves, with well-defined mental and physical stigmata of degeneracy and inbreeding. The average of their intelligence is woefully low, whilst their annals reek of overt viciousness and of half-hidden murders, incests, and deeds of almost unnamable violence and perversity. The old gentry, representing the two or three armigerous families which came from Salem in 1692, have kept somewhat above the general level of decay; though many branches are sunk into the sordid populace so deeply that only their names remain as a key to the origin they disgrace. (Lovecraft 1963, 162)

This—and not the kind of "racism" that critics hope to see more of—is the real underpinning of the hidden Lovecraft cultural mythos. Frequently, Lovecraft represents these people as New England rednecks, with atrocious dialects and degenerate habits and customs. It is these people who Lovecraft sees as delving into the worship of the Old Ones and mixing with the Deep Ones. Lovecraft's pages absolutely ooze with examples of dysgenics and cultural and "racial" degeneracy. By no means was Lovecraft an oddball when it came to these attitudes: they were firmly a part of the educated establishment of the day. Hitler got most of his ideas about eugenics from American programs aimed at this purpose and Henry Ford was the Führer's hero when it came to anti-Semitism, as well as building cars "for the people"—hence the *Volkswagen* ("people's car"). The book *White Trash* (2016) by Nancy Eisenberg outlines this aspect of late nineteenth- and early twentieth-century American culture in a way that betrays typical ideological bias, but which is nevertheless factually informative for our purposes here. The American eugenics movement was enormous and well established, and fear and demonization of rural poor, uneducated Caucasians equally well entrenched. Lovecraft's attitudes toward genetic degeneracy raising the specter of monstrous and hideous defects in the bodies and societies of America were not unique, but his folding of these ideas into the narratives of weird tales with occult overtones was a marvelous stroke of genius.

Another factor is that Lovecraft seems to project his anxieties onto the outside world, onto the dimensions of unspeakable chaos and obscene angles, whereby this realm is invited and drawn toward our world by degenerate amphibian half-humans, and that this fear of degenerate madness may have been something he actually felt could be a hidden, repressed part of himself. His parents each spent time in a mental institution, and both actually died there. He himself had suffered from mental breakdowns, such as the one that prevented him from finishing high school. With his beliefs, these circumstances must have fueled a frightful imagination surrounded by the specter of belonging himself to one of those "decayed" families he describes in his stories.

The literary output of H. P. Lovecraft is in many ways similar to the character of what I have ascribed to the horror films of the early twentieth century. They are a sort of self-created Rorschach Text: unfiltered contents of the unconscious expressed on the page in the form of a crafted tale within the context of a self-created, artificial mythology. Although perhaps Lovecraft did not invent the idea of an *artificial* mythology, and others, probably independent of him would use this idea later (e.g., J. R. R. Tolkien) his Cthulhu Mythos would prove to be the most widely inspirational mythology of its kind in the history of literature. Many important and influential writers, well established in their own right, wrote stories set in the Mythos. These include Clark Ashton Smith, Robert E. Howard, Frank Belknap Long, Robert Bloch, Fritz Leiber, Colin Wilson, Stephen King, and Don Webb.

The Essence of the Mythos

"Cthulhu Mythos" was not a term used by Lovecraft; it was later applied to the set of ideas he used as a backstory for his tales and which was picked up by his friends, students, and admirers, especially in the years following his death. Stories actually written by Lovecraft show a general informality toward the entities he describes, and he had to remind correspondents that they were entirely fictional, because he made them seem so real. His later followers coined the term "Cthulhu Mythos." He humorously referred to the system as "Yog-Sothothery."

Part of the way in which Lovecraft's artificial mythology worked, and became so believable to some people, is that he also insinuated his mythic features into the writers whose stories he either edited or with whom he collaborated (e.g., Hazel Heald, Zealia Bishop, C. M. Eddy), and then, or course, his friends (such as Robert E. Howard and Robert Bloch) began to include these elements themselves. In the end readers were seeing these elements, for example the Necronomicon, showing up in the works of a dozen writers contributing stories to a variety of competing magazines. The real and imaginary were cleverly mixed: Agrippa and the Necronomicon would be mentioned together, so when the reader discovers that Agrippa was a real person, well, then why couldn't Abdul Alhazred also be real?

Lovecraft was a voracious reader and was nicknamed "Abdul All*Has*Read" by the family lawyer. He worked historical

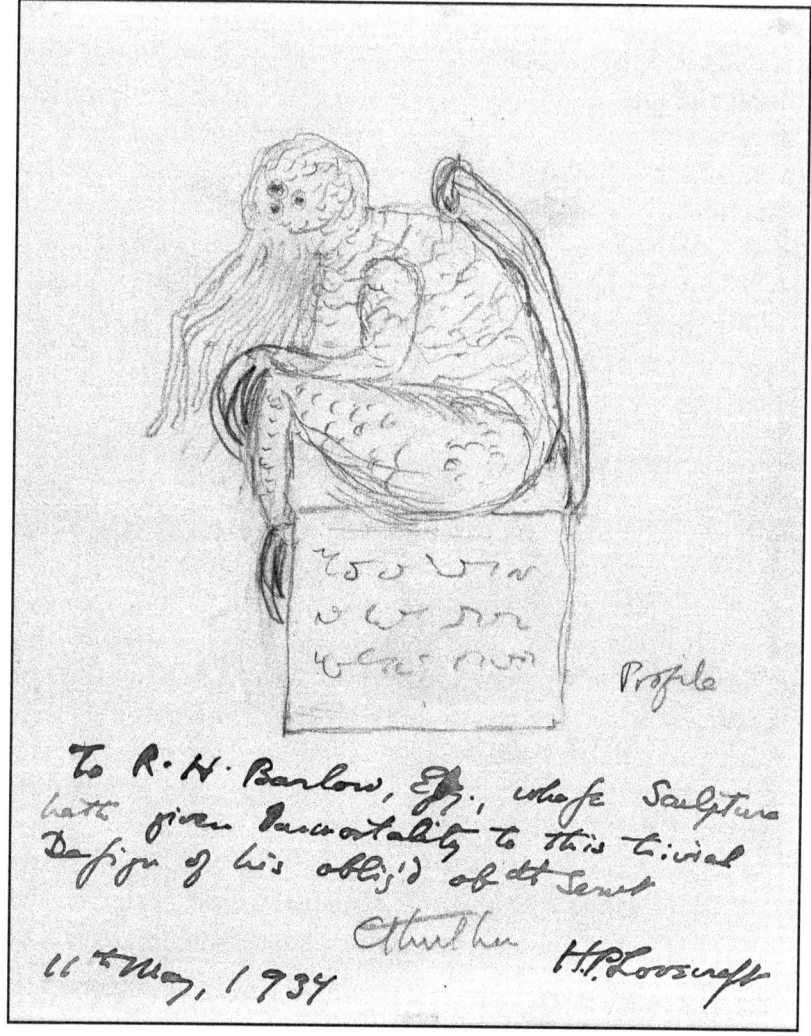

Pencil sketch of Cthulhu by Lovecraft, 1934.

details into his writing that later act as "depth charges" to his readers. The average reader of *Weird Tales* probably didn't know that Tibet is called Leng, that Nan Madol had extensive oddly angled megalithic architecture, or that Rhode Island (unlike the rest of Puritan New England) had an "occult scene" in the 1600s. Lovecraft planted these facts in his tales in a manner that gave a feeling of uncovering a conspiracy to his more educated readers. This eventually led to very strange waters in the 1950s when some

French eccentrics began producing a fusion of Lovecraft, UFOs, Nazi occultism, and Gurdjieff in *Planète* magazine—attaining its zenith in a book entitled *The Morning of the Magicians*. One of the fringy guys of the time, Dr. Jacques Vallee, met the American Satanist Anton LaVey just after LaVey began tinkering with Lovecraftian themes. So, the shadowy realm of pseudoscience and fringe history was again remixed and served up fresh.

The broad outlines of his mythic structure are this: that we live in a world that should be ruled by logic and reason, but that there is an abysmally older chaotic realm which existed in the past, and which still exists in another dimension of space/time which constantly tries to reassert itself. This realm and its inhabitants are for the most part entirely indifferent to the existence of human beings. Yet there are examples here and there where humans are so degenerate that they come into a sense of alliance with the chaotic realm. These form cults and try to aid the Old Ones in their attempts to return.

In a sense, Lovecraft was philosophically betrayed by some of his followers, such as August Derleth. Because Lovecraft was a materialistic atheist, a cosmicist in his terminology, and Derleth was a Christian, the two views did not make for a harmonious philosophical relationship. Not only did later writers try to create a formality surrounding the structure of the mythology and the entities that inhabited it, they also inserted ideas of good versus evil into the pantheon of entities. For Lovecraft the "good" consisted of logical, straightforward, scientific thinking, and whatever was "degenerate" or caused something to be "degenerate" was frightening and repulsive. His narrative genius created protagonists who were logical in their thinking, but had to realize, usually only gradually, that the other realm or dimension with its inhabitants *actually exists*.

Conclusion and Aftershocks

Although Lovecraft's own attitudes and ideas on politics, culture, and the writing of weird fiction are fairly well documented, contemporary fans and fantasists have often ascribed a more mysterious and sinister value to his works. The idea that

Lovecraft's mythos conceals and reveals some esoteric *reality* is commonplace among some groups and with some individuals. The attitude toward this aspect can run the gamut from the playfully imaginative (as in the case of Michael A. Aquino) to the deadly serious (as with Kenneth Grant). The great cosmic moment for this breakthrough seems to have come around the year 1972.

Although Kenneth Grant was the first to write about Lovecraft as if he had articulated a coherent esoteric and magical philosophy, albeit perhaps unconsciously produced, Michael Bertiaux was the first to make Lovecraftian ideas part of an active working magical system in conjunction with his "Monastery of the Seven Rays" during the 1960s. Both of these writers were, however, preceded decades earlier by one Morris Doreal in the 1920s, whose writings for the Brotherhood of the White Temple made use of various themes gleaned from the pulp magazine *Weird Tales* and elsewhere, including the name Yog-Sog-Thoth (apparently reconfigured by Lovecraft into Yog-Sothoth). Anton LaVey utilized Doreal's material, drawn from his work *The Emerald Tablets of Thoth the Atlantean* in creating the quasi-Lovecraftian ritual masterpiece known as "Die Elektrischen Vorspiele," published in the 1972 book *The Satanic Rituals*.

In many regards, Lovecraft spawned a set of ideas that are very much akin to a *religion*. We see this same phenomenon today in popular culture from Lord of the Rings to Harry Potter, and from Star Trek to Star Wars. Lovecraft's visions were, however, more similar to real mythic content, in the sense that individuals were left to innovate and evolve the mythos to suit their predilections throughout time.

One of the most interesting innovators in the genre of Lovecraftian esotericism is the aforementioned Michael A. Aquino, who wrote all of the explicitly Lovecraftian sections of the infamous *Satanic Rituals* book. He would later elaborate on the construction of these rituals in subsequent publications. An insider's view of the history behind the production of these rituals is contained in Aquino's two-volume work, *The Church of Satan* (2013). Aquino habilitated—or revalorized—the

Lovecraftian gods into tutelary beings who inspire their seekers to risk madness to gain great knowledge. The rituals he wrote are actually participatory philosophical treatises in the guise of "nameless and obscene" Lovecraftian rites. The most resent blossom on this unspeakable spawn of Yuggoth is *Infernal Geometry* by Toby Chappell (2019).

An insightful study of Kenneth Grant's ideas on Lovecraft is supplied in the book *The Necronomicon Files* by Daniel Harms and John Wisdom Gonce III (2003), where it is made clear that Grant believed that Lovecraft was accessing some other dimension (through his dreams most especially) and that this other plane of reality was somehow akin to, and contained correspondences with, the magical world of the English magician Aleister Crowley, of whom Grant had been a student.

All objective research indicates that Lovecraft had no special knowledge of, nor certainly no active interest in, the practice of magic or the occult. His use of these ideas or themes were just part of a viewpoint that thought of these things as degenerate and backward—and hence to his sensibilities, especially *frightening*. But again, Lovecraft was a genius and in this regard his genius shone though in his unconventional (and, for the time, pseudoscientific) description of "magic." There was the famous "grimoire" called the *Necronomicon*, supposedly compiled by the "mad Arab" Abdul Alhazred, which might be considered conventional enough as a theme by itself, but having it weave in and out of stories makes it almost like a character unto itself (this feature was borrowed from Robert W. Chambers's *The King in Yellow*). But it was the idea of entities specifically entering from other dimensions of space/time—and doing so by means of something described as an obscene geometry of strange non-Euclidian angles and planes in conjunction with arcane rituals—that really sparked the imagination of readers (and fellow writers) in new ways. This was not just medieval-style sorcerers making pacts with devils, this was something *new*—and hence far more "believable" and therefore more frightening to contemporary readers.

Those who wrote the screenplays of the early adaptations of

Lovecraft's works certainly read his works to a greater or lesser extent. *The Haunted Palace* and *The Dunwich Horror* especially demonstrate some understanding of the principles of Lovecraft's universe. This was less so with *Die, Monster, Die!*, and *The Shuttered Room* did not really reflect much of core Lovecraftian ideas. But in all cases at least some of the mythos came creeping through, despite efforts—conscious or commercial—to dampen them down. That, if nothing else, is a testimony to the power and persistence and strength of the Lovecraftian dream.

I'A RY'GZENGRHO

VII

The Mysteries of Edgar A. Poe

And while I thus spoke, did there not cross your mind some thought of the physical power of words? Is not every word an impulse on the air?
—Edgar A. Poe, "The Power of Words" (1845)

As a Monster Kid, I stood in line in front of the Casa Linda movie theater in Dallas, Texas in the early 1960s on many a Saturday morning to see the latest—usually American International Pictures—release. Many of these had their titles preceded by "Edgar Allan Poe's ———." If Poe's name could be attached to a film in any way, it was. Sometimes these were very tenuous or even nonexistent connections. But in any case, Poe's name was thought to be box-office gold. This gold bug had been around since the 1930s when Universal made three films based on or "inspired by" Poe: *Murders in the Rue Morgue* (1932), *The Black Cat* (1934), and *The Raven* (1935). All of these also became parts of the Shock Package that played on the Saturday night monster shows. But a more mature look at things would reveal that Poe's creativity and genius expresses a gold of a rather more refined sort.

In the general estimation of the rest of the world, Poe is one of the two truly great American writers. The other is Mark

Twain. Poe is best known to us as a "horror writer" but he was and is much more than that. He virtually invented the detective story (with "The Murders in the Rue Morgue," 1841) and the genre of science fiction. The investigation of Poe, as with so many other cases of these Gothick Meditations, reveals results far different than would have been expected by that eleven-year-old boy waiting to see the next horror "suggested" by Mr. Poe.

We will discover that Poe was, first and foremost, an investigator of the unknown—one who showed the way to investigate, and who imagined new ways of investigating the hidden realms of nature and the mind. Poe was a true Romantic in the greatest sense. He saw the inner consciousness of the individual as a determinative factor in one's experience of reality. But this apparently subjective approach was, to his way of thinking, an essential component of the only road to true discovery of objective truth. We will discover that in his own estimation his masterpiece was not "The Raven" or "The Fall of the House of Usher," but rather a little-known and usually ignored work of apparent nonfiction—or even science fiction, or pure philosophy—entitled *Eureka*, which he published in 1848.

Poe generally preferred to represent himself with the name "Edgar A. Poe," as he never felt loved or supported by Mr. Allan.

The Life and Death of Edgar A. Poe

Edgar Poe was born on January 19, 1809, and virtually orphaned three years later and sent to live with his godfather, John Allan, who did not adopt him. Edgar spent some of his childhood in England where his godfather was trying to do business. Back in the USA, Poe attended the University of Virginia for a year and was involved in love affairs, gambling, and drinking bouts. He joined the US Army under the assumed name Edgar A. Perry, but that did not work out. He eventually received an appointment to West Point with his godfather's influence, but got himself expelled. Poe had three volumes of poetry published, but with little success. In 1831 in Baltimore he embarked on a career path that would carry him forward—he began to write short stories (or "tales"), literary criticism, and edited magazines. His

The Mysteries of Edgar A. Poe

A photograph of Poe taken on November 9th, 1848.

was a tumultuous life, full of drinking problems, various affairs, and strange liaisons with women (including an arranged, and apparently never-consummated marriage to Virginia Clemm, when she was thirteen years old), conflicts with fellow writers, and constant financial difficulties. He achieved some fame in 1845 with the publication of his poem "The Raven." Virginia died in 1847 and Poe was diagnosed by a doctor as having a "brain lesion"—what we would know today to be a brain tumor. The next year he published what he considered his crowning achievement, *Eureka*. That year, 1848, he also lived for a time in Providence, Rhode Island. Back in Richmond his life entered its final, puzzling phase.

Poe's death in 1849 is seen by some to be as mysterious as many of his stories. He was supposed to have left Richmond to go to Philadelphia to edit some poetry. But he never arrived in the City of Brotherly Love. He departed Richmond on September 27th. On October 3rd, he was discovered in Ryan's Tavern in Baltimore, Maryland in a state of delirium. A note written by someone trying to get help for Poe read in part: ". . . and I assure you, he is in need of immediate assistance." Poe was dressed in shabby clothes, apparently not his own. He was taken to Washington College Hospital where he was kept in prisonlike conditions. It was assumed he was intoxicated, but this "intoxication" went on for days. Poe did not die until the early morning hours of October 7th.

Many theories exist about the cause of Poe's death. To me, the most likely explanation relates to his brain tumor. This would account for two facts: that he had no tolerance for alcohol, which is a symptom of some brain tumors; and when his body was exhumed for reburial many years after his death, it was reported that some "mass" was rolling around inside the skull. This could not have been his brain, as it would have been among the first parts to disintegrate, but a tumor would likely calcify and remain as a hard mass. But mysteries still abound in the circumstances surrounding his death. As we have seen, Poe's life and ideas are also obviously full of mysteries.

In a professional writing career that spanned less than twenty years, Poe was able to carve out a niche for himself as one of the greatest writers in the history of American letters. As noted, he is one of the few American literary figures regarded by the rest of the world as being among the immortals of letters, on the level of Goethe and Dante. In his home country, American academic critics have not been as kind as the rest of the world. This lack of consideration stems from various (illegitimate) sources: Rufus Griswold, whom Poe had tragically made his literary executor, engaged in a systematic defamation of Poe and his character

The Mysteries of Edgar A. Poe

A daguerreotype of Poe taken in the spring of 1849.
(Getty Museum Collection)

after his death; the mistaken idea that he was a "drunkard"; the general perceived subject matter of Poe's tales and poems ("supernatural horror"); and his poetic and sometimes difficult style of writing. This last point is something we encounter with Shelley's *Frankenstein* as well. Fewer and fewer contemporary readers have the patience to read these works that belong to the Romantic period of literature.

It should also be noted, as far as Poe's original literary genius is concerned, that he virtually invented the detective/mystery story, especially with his three C. Auguste Dupin tales: "The Murders in the Rue Morgue," "The Mystery of Marie Rogêt," and "The Purloined Letter." And he was probably the first author to develop science fiction as an independent genre of literature with stories such as "The Unparalleled Adventure of One Hans Pfall," "The Balloon Hoax," and "A Descent in to the Maelström." He became a hero and literary influence for several generations of writers from around the world, including Charles Baudelaire, Oscar Wilde, Fyodor Dostoyevsky, Robert Louis Stevenson, Arthur Conan Doyle, Jules Verne, Hanns Heinz Ewers, Jorge Luis Borges, Ray Bradbury, H. P. Lovecraft, and Stephen King—just to name a few.

One of the most thoroughly esoteric dimensions of Poe's work is the degree to which it is immersed in, and is an expression of, a unique and ingenious cosmology and psychology. It seems that Poe was first and foremost a cosmologist and philosopher of a mysterious world—not a merely writer of horror stories! This cosmology will be discussed presently.

Film and Literature

The body of cinematic material we will focus on here is made up of some of the films produced by Roger Corman in the in the early 1960s. I think that because Poe is very much an artist of the interior world, his stories are often not good material for adaptation to film. But because his name had become so lucrative at the box office in the middle of the twentieth century, his name and stories were used—especially by Corman, whose work spurred more interest in Poe than ever before.

Roger Corman is an accomplished film producer and director who is famous for getting the most quality (and profit) out of the fewest resources, under budget, and on time. He was a mentor to such up-and-coming filmmakers as Francis Ford Coppola, Ron Howard, Martin Scorsese, Peter Bogdanovich, Joe Dante, Nicholas Roeg, Jonathan Demme, and James Cameron, among others. Corman began his film carreer in the early 1950s after earning an engineering degree from Stanford and studying English literature at Oxford. It is widely perceived that his collective masterpiece consists of his eight adaptations of Poe stories for American International Pictures, beginning in 1960 with *House of Usher*, starring Vincent Price. The scripts for these films were completed by a variety of writers (e.g., Richard Matheson, Charles Beaumont, and Robert Towne). In 2010, Corman received a special Academy Award for his lifetime work.

Poe's name was so powerful in marketing in the 1960s that sometimes films would just use a title or a single line of poetry as a hook (e.g., *The Conqueror Worm*), or would employ a title to a poem (e.g., *The Haunted Palace*) in a similar way. In the case of the latter film, the story was actually based on material taken from H. P. Lovecraft (*The Case of Charles Dexter Ward*), whose name would only later be treated in a way similar to the manner in which Poe's had been "marketed" in the 1960s. For purposes of these meditations, I will also address another quasi-masterpiece of cinema based on a Poe story: the 1932 Universal production *Murders in the Rue Morgue*, starring Bela Lugosi.

"The Murders in the Rue Morgue"

As we have noted, many films were made which were supposed to be versions of Poe's stories, or at least "inspired" by his work. One of the earliest was *Murders in the Rue Morgue* (1932) with Bela Lugosi. Poe's tale "The Murders in the Rue Morgue" (1841) is often cited as the first detective story. Certainly, it was a major point of departure for the genre. The important thing is that the story links into Poe's general philosophy that runs through many of his stories. "Murders" begins with a prologue about the very method of "ratiocination"—what would later be called "detective work." The story then turns to C. Auguste Dupin's solving of a double murder case in which a certain Madame L'Espanaye and her daughter have been found dead. The mother's body was found behind the house with multiple broken bones and her head almost cut off. The daughter had been strangled and her body stuffed up the chimney. These murders took place in an apartment on a fourth floor, with the door locked from the inside. A bloody straight razor was found inside the apartment. Also found were tufts of hair and two bags of gold coins. Witnesses claim to have heard voices, but the language spoken by the other voice is heard by a variety of witnesses from different countries—each identifies the language spoken by the

Murders in the Rue Morgue (1932)

other voice as something other than their own language and as a language of which they themselves have no knowledge. (A scene depicting this is comically portrayed in the 1932 film version.) Dupin concludes that the language of the other voice was not human, that robbery was not the motive, as the gold coins remained behind, and that the killer must have had superhuman strength to stuff the body up the chimney. Also, the route of escape used by the murderer, and all the other evidence point to the killer being an "Ourang-Outang" (orangutan)! Dupin puts a notice in the newspaper asking if anyone has lost such an animal. He gets a response from a sailor. The sailor says he would pay a reward for the ape and Dupin hears the story of how the sailor captured the orangutan in Borneo and brought it to Paris. But the ape was hard to control. It had learned certain habits from watching the sailor, and took his straight razor and escaped from the sailor's apartment. It went down the Rue Morgue, climbed up into a building, and forthwith committed the murders of the two women. Thus, the murders are solved. The conclusion of the story is a testimony of how different "justice" was in those days: the sailor sells the ape and the story is told to the prefect of police, who responds that people "should mind their own business."

The 1932 screen adaptation of the Poe story "The Murders in the Rue Morgue" starred Bela Lugosi (fresh off of his triumph in *Dracula*) and is directed by Robert Forey. The team of Lugosi and Forey had been scheduled to work on *Frankenstein*, but that project was given to Boris Karloff and James Whale. The film departs in significant formulaic ways from the Poe story and tells the tale of a sideshow performer who moonlights as a mad scientist, Dr. Mirakle (Lugosi). The events take place in Paris, 1845. The film opens in a carnival scene where we meet Pierre Dupin, a young medical student and amateur detective; he is with his fiancée Camille and they are accompanied by Paul and Mignette. They are overawed by the strangeness of the shows. The sideshow they attend is that of Dr. Mirakle, who exhibits an ape named Erik. Mirakle claims that Erik is approaching human status and insists that he can communicate the animal "in his language." Both the ape and the doctor take an interest in Camille. Dr. Mirakle invites Camille to take a closer look at Erik; the ape snatches her bonnet and, when Dupin tries to get it back, Erik begins to strangle him. The doctor controls Erik and offers to replace the bonnet. Camille does not want to tell the creepy doctor where she lives, but Mirakle has his servant follow her to discover the location of her home.

The most effective sequence in the film, which is generally a wonderful piece of German-style cinema, photographed by Karl Freund, is the segment where Mirakle abducts a streetwalker and binds her to a Saint Andrew's Cross. He is injecting the women he abducts with blood from the ape, testing them to see if the mixture is working, which it does not—so he disposes of them in the river through a trapdoor beneath the cross. We discover that it is Mirakle's plan to breed Erik with a human woman to create a new race of beings. In the scene the prostitute is played by Arlene Francis (who would later become a household name in America for her regular appearances on the panel of the game show *What's My Line?*). She is retrieved from the river later and taken to the morgue. Dupin contrives to test her blood and discovers that it contains the same foreign elements he has found in other victims. In the meantime, Mirakle tries to have Camille visit Erik again; when she refuses, he sets about getting the ape to kidnap the girl. Dupin is nearby and hears the screams, but when the police arrive, they arrest Dupin. Upon gaining access to the apartment, they find Camille's mother dead, stuffed up the chimney. She is clutching some strange fur that Dupin thinks belongs to Erik. But Camille has disappeared. The police interview those three foreigners who cannot agree on what language they heard the kidnapper speaking. Dupin and the police go to Mirakle's hideout. The love triangle of Mirakle, Erik, and Camille turns violent as Erik finally kills his master in a jealous rage and makes off with his prize in a chase scene over the rooftops of Paris. Dupin eventually corners Erik on a rooftop and shots him, saving his girl.

This theme of evolutionary horror was one seriously held by the Austrian eccentric Jörg Lanz von Liebenfels (1874–1954), who believed humans had bred with apes in the dim past and in remote areas of Africa. Certainly, a whole study could be done on the terrors connected with evolution as expressed in a large number of ape-oriented films over the decades.

Murders in the Rue Morgue (1932)

The Poe Wave of the 1960s

The best-known adaptations of Poe's stories are the ones done under the direction of Roger Corman in the early 1960s. Here I would like to discuss five of these: *House of Usher* (1960); two segments of *The Tales of Terror* (1962) (based on "Morella" and "The Facts in the Case of M. Valdemar"); *The Masque of the Red Death* (1964); and *Tomb of Ligeia* (1964), based on Poe's story "Ligeia." As always, Hollywood takes liberties with the stories as they were written by Poe, but quite often the spirit of the old master manages to shine through from beyond the veil. The main "problem" with adapting Poe stories to the screen is that the author works so much from within the perceptions of the protagonist, in a manner that in many ways anticipates the Expressionist mode of narrative, that there is often only the barest outline of what we might call a "plot" or narrated action. Since films can hardly exist without these elements, screenwriters were pressed to provide them. In all cases Corman worked with accomplished screenwriters and cinematographers to produce a signature look and feel to his final films.

The House of Usher

Poe's original tale "The Fall of the House of Usher" was published in 1839 and is considered one of his greatest masterpieces. In it, the anonymous narrator visits his old friend Roderick Usher who suffers from various maladies of both physical and mental etiology. Roderick believes, for example, that the house he lives in is somehow alive. Tragically, Roderick's sister, Madeline, has recently died and is entombed in the family crypt. The narrator tries to encourage his friend by reading him tales of Germanic heroism, but on a stormy night his thought-to-be-dead sister is at the door and she attacks Roderick and they both fall to the floor dead. The narrator escapes the crumbling house, to watch it sink into the ground ". . . and the deep and dank tarn closed sullenly and silently over the fragments of the 'House of Usher.'" The story has been used as inspiration for six films over the years as well as four operas.

House of Usher (1960)

Corman's 1960 film version, *House of Usher*, was the first of his Poe-based projects. The screenplay was completed by the great Richard Matheson and the cinematography by Floyd Crosby, with whom Corman worked on the majority of his Poe-related films. The story concerns the arrival of one Philip Winthrop to the house where his fiancée Madeline Usher lives with her brother, Roderick (Vincent Price). The formerly stately house is in a swamp and is slowly falling apart. Roderick opposes Philip's engagement with his sister on the grounds that the Usher family is afflicted with madness, a trait that Roderick himself seems to demonstrate. During an emotional argument with Roderick, Madeline dies suddenly—or so Roderick would have Philip believe. After her entombment in the family vault, Philip is preparing to depart when he discovers that Madeline actually was known to suffer from catalepsy. He rushes to open her coffin, only to discover it empty. She is now wandering though the crypt having been driven insane by her experience of being entombed alive. When she finds her brother, she attacks him and both are consumed by flames that destroy the house. Philip escapes only to see the house sink into the swamp.

Tales of Terror

Tales of Terror is an anthology of three short films, all written by Richard Matheson and directed by Roger Corman. It was released in the summer of 1962 and played as half of a double feature with *Panic in the Year Zero* about the aftermath of an atomic blast. This latter film was a clear and present horror in our lives in 1962, living as we were on the eve of the Cuban Missile Crisis and when we were regularly engaging in "duck-and-cover" drills at school. The Corman film consisted of three stories: "Morella," "The Black Cat," and "The Facts in the Case of M. Valdemar."

Poe's 1835 tale "Morella" has a nameless narrator who tells of his marriage to a woman named Morella, who is highly educated (at the University of Pressburg in the Austrian Empire) and intelligent. She schools him in philosophy, especially that of the

The Mysteries of Edgar A. Poe

Vincent Price with a replica of Peter Lorre's head in a promotional shot for *Tales of Terror* (1962).

German Romantic philosophers Fichte and Schelling on the idea of identity and immortality of the soul. She is physically weak and ill, and dies giving birth to their child—but not before delivering a prophecy that "when my spirit departs, shall the child live." The daughter born to them was given no name, but as she grew, she looked more and more like her mother. On her tenth birthday, the narrator decides to have the girl baptized. When the priest asks the name of the child, the narrator whispers "Morella." The girl calls out "I am here!" and falls back on the floor, dead. When the narrator takes the girl's body to the tomb, to be placed beside the body of his wife, he reports: "I laughed with a long and bitter laugh as I found no traces of the first, in the charnel where I laid the second Morella."

In the film adaptation of "Morella," we see a daughter named Lenore Locke return to her ancestral home to confront her father (Vincent Price). Lenore's mother had died soon after giving birth to Lenore and the mother blamed "the baby" for her sickness and untimely death. Locke had fallen into a deep, lifelong depression after that and had preserved Morella's body in her deathbed. Locke sent the girl away and never saw her again. Now, twenty-six years later, his daughter had returned—to tell him that she herself was dying of an unspecified malady. They reconcile, for a moment at least. One night Morella's spirit appears to leave her dead body and attack Lenore—causing her death. Morella has been "avenged." Locke is grief stricken, and horrified to discover his wife—rejuvenated and reanimated—risen up from her deathbed. In shock, he drops a lamp, igniting the bed and the room as Morella attacks and strangles him. As the room and house go up in flames, the last shot shows Lenore clutching her father's neck.

Although the stories of the film adaptation and the original tale have little in common, Matheson does an admirable job at depicting a Poe-like mentality. Poe's original story is one of metempsychosis, or "reincarnation" (a favorite theme also found in other of Poe's tales). The original text bears many conceptual connections with the ancient idea of rebirth found in Germanic lore, where the posthumous child is considered to be the parent reborn. I explore this esoteric and mythic concept in my book *Sigurðr* (Lodestar, 2015). The film adaptation, however, clearly makes use of Poe's also often-found concept of madness, shifting perceptions and distortions of reality based on these subjective phenomena in the consciousness of the individual.

"The Case of M. Valdemar," also part of the *Tales of Terror* trilogy, tells the story of a painfully dying man, Valdemar (Price), who is being treated by a Mesmerist named Carmichael (Basil Rathbone) to alleviate his pain. Valdemar's attending physician and friend objects to the treatment as quackery, but his loving and loyal wife, Helene (Debra Padget), supports her husband. Valdemar agrees, over his doctor's objections, to allow Carmichael to Mesmerize him at the very moment of death as an experiment. Valdemar expresses his wish to his wife that she should marry the physician after his death. So, Valdemar is indeed

Mesmerized at the moment of his death. This is accomplished with the aid of an infernal contraption made up of a rotating machine that emits kaleidoscopic colors. This allows Valdemar to continue to communicate from beyond the veil. The trance holds his active mind in his dead body for some months. One evening the physician and Helene arrive at the house, where Carmichael seems to have taken control, and they demand that Valdemar be released from the trance. Carmichael has Valdemar communicate that he wishes Helene to marry Carmichael. The physician leaves the house and Carmichael makes his move on Helene. This is just too much—even for a dead man: Valdemar rises up out of his bed and, as his body is rotting away before our eyes, he kills the sinister Mesmerist.

Poe's story, titled "The Facts of M. Valdemar's Case," is quite different. It takes the form of a report by the unnamed Mesmerist himself on the case of M. Valdemar, who allows himself to be Mesmerized at the point of death and, in a Mesmerized state, the patient continues to exist for seven months. After this span of time, the Mesmerist determines to try to awaken Valdemar. When he does so, the patient enters into a state of acute distress and pleads:

> "For God's sake!—quick!—quick!—put me to sleep—or, quick!—waken me!—quick!—I say to you that I am dead!"

The Mesmerist does awaken him, and the result is that his body quickly becomes a "nearly liquid mass of loathsome—of detestable putridity" (Poe 1935, 223).

This story was widely reprinted, and often in ways that made it appear to be fact, not fiction. As Poe wrote it, it perhaps belongs to his corpus of science-fiction tales. During Poe's lifetime, Mesmerism (founded by the German physician Franz Anton Mesmer, 1734–1815) was taken quite seriously and it is something which lies at the root of many accepted scientific and medical practices today, such as hypnotism.

The Masque of the Red Death

Poe's original story is highly descriptive, atmospheric, and poetic in style, and simply tells the tale of Prince Prospero in whose realm a plague, called the red death, is raging. He retires into a specially designed abbey to hold a masquerade ball for members of his court. They seal themselves into the structure, safely within, leaving the plague outside. The building is fitted with seven chambers, each of a different color, with the last and seventh being black and fitted with a great ebony clockwork. Clearly,

The Masque of the Red Death (1964)

these are emblematic of the seven planetary spheres, with this last one corresponding to Saturn. In the end a figure appears among the revelers who is in fact an embodiment of the Red Death, which has entered the structure and lays waste to all who are gathered there. It ends with the words, "And Darkness and Decay and the Red Death held illimitable dominion over all."

Corman's cinematic version had to create many more plot elements to carry the story of a film. The screenplay, which adds much in the way of plots and even a subplot based on another Poe tale ("Hop-Frog"), is by the talented and all-too-soon-departed Charles Beaumont. Poe's visual imagery is also vividly evoked by cinematographer Nicholas Roeg. The film tells the story of Prince Prospero (Vincent Price), who is the leader of a Satanic cult and who fortifies himself and his followers in his palace against the Red Death ravaging the countryside without. Prospero tries to recruit a beautiful village girl, Francesca, to the Satanic fold but is foiled in his efforts. In the end, a masked figure robed in red enters and reveals himself as not being a servant of Satan as, "Death has no master." The figure tells Prospero his Satanic beliefs will not save him and declares: "Each man creates his own God for himself—his own Heaven, his own Hell." When the prince rips away the figure's mask, his own face is revealed, dripping red. The film ends as does Poe's own story. The figure of the Red Death in the countryside reading Tarot cards is heavily reminiscent of Ingmar Bergman's chess-playing figure of Death in *The Seventh Seal* (1957).

Tomb of Ligeia

Poe's original 1838 story entitled "Ligeia" is substantially different from the film that it inspired a hundred and twenty-six years later. The tale is considered one of his greatest and is crafted in such a way as to leave the reader able to interpret the narrative in a variety of different ways. It bears conceptual similarity to "Morella." The story is told from the perspective of an anonymous narrator, who is married to a remarkable woman named Ligeia. She is a woman of great genius, indomitable will, and great beauty. She unfortunately dies and the narrator remarries, this

Tomb of Ligeia (1964)

time to a woman named Rowena, who is the opposite of Ligeia in every way. She too sickens and dies, but on her bier the spirit of Ligeia momentarily takes possession of the dead Rowena. The whole story can be interpreted as a supernatural tale of metempsychosis. Or perhaps the qualities of Ligeia exist only in the narrator's subjective universe and her return from the dead too is merely in his deluded mind. Or Rowena is real, but Ligeia is a figment of the narrator's imagination. This latter motif is reminiscent of the Celtic idea of the fairy wife, the notion that a man is married to a real woman but also to a woman from the underworld or otherworld—a sort of parallel universe—and this causes all manner of confusion and inner conflict.

Corman's film version called *Tomb of Ligeia* was made right after *The Masque of the Red Death* and originally played on a double bill with Mario Bava's *Black Sabbath* in the winter of 1964. The film tells the story of Verden Fell (Vincent Price), whose wife, Ligeia, has died. She was an atheist and blasphemed against God, and Fell feels haunted by her. He marries Rowena, a young woman again very different from Ligeia. The house they live in seems haunted by Ligeia and there is a cat always lurking about, which he believes may be possessed by the dead woman. In the end Fell has a final confrontation with the cat/Ligeia and manages to strangle it, but the whole structure burns down due to an accident. Rowena goes off to be happy with another man. Overall the film suffers from a reliance on ailurophobia—which seems very un–Poe-like.

Cats play a part in one way or another in several of Poe's stories and adaptations of his stories. In real life Poe was a great lover of cats, as was one of his great admirers, H. P. Lovecraft. Poe's beloved tortoiseshell cat named Catterina, who sat on his shoulder as he wrote and kept his wife warm in her illness, is said to have died at the precise moment of Poe's own death, a hundred and fifty miles distant.

Understanding Poe

Edgar A. Poe as a thinker, author, and human being is not an easy topic to understand in totality. He remains, on many counts, a mystery. Books have been written about him, museums established in his memory, and he has remained an inspiration to generation after generation of authors. Some of the difficulty in interpreting the meaning of the man and his work stems from the fact that so much has been said about him (often not always positive or in a helpful spirit) and works—including the films we have discussed here—merely inspired by him are sometimes taken as representative of his work itself. Most of these phenomena are wonderful. They remain a testimony to the power of his creativity and inspiration. Poe is more than a writer of weird stories—he is a cultural icon and important feature of American culture.

This work of mine cannot hope to unravel the mystery of Edgar A. Poe as a revelation for all suddenly to be enlightened and understand what is hidden within in some new and intelligible way. This, we assume in the end, is impossible. The Mystery is just too great. This can, I think, be said: Poe himself should be seen first and foremost as an investigator of the unknown, one who himself investigates the Mysteries. This can be observed both in his personal obsessions as well as in the themes of his best works of fiction, and in his enigmatic work called *Eureka*.

One of the most important factors in Poe's thought is the role of the perspective (inner consciousness) of the individual thinker as that which determines experience and opens the door to the discovery of hidden truths or reality itself. This path can be seen to be a dangerous one, however, as it can lead to madness as well as the discovery of a higher poetic reality. As an artist, Poe directly confronted the reality that ultimate inner truths can be expressed in words only with extreme difficulty and with the requirement of supreme talent.

As we have noted earlier, the eminent American writer of weird fiction, H. P. Lovecraft, was a great admirer of Poe. Many critics have noted that Lovecraft intentionally tried to imitate Poe's literary style, except the times had (supposedly) long since passed that style by. But it is also possible that Lovecraft, perhaps unconsciously, imitated Poe in a more profound sense as well. The genius of Lovecraft, as we see in Essay VI of this collection, was in his creation of an underlying artificial mythos in which his weird tales somehow "made sense." Poe worked from a similar premise. He revealed this underlying theory in his "prose poem" entitled *Eureka*, published in 1848. This work purported to explain the mysteries of the universe. Whether it succeeds or fails in achieving that goal is not for me to say. But we can be absolutely certain that it explained the subjective universe of one Mr. Edgar A. Poe, and in turn it becomes the key to understanding the creations of that subjective universe—the literary works of that same Poe. I am certainly not the first one to think that the contents of Eureka could help explain Poe's fictional output. Some have mistakenly thought that *Eureka* was the basis for his stories—which cannot be exactly true as he wrote down the text of *Eureka* near the end of his life. But the underlying ideas laid out in the text were doubtless unexpressed underlying beliefs and assumptions of the author, which had been acquired at a much younger age. In any event, the best, most authentic interpretive touchstone for Poe's work is certainly this unique text. The title of this work is taken from the Greek term *eureka*, meaning "I found (it)," which is said to have been uttered by Archimedes when he stepped into his bath and realized the volume of water displaced, measured by the rise of water in the tub, is equal to the volume of the part of his body submerged in the water. The word becomes a formula to express that moment of sudden discovery of any great truth or thing.

It is fascinating to observe how the persistent power of the ideas expressed in Eureka permeate the fictional work of Poe, but even more astounding to realize how many of these concepts penetrate right into the films based, no matter how imprecisely, on the mentality of Poe. The best and most convenient edition of *Eureka* is the one provided by Harold Beaver in the Penguin edition found in *The Science Fiction of Edgar Allan Poe* (1976). This edition contains notes and some cross-references to the literary works of Poe as well.

Summary of Some Ideas Contained in Eureka

The book *Eureka* was Poe's longest nonfiction work and it was his last major publication before his death. It is based on a lecture he presented on February 3, 1848, called "On the Cosmography of the Universe." Some of his conclusions are startling (e.g., that "space and duration are one," and that "matter and spirit are made of the same essence"). *Eureka* shares in themes persistently found in Poe's fictional work. Among these are attempts to break beyond the barrier of death, a theme that we see in "The Fall of the House of Usher," "Ligeia," "The Facts in the Case of M. Valdemar," "Morella," and many others.

The 1864 French edition of *Eureka*, translated by Charles Baudelaire. (Bibliothèque nationale de France)

Poe sees the universe as something akin to a written work of fiction by an author most people call God. In *Eureka*, Poe takes on the role of a detective employing his method of ratiocination and trying to solve the mystery of a case called "the universe." He concludes that it, like a good short story, is a self-contained system. Poe is of the belief that truth can be captured through language, which often finds itself enmeshed in what he would call cryptography—the use of language to encode meaning, and by extension a method of decoding mysteries. Because people have a tendency to believe their souls to be infinite, Poe concludes that this stems from the fact that the human soul was once part of God, and it is back to this God that the individual human soul will eventually return. Individual souls are sent out from and, in the end, will return to, the center. Similarly, the whole cosmos is constantly expanding and contacting, akin to a cosmic heartbeat. In this way, the cosmos is always renewing itself and is in a sense deathless, with the human soul being an integral part of God. Although the book appears to be a treatise on something like physics, Poe insisted that it is to be considered only as a work of art, not one of science. It would appear that Poe is simply using the jargon of science to make what is actually a point about aesthetics or art. In the final analysis, Poe saw that intuition is the basis or genesis of all of what is called "science." Poe, like Shelley, was a typical Romantic critic of the arrogance of what was coming to be known as modern science, based as it was, at least in its own estimation, on nothing but objective data and pure reason. The contents of *Eureka* can be compared to other nineteenth-century works such as those of Joseph Smith, Helena Blavatsky, and Mary Baker Eddy.

The Mystery of Poe

Poe's motivation was the uncovering of the unknown by means of some inspired reasoning, by a method akin to Plato's noesis—"rational intuition." The correct and accurate application of this theory results in the substance of his ratiocination stories, such as "The Murders in the Rue Morgue," but the perverse and equally possible dysfunction of this faculty results in the delusions and false perceptions so common in Poe's tales.

If Plato was lurking behind it in any way, it should also be noted that the old philosopher was not above spinning a yarn or two that bordered on the fantastic with his "Myth of the Cave" and his science-fiction tale of the Lost Atlantis.

Everything that is horrific in Poe's fictional universe—and by that I mean the universe he coherently depicts in his tales of mystery and imagination—is the result of misperception. People misperceive the state of life and death, which results in his well-known and much-exploited fear of premature burial. Tales are often told from the perspective of anonymous first-person narrators whose perceptions are skewed by psychological or physical conditions, but because the narrator provides the only information to which we are privy, we too must participate in this sometimes-insane view of the world. In this Poe is a clear and present precursor to the art form later known as Expressionism, which we discuss in the Essay XII on Caligari. By the same token, this mysterious subjective faculty of the human mind can, when correctly guided by genius, result in the discovery of hidden truths. Out of this idea a great deal of his work also blossoms. His stories of ratiocination, as well as his nonfiction works of criticism and analysis, including *Eureka*, belong to this category.

One of Poe's tales that often goes unread is the oddity entitled "The Sphinx" (1846), which describes how the narrator has mistaken a small insect for a monster due to his own optical perspective on it. It is a demonstration of the fact that the subjective perception of the mind can greatly affect what one sees as truth. The ability of the subject to intuit the truth about a situation is related to the level of quality of the observation made by the subject. Some observations lead to eureka moments, the objective and meaning of which transcend the momentary sensation, while others remain befuddled in illusion.

Today Poe is little heard about in the film industry. After the craze over him at the time of the Corman films of the 1960s, he has generally been allowed to rest in some semblance of peace. As noted earlier, film is perhaps not the best medium in which to experience the full genius of Edgar A. Poe. Perhaps the masters of the German Expressionist period would have been the best filmmakers to exploit the genius of Poe, as the trick of representing the subjective experience of the unstable mind is essential in the representation of the horrors Poe has to offer. As we will see in Essay X about the German decadent writer Hanns Heinz Ewers, who was an ardent admirer of Poe and defender of his reputation, wrote the screenplay for an Expressionist film inspired by Poe's tale "William Wilson" entitled *Der Student von Prag* (The Student of Prague). I will have more to say about "William Wilson" in the essay on Ewers. Taken as a whole, Poe's work is still largely underappreciated and often neglected in the American academy. There is much in it that still awaits elucidation.

> *The breeze—the breath of God—is still—*
> *And the mist upon the hill,*
> *Shadowy—shadowy—yet unbroken,*
> *Is a symbol and a token—*
> *How it hangs upon the trees,*
> *A mystery of mysteries!*

—"Spirits of the Dead" (1827)

VIII
Zombies
From the Cane Fields to Cosmic Ghouls

When I first envisioned this project, I did not conceive of a meditation on the zombie genre. But later, walking through a Half-Price Books store in September of 2016, I came across a whole display of books on zombie movies and the like, and was immediately struck with the absolute *necessity* of turning the lens onto this field of material. Zombies are *too popular* to ignore. In the down period of my life, I had to take a job at a fast food joint to pay the bills. The guys I worked with were deep into zombies. They played video games having to do with them, and *The Walking Dead* was their favorite show on television. I asked many of them whether they knew where the idea of the zombie came from. *None* of them knew. (By the way, all of them were African Americans.) So, while Zombies might be popular, they are just as mysterious as ever.

I think back to my Monster Party nights as a kid. One of my best shows was based on a "Nightmare Theater" showing of *I Walked with a Zombie* (1943). As I led the participants through the house, at one point they saw a girl lying in bed as if dead. I took my guests to another room and, once there, at a sort of weird zombie altar, I intoned the zombie chant from

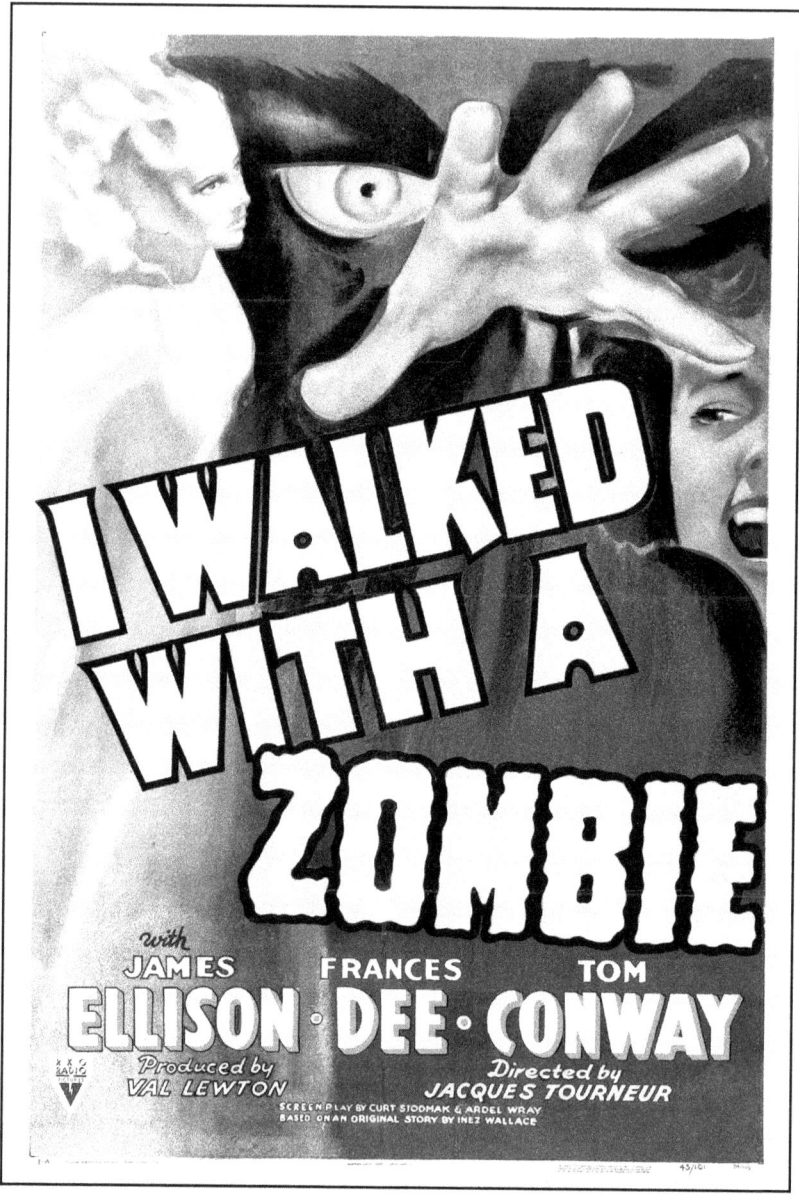

I Walked with a Zombie (1943)

the film: "*Ah-OO-ahhhh.*" With this bit of misdirection, the girl slipped away behind the participants unnoticed, only to reappear suddenly, as if by *magic*, walking outside the window in front of the house, all zombielike…

Zombies

My childhood zombie- or Voodoo-film experience encompassed *White Zombie* (1932), *I Walked with a Zombie*, the segment of the Amicus anthology film *Dr. Terror's House of Horrors* entitled "Voodoo" (1965), and the Hammer Films feature *Plague of the Zombies* (1966). I remember seeing this last film at a drive-in movie theater in Dallas when it came out in January of 1966. It was frigid that night and the theater rented car-heaters to keep the patrons from ending up as the frozen dead. *Plague of the Zombies* is a bridge between the Haitian Voodoo scene and the wider possibility of zombies appearing outside that context. The film posits a Haitian connection, but it is set in Cornwall, where a gentleman, who has learned the black arts in Haiti, plies his craft to get zombified miners to work his tin mine. As the title suggests, it is at least posited that the problems of the local young men dying is attributable to a *disease* of some sort.

The zombie or Voodoo genre, as small as it was before 1968, was not all that inspiring to me. Clearly, the horror angle was rooted in one similar to that of the vampire (i.e., a living dead person). But it was tinged with a sort of *ethnic* horror—because this was originally set in a world of Africans, in which white people were a minority, there was an implicit sort of "racial horror." (This was to some extent rooted in a sense of colonial guilt and anxiety over what came to be called "cultural appropriation.") None of this spoke to me much then or now. I remember going with my father on a business trip in about 1965 to Shreveport, Louisiana. I left the downtown motel by myself soon after we got there and walked around on the street. I realized all of a sudden: I am just about the only white person I can see around here. It was a psychological shock, and an interesting experiential lesson for my child's mind. Colonials in African or Caribbean lands probably felt something similar—and were obviously frightened by it on some level. My Eden ancestors from the Cayman Islands probably felt it before and even after 1835 when slavery was abolished in the islands. There, the syncretic Afro-Caribbean religion of Obeah is in evidence. Some colonialists were obviously fearful of the nonwhite peoples they were colonizing and enslaving, and on a deep level the idea that these people might possess some special magical powers was even more frightening.

Folklore and Religion

The facts about zombies lead in a direction that bears little relation to the way they are conceived in the current zombie craze. The lore of the zombie appears rooted in the Afro-Caribbean syncretic religion of *voudon*, or Voodoo, and seems to be mainly a part of the tradition in Haiti. The creation of zombies is *not* an essential part of this religion, to be sure, as it appears to be most closely connected to the Petro sect of it, which practices various sorts of malevolent magic and involves blood sacrifice. In essence the creation of zombies is intimately connected to the ideology of slavery, being a way for planters to acquire cheap labor by exploiting the magical frame of reference of the common folk. It also seems that "zombification" was used as a way to punish individuals for various crimes against the community or insults against the local *houngan* or *bokor* (i.e., "priest" of the religion).

The folklore of the creation of a zombie is rooted in African beliefs about the soul. The word upon which "zombie" is based was first mentioned in the written record in English in Robert Southey's three-volume work, *The History of Brazil* (1810–1819). The word is of West African origin. For the West African, the individual has four distinct souls: an immortal soul (*zonbi*), a bush-soul, a shadow-soul, and a dream-soul. The immortal soul governs the others and gives life to the body. It is allotted a certain time on earth. If an individual dies (usually by violence or unnatural causes) before the allotted time of the *zonbi*, it becomes a fifth sort of soul: a wandering soul. It seeks a new abode, preferably the body of a newborn child. However, through the application of sorcery, the *bokor* is able to snatch the soul as it hovers near the body and capture it in a bottle or some other container. He uses this to reanimate the corpse as a living dead. This process explains how the term for the "soul" became a designation for the living dead.

The Bantu term *nzambi* or *zonbi* is used to designate the immortal soul, but is also a conception of the absolute

Zombies

deity—either as the creator god or goddess. The lore of the zombie actually belongs to a complex and profound metaphysical universe rooted in African religion. It should not, however, be assumed that such lore is unique to Africa. Although each culture has its individual aspects, there are similar ideas found in Northern European pagan traditions. The Norse world knows of an entity called the *draugr*—a living corpse that often guards the contents of its own grave. There are *aptrgöngumenn* (literally, "men who come back," revenants) who stalk pastures and farms after dark and cause all sorts of mischief. There are also examples of sorcerers raising the dead to act as fighting men for undermanned armies. The metaphysic in most cases is strikingly similar: an animating principle, which usually departs from the body permanently, is caused by circumstance or magic to return to the dead body, reanimating it.

There are unique aspects to the Afro-Caribbean phenomenon of zombies that have recently become more well known. Wade Davis's 1985 book *The Serpent and the Rainbow* and the 1998 film based on it delve into the whole process of zombification, which proceeds on several levels: pharmacological, psychological—and yes, of course, magical. We will look a bit deeper into this below.

The Zombie Tradition and the Written Record

The zombie craze in films was rooted in the book *The Magic Island* written by the adventurer and occultist William Seabrook (1884–1945). His book appeared in 1929 and caused quite a sensation. The first zombie film, *White Zombie*, was released in 1932, and is said to have been directly inspired by Seabrook's book. Seabrook offers the following description:

> It seemed ... that while the *zombie* came from the grave, it was neither a ghost, nor yet a person who had been raised like Lazarus from the dead. The *zombie*, they say, is a soulless human corpse, still dead, but taken from the grave and endowed by sorcery with a mechanical semblance of life— it is a dead body which is made to walk and act

William Seabrook in front of a Voodoo altar.

and move as if it were alive. People who have the power to do this go to a fresh grave, dig up the body before it has had time to rot, galvanize it into movement, and then make of it a servant or slave, occasionally for the commission of some crime, more often simply as a drudge around the habitation or the farm, setting it dull heavy tasks, and beating it like a dumb beast if it slackens. (Seabrook 2016, 93)

When Seabrook asked his informants about vampires and werewolves and zombies in Haiti, they were ready to admit that the first two may be imaginary, but were deadly serious about the actual existence of *zombies*. That zombies are taken seriously is actually recorded in the law of Haiti. Article 249 of the *Criminal Code* of the Republic of Haiti reads:

> Also shall be qualified as attempted murder the employment which may be made against any person of substances which, without causing

actual death, produce a lethargic coma more or less prolonged. If, after the administering of such substances, the person has been buried, the act shall be considered murder no matter what result follows. (Seabrook 2016, 103)

This, and other pieces of evidence and research, led the Harvard ethnobotanist Wade Davis to discover and make known to the wider public this truth behind the zombification process. Regardless of the composition of the substance used, the *bokor* administers a potion to the victim, who goes into a deep, coma-like trance, is buried and later dug up and awakened to a semiconscious state, and informed that he or she has become *zombie*. Given the cultural and psychological frame of reference in which the victim lives, this suggestion is overwhelming and becomes a fact of life (or half-life) for that individual. They have really become a *zombie*, subject to the will of the *bokor*.

Before our target year of 1975, there was virtually nothing in imaginative horror literature about zombies, or at least certainly not by that name. The zombie genre of horror seems to have been a cinematic phenomenon from the beginning.

Zombie Films

To date over 450 films have been made that feature zombies in one way or another. Most of these were made after George Romero's re-envisioning of the zombie in 1968 and they have left their Haitian roots far behind. The initial phase of zombie films had but few entries and spanned a time between 1932 and 1943. The first of these, as we have said, was *White Zombie*, starring Bela Lugosi as a white Voodoo master named Murder Legendre who is enlisted by a wealthy planter to take a woman away from her fiancé. Legendre, who runs a crew of zombies at his sugarcane mill, convinces the planter that the women must be turned into a zombie with a potion he provides. The potion is delivered and the woman appears to die, and she is buried in a tomb. Legendre and a troop of zombie servants enter the tomb

White Zombie (1932)

and remove her body and take it to the Voodoo master's castle where the woman is revived as a zombie. When the planter sees the woman in zombie form, he begs Legendre to return her to life, but the master refuses and demonstrates his power over her. The Voodoo master then slips the planter some of the potion as well. It soon becomes clear that the Voodoo master has his own plans for the woman. In the end the fiancé, now husband, enters the castle and saves the day. The spell is broken with Legendre's death. The woman reports: "I dreamed." *White Zombie* is a mixture of Haitian folklore and Gothic horror. The follow-up to *White Zombie* was *Revolt of the Zombies*, which relocates the idea of zombies to the Far East. An expedition from Western countries with colonial interests are dispatched to Cambodia to discover and then destroy the so-called Secret of the Zombies. *King of the Zombies* is a half-comedy, half-propaganda film made

Bela Lugosi in *White Zombie*.

in 1941. Because *King of the Zombies* was produced and released before the USA entered World War II, the vague anti-German subtext was not made entirely explicit. Such was not the case a few years later when *Revenge of the Zombies* was released in 1943 with its villain Dr. Max Heinrich von Altermann, played by John Carradine. Both *Revolt* and *Revenge* featured the common trope of Axis spies communicating with "headquarters" using a radio. Some semblance of quality was returned to the genre with Val Lewton's production of *I Walked with a Zombie* in 1943. This film was directed by Jacques Tourneur, and written by Curt Siodmak and Ardel Wray. Lewton instructed the writers to use the Gothic novel *Jane Eyre* as a narrative structure for the story. The title and general idea of a zombie theme was suggested by a nonfiction

I Walked with a Zombie (1943)

article by the same title written by Inez Wallace for the *American Weekly* newspaper supplement—an article that was optioned by Lewton. The Siodmak/Wray script tells the story of Betsy, who is hired to care for the ailing wife of a sugar plantation owner named Paul Holland. The island where the plantation is located is inhabited by a few white people and the descendants of African slaves. Holland's wife, Jessica, has supposedly contracted an illness which has damaged her spinal column and left her devoid of willpower to act on her own. Although Jessica's condition and its cause remains at first mysterious, Betsy tries to find her a cure through Voodoo when a housemaid tells her that a priest of the religion cured someone in a similar condition. She secretly guides Jessica through the cane fields by night, where they come upon a crossroads guarded by the Carre-Four. They make their way to the *houmfort*, a sort of temple for Voodoo gatherings. There Betsy discovers that the head of the cult is one of the white residents at the plantation, who tells Betsy that Jessica cannot be cured. As they leave, Jessica is stabbed with a sword—but because she does not bleed, the practitioners see that she is, in fact, a zombie. It is revealed that she was turned into a zombie to prevent her from leaving the plantation. The Voodoo practitioners try to draw Jessica back out to them, but she is killed by one of the plantation residents, who carries her body out to sea. *I Walked with a Zombie* had much more of an authentic air about it, due to its roots in the Inez Wallace article, which tells the story of a man who had a relationship with a native girl in Haiti, but then married a white woman. The bride was supposedly then killed and zombified by the locals in revenge. This was the last and best of the traditional zombie films.

The New Wave of Zombies

As attested by my buddies at the fast-food joint, most current zombie enthusiasts have little to no idea about the Haitian origin of the zombie myth and magic. The ultimate genius behind this transformation in zombie culture is the great Richard Matheson, who in 1954 published a novel entitled *I Am Legend*. From this point on, the genre began to evolve in a new direction.

In a manner of speaking, Ed Wood's *Plan Nine from Outer Space* (1959) can be counted as a zombie film of this new genre. Instead of the traditional Voodoo-based, magical rationale for how the dead are resurrected, it substitutes a science-fiction one. As such, Wood may have been influenced by Matheson's *I Am Legend*. In that regard, then, Wood was perhaps the first to introduce the science-fiction element to the zombie genre. This science-fiction dimension would continue to grow over the years.

In 1964 Matheson's story was finally turned into a film entitled *The Last Man on Earth*, produced by an Italian/American company in Rome and starring Vincent Price as Dr. Robert Morgan. Matheson actually worked on the screenplay, but was dissatisfied with the result and appears in the credits as Logan Swanson. This was one of the many horror films I saw at the Saturday matinee at the Casa Linda Theatre in Dallas. It tells the story of Morgan, who relentlessly hunts the vampiric zombie-like creatures that are taking over the whole world as a result of some sort of bacterial infection. As in the original story, these creatures share many of the characteristics of the traditional European vampire. In the end, Morgan is killed by the vampire/zombies, apparently the last actual human being. Two years later the aforementioned *Plague of the Zombies* appeared from Hammer studios. And then two years after that came the cataclysmic breakthrough with *Night of the Living Dead*.

This landmark film was made on a shoestring budget ($114,000), but Romero turned this deficit into a strength of the picture by shooting it in black and white and giving it a "newsreel" ambiance. When I was a kid in Dallas, Channel 5 ran a fifteen-minute, late-night news summary from around the State of Texas, called the *Texas News*. This seemed to focus on gory footage and lurid stories. The film was silent and there was a droning narrator. *Night of the Living Dead* had the same feel. In 1968—especially, perhaps, in that year when the world appeared to be coming apart—the scenes of the *Night of the Living Dead*, too, seemed as if they could have actually happened. The story is simple and explains very little to the viewer. All of the action

Richard Matheson's novel *I Am Legend* (1954).

Zombies

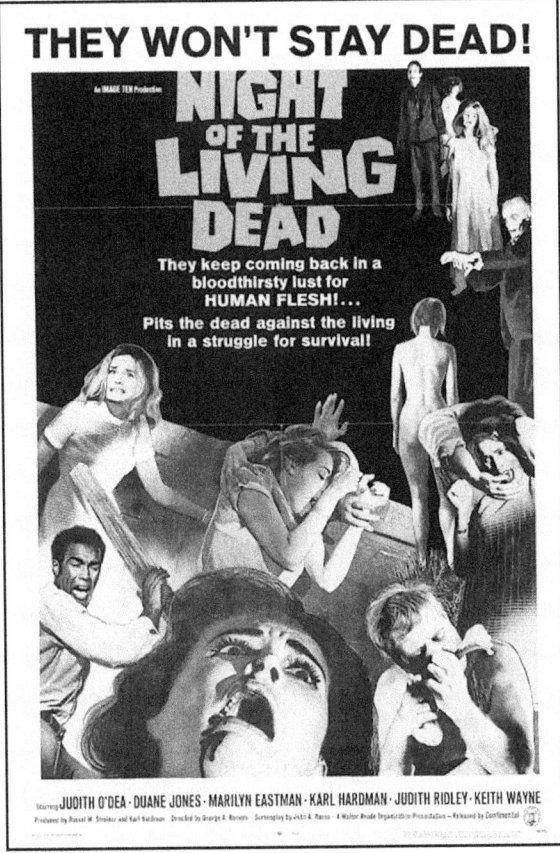

Night of the Living Dead (1968)

takes place in one night, fulfilling Aristotle's idea of the unity of time. A group of people take refuge in an old farmhouse to escape an onslaught of reanimated corpses bent on devouring them. Among the people is an African American man named Ben. He seems to be the best leader but is resisted by others. They barricade themselves in the house and fight the living dead off as wave after wave attacks, infecting most of the living in one way or another. Radio reports inform them that this plague of the undead is spreading over the eastern seaboard of the country. In the end only Ben is left alive, sealed in the basement of the house. The morning comes, authorities are clearing the area outside the house, Ben emerges and is shot at once in the forehead and his body thrown on a pile of zombies. This film instantly became a cult classic and quickly grossed two hundred and fifty times its production cost.

The Meditation

In some ways, the original zombie mythology closely mirrors that of the German Weimar-period obsession with the control of persons by some sort of magical or hypnotic spell. There the controller exercises power through the entity he controls: the somnambulist (Cesare in *Caligari*), the *golem*, Ultima Futura (the robotrix in *Metropolis*), Dr. Mabuse's ability to control events indirectly, and so on. Except the zombie in historical fact was generally a *worker*, a *slave* used to work the sugarcane fields in Haiti. This connection with the theme of German Expressionist films of the 1920s is actually most clearly reflected in the earliest of the American zombie films such as *White Zombie*, *Revolt of the Zombies*, and *King of the Zombies*.

In tradition, the fear factor in connection with the idea of zombies was not a fear *of* zombies, but rather a fear of *becoming* a zombie. After Matheson and Romero definitively, but inadvertently, modified the tradition, there was a definite fear *of* zombies, not based on their special strength or cunning, but purely as a corollary of their overwhelming number and insatiable appetites. In the Haitian lore the zombie is an empty vessel used by their masters for labor, and so on. After the Matheson/Romero reformation they become entities dangerous because of their numbers, the expansion of their numbers, and their one-pointed focus on consuming the brains of the living.

The transition of the character of zombies found in films was engendered in the world of literature, and what may at first seem to be a simple idea proves itself to be quite complex. The fairly compact corpus of zombie films of the 1930s and 1940s was given a whole new twist, in combination with the other kind of horrific living dead, the vampire, in Richard Matheson's 1954 novel *I Am Legend*. The novel tells the story of Robert Neville as the only survivor of a worldwide bacterial pandemic, which has turned the infected into beings much like traditional

Zombies

Night of the Living Dead

vampires. He seems to be the only one immune to the disease. He barricades himself inside his house while the vampires try to gain entry. Neville discovers more efficient ways of killing the infected and eliminates great numbers of them. He meets a woman named Ruth who seems to be uninfected and with whom he develops a relationship. But as it turns out, she is in fact infected, and has been sent as a spy by her fellow vampires. In this new world, the reanimated corpses are feral beings, but those infected while still living are capable of thought and are trying to build a "new society." The attacks on his house continue and Neville is eventually wounded and captured. He is put in a barred cell and condemned to be executed. Ruth visits him and provides him with drugs so that he will not have to experience his execution. In his final moments he comes to realize that he represents a type of being in this new world who has assumed the role of the vampire and that their desire to kill him is little different from the human desire to kill vampires. He further realizes that after his death he will assume the role of a "legend." This novel by the highly influential writer Matheson would be filmed three times: *The Last Man on Earth* (1964), *The Omega Man* (1971), and more recently, the film version *I Am Legend* (2007). Matheson's combination of the reanimated corpse of the zombie with the lethal feeding frenzy of the vampire was again tweaked in 1968 when the Pittsburgh commercial filmmaker George Romero made his super-low-budget classic, *Night of the Living Dead*. Clearly, this vision of the "zombie" (neither Matheson nor Romero originally used this word for their living dead menaces) became increasingly popular from that moment on. In point of fact, of course, the idea of zombies rising up out of their graves to overrun the world was originally part of that famous "worst movie ever made"—*Plan Nine from Outer Space* by the immortal Ed Wood. That film was originally entitled "Grave Robbers from Outer Space."

Romero, in a series of films that he produced following *Night of the Living Dead* between 1978 and 2009, makes his interpretation of the new genre quite clear. Not since the Red Scare subtext of the 1950s sci-fi films, with their plot line of "an unseen force from beyond is taking over our neighbors who are going to kill us and take over our society," has a genre's subtext been so transparent. Zombies were transformed from exploited workers into out-of-control *consumers*. These consumers are

George Romero's *Dawn of the Dead* (1978).

literally out to devour our *brains*. We are constantly surrounded by a horde of them—the unthinking, plodding, implacable masses—and we must hold off this horde in our desperate struggle for survival. The ironic part of it by now is that the zombie genre itself as itself become a sort of *zombie* in its own right. It is consuming the brains of those who watch the product and in nerdy fashion speculate about the physiology of zombies, the etiology of the "virus" that causes the zombie phenomenon, and the prognosis for a society that has undergone what is called a "zombie apocalypse." By allowing their brains to be consumed by this meaningless nonsense, they participate fully in the true zombie apocalypse overtaking our culture. Beyond this, in an economic sense, the consumer is *still* the zombie which transfers the fruits of its labor to the ruling masters, having succumbed to the magic spell of marketing and advertising.

Just as we noted that in the Weimar Period in Germany the theme of a mastermind controlling events through an instrument of his will was perhaps a forecast of things to come, certainly the now-dominating theme of the mindless masses motivated by an impersonal mental and physical disease process may be seen to be a similar forecast of those things to come. Or is it already here? We hope not.

"Cultural Appropriation"?

One of the films mentioned at the beginning of the essay was the segment of *Dr. Terror's House of Horrors* entitled "Voodoo." It has nothing to do with zombies as such but makes use of Afro-Caribbean culture in a special way. It is based on a novella called "Papa Benjamin" by Cornell Woolrich (writing as William Irish), published in a 1943 collection entitled *I Wouldn't Be in Your Shoes*. This story was adapted into other media as well: a radio broadcast (*Escape!*) and the television program *Thriller*. The original story takes place in the French Quarter in New Orleans and involves a desperate nightclub performer named Eddie Bloch who uses Voodoo elements to transform his flopping act. In the segment of the *Dr. Terror* anthology, we meet a British jazz musician who travels to the West Indies, where he steals a musical tune

I Walked with a Zombie

from a Voodoo ceremony he witnesses. Back in London, the musician starts to use the music in his jazz act, the cultists from whom he stole the music appear to manifest themselves and take vengeance on him for his theft of their sacred rhythms. The story interests us here as a textbook example of what has become known as "cultural appropriation." The appropriation in this case can be seen as a symbol for the general exploitation of people by colonial powers. I must note, however, that the notion is not very sophisticated, as all of culture and the history of human culture itself is based on these processes. Colonial empires have flourished and failed dozens of times over the globe since time immemorial—China, Greece, Persia, Rome, and so on—long before the British established their empire. Culture and the spread of culture is based on mutual influence (politically mislabeled "appropriation"). Everywhere that cultures interact, such influence inevitably takes place. Without *appropriation*, culture itself would be impossible.

Zombies

Aftershocks

In retrospect, the zombie genre of horror films should obviously be divided into two classes: the early and comparatively sparse Voodoo-based phase, and the huge and overwhelming phase that follows in the wake of *I am Legend* or *Night of the Living Dead*. Although tangentially related, they are substantially two different things.

The zombie craze of the twenty-first century has far surpassed anything previously produced. The idea of zombies and the "zombie apocalypse" have become as much a part of current popular culture as Frankenstein, Dracula, and the Wolf Man ever were in previous generations. Clearly, the initial impetus of the genre hinges on the anthropomorphizing of the idea of decay, disease, and aggressive-yet-lumbering destructive forces threatening the very existence of humanity. The popularity of the mythos seems directly connected to the AIDS epidemic and general fears of pandemics around the globe. Beyond this, however, there has been an even more profound twist, which has become increasingly well established under the influence of social criticism and certain academic theories: the turning of the zombies into an oppressed "Other." (We saw in our essay on the vampire how some have interpreted Stoker's vision of a vampiric invasion from Eastern Europe as a metaphor for the perceived increased immigration of Eastern European Jews to Britain in the late nineteenth century.)

IX

Cults and Covens

The word "cult" is greatly misunderstood. In usual and casual parlance, it means a religious or quasi-religious group that the speaker does not like. In point of fact, all religious organizations with a set of beliefs, rituals, and social organizational principles are technically cults. The term "cult" is derived from the Latin verb *colere*, "to care, cultivate," and directly from the adjective form *cultus*, "inhabited, cultivated, worshipped." At first the word was used to describe the acts of worship, not the group that did the activity. The Catholic Church is a cult, just as much as Krishna Consciousness or the Church of Satan. From a sociological or anthropological viewpoint, they are all equally "cults." Organized groups with dangerous, gruesome, and nefarious practices and motives have been a mainstay of horror films for a long time. Many of the essays in this book concern themselves with cultic dimensions (e.g., the cult of the vampire, Egyptian cults of living mummies, Voodoo, the Cthulhu-worshippers of Lovecraft, and the cults lurking behind some early German Expressionist films).

In my judgment, I was influenced to a significant degree in my later interests in life by early feelings evoked by horror and science-fiction films. I loved the scholarly camaraderie I saw in movies such as *Journey to the Center of the Earth* (1959) and *The Time Machine* (1960), but also the secret world of power expressed in ones such as *The Masque of the Red Death* (1964) or *Kiss of the Vampire* (1963). Eventually, as is documented elsewhere in the book, I would myself join several cults and create some of my own as well. These would span from the magical/initiatory to the religious, and to the sexual underground inspired by Sade and Sacher-Masoch. These phases of actualization of early feelings would only come well after my initial exposure to these films, however. They alone cannot explain the events of my later life.

On one level or another, cults of various kinds and descriptions play parts in many horror films. We have the secret band of vampire-hunters in *Dracula*, the Priesthood of Arkam in the Mummy series of the 1940s, the ancient initiatory background of the werewolf, Lovecraft's Cthulhu cults, and many others. However, just as often we find individuals operating alone to accomplish some visionary and usually unintentionally evil purpose, such as Frankenstein, Dracula, and all the mad scientists working in the mad labs throughout the history of the horror film.

The topic of cults and covens in horror films and their deeper significance is a complex one. They have psychological or esoteric meanings for individuals in which the cults and their members are metaphors for the inner workings of the mind and the pathway of individuals through the maze of the culture to which they belong. But they also reveal the matrix of meaning—deceptive though it is—which explains how a whole society can be caused to go into a panic, to lose its rational mind and revert to a mode of thinking that was thought to have been eradicated three hundred years before. Here we will see, among other things, how horror movies of the late 1960s and 1970s played a significant role in the real-life tragedy of what came to be called the Satanic Panic beginning in the 1980s. This is serious, if often dreary, material that has had to creep into our wonderful world of Gothick Meditations, but it is a story that needs to be told.

Cults have been a part of the religious landscape of worldwide

Early Christians conducting a ceremony in a catacomb, 50 C.E.

culture since time immemorial. Cults that are seen as dangerous threats to social and political order only really occur in societies which are in crisis and flux, and have lost their sense of internal integrity, solidarity and identity. Such a condition was common, for example, in the late Roman Empire. Some people have noted parallels between the late Empire and current Western civilization generally. Hostility toward cults, and fear of them, is indeed an ancient obsession. Here is an excerpt from one ancient Latin text:

> A child ... is set before the would-be novice. The novice stabs the child to death. ... Then ... they hungrily drink the child's blood, and compete with one another as they divide the limbs. Through this victim they are all bound together; and the fact that they all share this knowledge of the crime pledges them all to silence.
>
> On the feast-day they all foregather with their children, sisters, mothers, people of either sex and all ages. When the company is all aglow from feasting, and impure lust has been set afire by drunkenness, they twine the bonds of unnamable passion as chance decides. And so all alike are incestuous, if not always in deed at least by complicity.... Precisely the secrecy of this evil religion proves that all these things, or practically all, are true. (Cohn 1975, 1)

This description, which might have been taken from the pages of a tabloid in the time of the Satanic Panic, was actually written almost two thousand years ago by a *pagan* author describing a strange cult from the East that had infected the Roman Empire—*Christianity*. These observations about Christianity were certainly factually in error, but were based on the Romans' (well-founded) fear that this cult, which numbered many slaves and criminals in its ranks, whose founding hero was an executed criminal himself, and which was bent on taking over the Empire, met in graveyards and as a central part of their rite could be heard to exclaiming: "Eat ... this is my body! Drink ... this is the chalice of my blood!" It is rather logical for the Roman pagans to conclude that the Christians were ghoulish, cannibalistic libertines (with their "love feasts") and to fear them with equal logic. Later, once this cult had indeed taken over the empire, the Church would use these Latin texts, originally fashioned to accuse Christians of misdeeds, and substitute the names of heretical sects, such as the Bogomils. The general description of breeding babies for sacrifice and participation in sexual orgies, and so forth, would continue to be used from the Middle Ages right up to the Satanic Panic of the 1980s. The horrific fantasy of Roman philosophers about Christians continued on and became the delusions of modern believers.

In antiquity not all cults were necessarily considered evil or detrimental to public order. Some, such as that of Mithras or Orpheus, would be considered salutary and beneficial to society and to the health of the Empire. The designation "cult" today is very similar to the attitude of the ancients toward religions or other kinds of movements that were considered unhealthy and detrimental to the social, political, and economic order of the Empire. Good cults make men stronger, wiser, and more prosperous; bad ones make men weaker, more gullible, and less thoughtful.

Cults in Literature and Film

Literature has a wide range of cultic horrors, but it must be said that the cinematic versions of cult horrors appear more vibrant and obsessive. Lovecraft and his school (see Essay VI) were full of "Unspeakable Cults." For the purposes of this meditation, I will divide the history of cults in film into two phases: pre– and post–*Rosemary's Baby*. To the earlier period of the first phase belong *Seven Footprints to Satan* (1929) and *The Black Cat* (1934).

Our look at cults in horror films begins, then, with *Seven Footprints to Satan* (1929). Long thought to be a lost film, it is based directly on the A. Merritt book by the same title published in 1927. Abraham Merritt (1884–1943) was a successful writer and journalist who often wrote in the same publications as H. P. Lovecraft and Robert E. Howard (e.g., *Weird Tales*). The book is entirely serious in tone and leaves the reader wondering whether Satan is a supernatural entity who has taken on human form, or whether he is a criminal mastermind in the mold of Fu Manchu

Seven Footprints to Satan (1929)

or Dr. Mabuse. In the film, it turns out that Satan is the main character's rich Uncle Joe who wants to prevent the protagonist from going on a trip of exploration to Africa. Both the book and the film are highly entertaining in their own ways. The central feature of the story is that Satan has a sort of ceremonial game involving a platform of seven steps which leads up to his black throne; beside the latter is a golden throne, which will be taken by the one who wins the challenge. Four of the steps are chosen by a mechanical device as being "good" ones, while three others belong to Satan. If the challenger steps only on the four good spots, the golden throne is won and he has Satan as his servant—which brings untold wealth and power. If, however, the player steps on one of Satan's steps, a single favor is owed to Satan—with no questions asked. If two of Satan's steps are landed upon, the challenger has to serve him for a full year. But if three steps belong to Satan, the player's immortal soul is lost forever. As it turns out, Satan has rigged the game pretty well, so that the challenger virtually has no chance of winning.

The Black Cat was a film that all Monster Kids saw as a part

The Black Cat (1934)

of the Shock Package. It was directed for Universal by Edgar Ulmer, who had worked on films in Weimar Berlin before his immigration to the US. The film tells the story of newlyweds Peter and Joan on their honeymoon in Hungary when they meet a man, Dr. Vitus Werdegast (Bela Lugosi), and on a bus ride with him have a crash and have to go to the nearby home of Hjalmar Poelzig (Boris Karloff). It turns out that Poelzig had commanded a fort called Marmoros [pron. "MAHR-mor-osh"] on that site during World War I. Werdegast had been a prisoner in a Serbian camp for fifteen years, during which time Poelzig took possession of Werdegast's wife, Karen, and his infant daughter, also named Karen. Poelzig keeps the preserved bodies of women in glass cases on display. He plans to sacrifice Joan in a Satanic ritual during the dark of the moon. He is seen to be reading from a book called "The Rites of Lucifer."

During the ceremony, Poelzig recites a long Latin incantation, the full text of which reads:

> *Cum grano salis. Fortis cadere cedere non potest. Humanum est errare. Lupis pilum mutat, non mentem. Magna est veritas et praevalebit. Acta exteriora indicant interiora secreta. Aequam memento rebus in arduis servare mentem. Amissum quod nescitur non amittitur. Brutum fulmen. Cum grano salis. Fortis cadere cedere non potest. Fructu, non foliis arborem aestima. Insanus omnes furere credit ceteros. Quem paenitet peccasse paene est innocens.*

Surprisingly, this translates to:

> With a grain of salt. A brave man may fall, but he cannot yield. To err is human. The wolf may change his skin, but not his nature. Truth is mighty and will prevail. External actions show internal secrets. Remember when life's path is steep to keep your mind even. The loss that is not

Boris Karloff as Satanic priest Hjalmar Poelzig in *The Black Cat*.

known is no loss at all. Heavy thunder. With a grain of salt. A brave man may fall, but he cannot yield. By its fruit, not by its leaves, judge a tree. Every madman thinks everybody mad. Who repents from sinning is almost innocent.

Werdegast tries to stop Poelzig, but is thwarted. During this ritual, in which Joan is laid across a cross-like contraption, something unexplained happens and Joan is whisked away. Werdegast then discovers that Poelzig has killed his daughter and ties him to his own embalming rack, takes up a scalpel, and utters the famous words:

> *Do you know what I am going to do to you now?*
> *No?*
> *Did you ever see an animal skinned, Hjalmar? Ha, ha, ha.*

Karloff and Lugosi in a promotional photo for *The Black Cat*.

That's what I'm going to do to you now—tear the skin from your body... slowly... bit by bit!

Werdegast proceeds to begin this ghastly procedure in an artfully filmed scene. But in the process Werdegast is shot by Peter by mistake. Mortally wounded, Werdegast activates explosives to blow up Fort Marmoros. This destroys the building and Poelzig's whole "rotten cult." Joan and Peter escape to safety.

The genius of *The Black Cat* resides not so much in its plot or story, but in the atmospheric elements and attention to detail regarding everything from set-design, to wardrobe, to symbolic elements such as the Luciferian cult, to apparent sexual variations—sadomasochism, necrophilia, pedophilia, and homosexuality have all been ascribed to its sphere. Ulmer was a talented filmmaker, dedicated to his craft, but this was the only project he made for a major company. *The Black Cat* was Universal's top-grossing film of 1934. It appears to me that Ulmer brought something of the ambiance of post–World War One culture—the Weimar mystique—to the screen, just a year after its demise in 1933 when Hitler came to power in Germany. This culture is explored in more detail in Essay XII. It is perhaps true that the film was so disturbing on some vague level that it got him blacklisted, much as *Freaks* had done for Tod Browning. But there is more to that story. Ulmer fell in love with his script assistant on the project, Shirley Alexander, married to one of the company owner's favorite nephews. Shirley's marriage ended and she and Ulmer were then married. Ulmer left Hollywood for New York. There Ulmer embarked on a low-budget independent filmmaking career: this included Yiddish films (*Green Fields*, 1937), an all African American–cast film (*Moon over Harlem*, 1939), a Ukrainian one (*Cossacks in Exile*, 1939), and an exploitation film, *Girls in Chains* (1943). Other notable contributions by Ulmer to the world of cinema were his noir masterpiece *Detour* (1945) and a weird but meaningful little science-fiction picture, *The Man from Planet X* (1951).

The Seventh Victim (1943) was produced by Val Lewton and directed by Mark Robson. The script was revised by DeWitt Bodeen, who included the element of a Satanic cult inspired by a group he claimed to have known about in New York City. The story is somewhat enigmatic and subtle, and the film depends heavily on its atmosphere and aura of mystery. It concerns a young woman named Mary, who is obliged to leave her Catholic boarding school because her sister and only relative, Jacqueline, has gone missing and has not paid Mary's tuition. Mary sets out to find her sister in New York. When Mary arrives in New York, she finds out that Jacqueline had sold her cosmetics business eight months prior, but Mary learns from a former

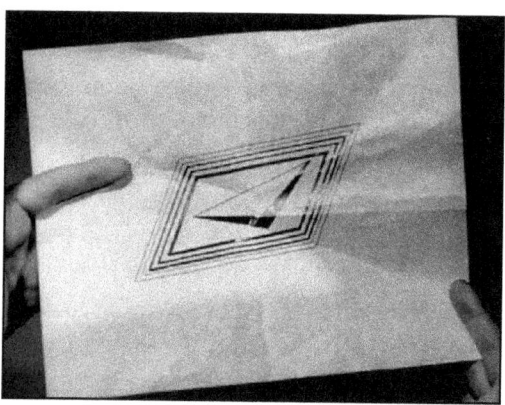

The Palladists' parallelogram in *The Seventh Victim* (1943).

employee, Frances—who claims to have seen Jacqueline a week earlier—that she might find out something at Dante's, an Italian restaurant in Greenwich Village. Mary goes there and discovers an apartment above the restaurant that her sister had rented, but never moved into. The rooms of the apartment are empty except for a wooden chair, over which hangs a noose from the ceiling. Mary meets her sister's secret husband, Gregory, along with a few other people, and learns that her sister is a member of a cult called the Palladists. Mary eventually finds Jacqueline, but she is later kidnapped by the cult and condemned to die for revealing the existence of the organization. They do not kill her directly, however. The deed is done by means of magic: using concentration on the cult's unique symbol, a parallelogram, Jacqueline is caused to enter the apartment she had rented, and to hang herself with the noose hanging from the ceiling and the chair provided. It is noted that Jacqueline was suicidal anyway, so the cult just pushed her in a natural direction. This is an example of what Anton LaVey called the Balance Factor. This factor stipulates that magic works best if it takes advantage of

Curse of the Demon (1957)

preexisting conditions or tendencies in a person's character or in the probability of events occurring.

A sort of interesting romantic comedy also about a witches' coven in Greenwich Village is the 1958 film *Bell, Book and Candle* starring James Stewart and Kim Novak. The cult and the magic are all depicted as real, but it is lighthearted, with a happy ending.

A favorite of most horror aficionados is *Curse of the Demon* (1957; called *Night of the Demon* in Britain). It is adapted from M. R. James's 1911 short story "Casting the Runes." The film was directed by Jacques Tourneur of *Cat People* fame and starred Dana Andrews, not an actor normally associated with horror films.

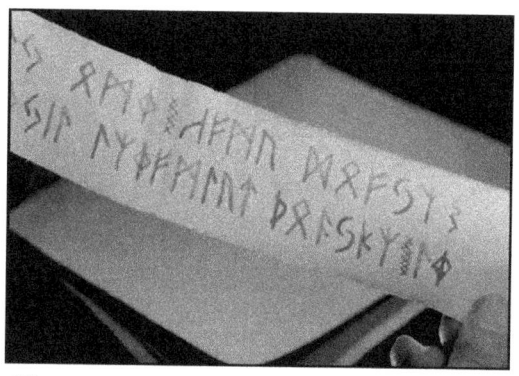

The runic incription in *Curse of the Demon*.

ᛉ ᚱᛗᛠᛚᚠᛗᚾ ᛘᛉᚠᛉᛟᛇ
ᛉᛁᚱ ᚱᛟᛠᚠᛗᚱᚾᛏ ᚦᛉᚠᛉᚲᛟᚼᛚᚱᚢ

The film's runic inscription, transcribed with some semblance of accuracy as above, shows that it is merely a jumble of runic and rune-like symbols. It is, for example, a mixture of the Older Futhark and the Anglo-Saxon Futhorc that bears no authenticity from a runological perspective, nor does it make any sense linguistically.

This film is marked by its excellent production values and design. It can also be ascribed to a small group of films that have been dubbed "Folk Horror." Instead of using standard Satanic imagery and logic of a cult opposed to orthodox Christian values, it steps totally outside this model to present the idea of an ancient, pre-Christian cult that has continued to the present day. Some other older films that belong to this genre are *Witchfinder General* (1968), *Blood on Satan's Claw* (1971), *The Virgin Spring* (1960), and *The Wicker Man* (1973). The genre of folk horror is at present a growing one. Folk horror can be more disturbing to the average audience because it implies that the narrative is not rigged in the sense that standard Satanic narratives always suggest that the Devil must be defeated in the end because the Bible says so. If the underlying mythology is drawn from the Christian narrative, then it must logically follow the narrative mandates of that myth. But folk horror usually has no such Christian mythic narrative driving it. Rather it says: the old ways have never been destroyed, and cannot be destroyed. They will rise up and atavistically reassert themselves, inevitably.

The exemplary folk-horror film is perhaps *The Wicker Man*, which was hailed at the time of its release in 1973 as the "Citizen Kane of horror films." Narratively, it is framed as a sort of mystery

Christopher Lee as Lord Summerisle in *The Wicker Man* (1973).

story in which a police officer investigates the disappearance of a little girl, suspecting that she is to be sacrificed by a community of druidic-type cultists led by Lord Summerisle (Christopher Lee). In the end, it is revealed that the cop, a virgin prig, has been lured to his death as the actual sacrifice of the cult, to be burned alive in the wicker man to ensure the fertility of the island on which the cult lives near the coast of Scotland. It's all very pious and merry. Pagans love it, Christians are scared witless. The idea of sacrifices being burned in effigies of men made out of wicker is drawn from classical descriptions, especially as recorded by Julius Caesar in *De bello Gallico* (The Gallic War) concerning practices in Gaul (present-day France). It is uncertain as to whether such practices actually took place. Human sacrifice was certainly engaged in by the Druids, but the one sacrificed was preferably a criminal or prisoner of war, or perhaps a noble volunteer.

The New Satanic Age in Film

The most revolutionary and influential film about cults was released in 1968—*Rosemary's Baby* directed by Roman Polanski. The film is based on Ira Levin's bestselling 1967 novel of the same title. Due to the general story and theme, coupled with its high-quality production and the media attention it garnered, this film changed the whole cult movie genre, spawning dozens of other films inspired by some of its themes and concepts. It can be said that a new phase of the depiction of cults in horror films was ushered in by this film. It tells the story of Rosemary and Guy Woodhouse, who live in a large exclusive apartment building in NYC. Guy is a struggling actor. They befriend an elderly couple, Roman and Minnie Castevet. Guy becomes friendly with them and his acting prospects take a miraculous turn for the better. Roman and Minnie enter into a conspiracy with Guy to have Rosemary become pregnant with Satan's child—the Antichrist. After the child is born, Rosemary at first rejects it, but it is the cause of a great gathering of Satanists from around the world in the apartment building, who exclaim at one point during a celebratory party: "Hail Satan! To 1966, the Year One!" In the final scene Rosemary sees the child, and is at first horrified by his eyes. She asks, "What have you done to his eyes!?" Roman calmly answers: "He has his father's eyes." At last Rosemary accepts and begins to love her son. It was widely rumored that Anton LaVey had been a technical advisor on the film, and that he had even played Satan in the scene where the Devil impregnates Rosemary. This rumor was made all the more believable for some due to the proclamation in the film that 1966 is the Year One, as this is the doctrine of the Church of Satan, which was founded in 1966. Film historians reject the idea that LaVey had anything to do with the film. He did make an appearance at the premier of the movie in San Francisco, and that was the moment when Michael Aquino first saw LaVey. The phrase "Rosemary's Baby" later became an insider's code name for the Church of Satan itself.

The effectiveness of *Rosemary's Baby* hinges on its theme of cosmic horror (the birth of the "Antichrist"); the entanglement of an average, innocent, and virtuous woman in the process; and the details of how she was unwittingly drawn into the trap of becoming a vessel for the manifestation of His Satanic Majesty.

Rosemary's Baby became a springboard for a whole new genre of Satanic cult films. This genre has only grown over the

Rosemary's Baby (1968)

years. Some took up the Antichrist themes (e.g., the *Omen* series [1976–1985]), while many others were concerned with the fascinating theme of recurring rejuvenation though magical/Satanic rites (e.g., *The Mephisto Waltz* [1971] and *The Brotherhood of Satan* [1971]). This latter theme is very intelligible at the dawn of the "Me Generation" and in a society becoming increasingly youth- and beauty-oriented. The essential component of the immortality and rejuvenation themes is the focus on the survival of the carnal ego of the individual.

A perhaps unexpected entry here is *The Devils* (1971) by Ken Russell. It is based on Aldous Huxley's historical novel *The Devils of Loudun* (1952) and tells the story of Urban Grandier, a priest who was burned at the stake for having made a pact with the Devil and bewitching the nuns in the nearby Ursuline convent. Grandier, played by Oliver Reed, is accurately portrayed as a libertine philosopher, protective of his town and questioning of the Church. He is eliminated by Church and State for political purposes. Here it is clear that the nefarious cult being discussed is not a "Satanic" one—but the Roman Catholic Church itself. It creates scenes every bit as horrific as any supposedly diabolical cult, and does so with the complete aura of acceptability and virtue! *This* is the true horror of history.

The Exorcist (1973) might well be included in this category, but it is really a straightforward orthodox story that seems to assume that all of the ideas about demons and demonic

The Devils (1971)

possession inherited from the Middle Ages are somehow true and real. As weak as that premise might seem at first, the story is told so well, and the effects so well done, that it clearly had a transcendent effect on many audiences. I knew several people who, after spending the evening in a line to get the newly inflated ticket prices, spent the night unable to go to sleep because they had been convinced that "something like that might be possible." The film was so well crafted that it made believers—even if only for the night—out of all sorts of people. It is my belief that the use of borderline subliminal shots used in the picture were responsible for some of its exaggerated psychological effects. The impact of *The Exorcist* can be seen as a catalyst for the conclusion of the first great age of the supernatural horror film, just as *The Texas Chainsaw Massacre* (1974) can be seen as the end of an era in the psychological "slasher" genre. In both cases even bigger box-office receipts were on the other side, but as an art form, these two films marked the ultimate expressions of their kind.

Interpretation

When looking at the idea of cults in horror films, one must realize that the element at hand is a social, or sociological one. Cults are social groups. They have an internal structure; typically, this is hierarchical. They usually hold out the promise of some sort of gain to the members of the cult: success, wealth, long life, untold pleasures, wisdom, knowledge, and so on. On the other hand, cults are often seen as being antisocial with regard the more general culture in which the cult exists. It may work at purposes contrary to the general interests of the host culture.

Since cults themselves represent a sociological phenomenon, it would appear that their hidden meaning as expressed in early horror films would also have a strong sociological dimension. Cults can be seen as institutions that bolster or threaten one's own social class or group. The pagan Romans of antiquity saw the Christians as a gang of criminals who had bloody orgies and practiced cannibalism, but by the same token, poor fundamentalist rural people today might see their problems rooted in that damned Bavarian Illuminati and all those egghead professors.

The cult forms a double-edged sword in the horror genre. Some people fear cults. They are obsessed and frightened by the idea that behind an apparent facade of normalcy there lurks an organized and powerful, evil and nefarious group that threatens conventional people's sanity, position, and their very lives. On the other hand, there are people who are fascinated with the idea of *belonging* to such a cult. Based on purely anecdotal evidence and my own personal experience, I would venture to guess that the average Monster Kid of the 1960s was a fairly marginalized outsider in his school and social environment. To such an outsider, the idea of belonging to a powerful, sexy, and wealthy group of secret *insider* cultists would be pretty appealing. Although the cult is almost always destroyed at the end of the film, for the moments in-between, when the cult is presented in all its frightful glory, the image can be seductive. This allure, coupled with some knowledge of actual history, make the viability of such cults even more attractive. Of course, for most Monster Kids such ideas remained only in the realm of fantasy …

Beliefs surrounding the idea of a cult engaging in a conspiracy to overthrow the existing cultural norms or the political establishment have been around for millennia. As we saw, the ancient Romans actually pioneered this belief in connection with their (well-founded) suspicions that the Christians constituted just such a deviant cult from the East. In horror films this cultic scenario is rather common, as is the idea of a mad individual (a scientist or magician) who has discovered some secret power with which he threatens to alter the world in similar ways. All of this is mirrored in the common American mythic obsession with the archetype of the "Lone Nut" *versus* the myth of a vast right-wing or left-wing conspiracy—lefties see the Klan and the Nazis behind every event, whereas the extreme Right remains fearful of the Illuminati or the Zionists, and everyone can be terrified by the possibility of some sort of Plan from Outer Space.

Certainly, one of the most pronounced attractions to the idea of a cult is the power of *belonging*. This is especially true for people who feel that the conventional society around them is repressive and full of erroneous assumptions. The individual who has arrived at inner conclusions that deviate from the consensus reality, as expressed among the people all around him or her, longs in a sense for the companionship and even mentorship of those who share in this alternative view of reality. This impulse is often used as a mode of manipulating insecure individuals and this is the usual story where cults are involved. But again, all cults are not the same. Some encourage individual development and the strengthening of the individual will and consciousness. At the same time, the work of cults can also be seen to be involved with the revolutionary activity of destroying the status quo of a society in order to take its potential to a higher level. Success in this regard is rare, but where radical changes have been made in the world—whether through the Italian Renaissance or the American Revolution—certain "cultic" characteristics were nevertheless present.

Formal Satanism's influence on film was rather sparse. By formal Satanism I mean one of the recognized and official Satanic or left-hand-path organizations, such as the Church of Satan or the Temple of Set. But where it did occur it certainly lent an air of authenticity and power to scripts that might have otherwise been lame in the extreme. One notable example of this is when then Priest Michael Aquino of the Church of Satan wrote a ritual passage for the independent film *Asylum of Satan* (1972). The ritual part of the script read:

> **Martine:** In the name of Satan, Arch Dæmon and Lord of Infernus, I call for the Gates of the Dark Realm to crash asunder, that my commands shall ride the whirlwinds of the Abyss! Azazel, Herald of Hell, Behold! I speak the keys of the nine Angles and I summon the High Dæmon who doth unleash the Apocalypse: Abaddon–Typhon–Lord of the Seven, whose name is and shall be death! Through the blazing angles of the Shining Trapezoid... Come! By the Tenth Key

Lobby card for the German release of *The Devil's Rain* (1975).

thy doom hath been spoken, for we are the same—the true worshippers of the highest and ineffable King of Hell!

Hark, Abaddon! The rites are spoken. Met are thy terms of acridian fire, serpent, and dismemberment. Loose the Hounds of the Barrier and attend us, for the Bond of Satan hath been sealed by Asmodeus, by Astaroth, by Belial, by Leviathan.

Arise! Move, and appear! Leave now thy ruined and blackened temple beyond the stars. Behold before thee the goat without horns, unblemished according to thy desire. By the covenant of Satan, sealed in the Black Flame, open the mysteries of creation!

All: Ave Satanas! Rege Satanas! Hail, Satan!

This ritual text shows elements from the leading edge of

Cults and Covens

Satanism as it was being practiced in the grottos of the Church of Satan at that time. Note the elements drawn from Lovecraftian imagery and ritual.

In 1975 the film *The Devil's Rain* appeared, in which Anton LaVey acted as a technical advisor and even had a minor role in the film itself. He designed certain aspects of the rituals and certainly of the ceremonial symbolism. His hand is directly visible in the set design of the ritual chamber, with its impactful trapezoidal pentagram device:

LaVey-designed trapezoidal pentagram in *The Devil's Rain*.

Conclusion and Aftershocks

Most films merely create aftershocks within the genre of horror films or in other avenues of art and popular culture. In the case of films about Satanic cults, and most especially *Rosemary's Baby*, it can be argued that effects were created and reverberations felt in the realms of religion, politics, law, and general culture. It spawned a whole series of imitations the images and ideas of which influenced an impressionable generation. These films appear to have had a direct effect on what was to be called the Satanic Panic 1980–1992.

Roots of the Satanic Panic: The Pentagram of Deception

If we look back critically at the time period before the Satanic Panic began around 1980, we will discover what I call the Pentagram of Deception—five elements that when taken together put a spell over the minds of many Americans and others worldwide. It would all be so amusing—if so many people had not been hurt by the activities of legal entities which had the power to harm innocent citizens: law enforcement, clergy, and therapists. The Pentagram of Deception is formed by the following points:

1. Medieval Foundation
2. Traumatic Contemporary Events (assasinations, Vietnam, Watergate, Manson)
3. Horror Films
4. Dungeons and Dragons
5. Heavy Metal

Some of these points are real and concrete influences, while others are the misinterpretation or vehicles of mere entertainment of people who had for whatever reason lost their ability to distinguish fact from fiction. In no way do I wish to have the reader misconstrue the Pentagram of Deception as a description of what caused some sort of actual Satanic cult to come into existence or cause crimes to be committed. To the contrary, I stress here that these factors only led a good number of our unfortunate fellow citizens to be deceived into *believing* that such things were happening. It was estimated that around seventy per cent of Americans believed that Satanic cults were committing crimes "in the name of Satan" around the country in the 1980s. They had worked their fragile minds into believing they had a role in a horror film of their own making. It was so exciting to be able to think: "This is not a dream, it is really happening!"

The first point of the pentagram is the medieval substratum of surviving Christian culture. It is based on medieval ideas that included belief in the existence of nefarious cults (e.g., Bogomils,

Cathars, Paulicians, witches, pagans, and most especially, the Jews) which sought to undermine the hegemony of Christendom. From the Middle Ages into the Nazi era in Germany, Jews were accused of many of the standard medieval charges the Christians made against cults—being in league with Satan (the Synagogue of Satan), sacrifice of children and using their blood for Passover rituals, poisoning water, and so on. All of this formed a general cultural underlay, waiting to be atavistically revived if and when the right stimulus was applied.

The second point constitutes contemporary events: the assassinations of JFK, MLK, and RFK; the Vietnam War and its failure; the Watergate scandal and the resignation of the President; the headlines surrounding the Manson Family; and many other happenings in the turbulent Sixties and early Seventies. (Culturally, I think it can be said that the *real* 1960s date from between the election of JFK to the resignation of Nixon: 1960–1974.) These traumas put people in the mood to regress to the medieval thinking. Such a thing is not rare: in the twentieth century alone, we saw Germany do so (1933) and Iran as well (1979).

Thirdly, horror films in general, but especially those depicting forms of Satanism and cultic activity, both gave vent to the fears and anxieties of the age and provided a template for the imaginations of individuals under the stress and strain of the traumatic cultural changes that were taking place. Most used the films as they were intended, as cathartic release. Others, disabled by medieval superstitions and rattled by ongoing social change, simply let reality get away from them and began to believe that "it is really happening."

The fourth point, the activity known as fantasy role-playing games (RPGs), often known by one of its brand names, *Dungeons and Dragons*, took hold in the culture around 1980, although it actually goes back into the 1970s. This form of recreation allowed people, especially kids, to create alternative universes and immerse themselves in them. Outsiders to the activity, especially the parents of these kids, sometimes saw the game as dangerous and "cultic," or "occultic." When one enthusiast of

RPGs committed suicide, his mother blamed the RPGs he was playing, linked them to Satanic cults, formed a pressure group called BADD—"Bothered About Dungeons and Dragons."

The final point of the pentagram is so-called heavy metal music, a genre in part inspired by horror films. Again, the noise created by these bands was no doubt very annoying to parents of kids who loved its iconoclastic messages (just as parents of the Monster Kid generation hated rock and roll), yet this, too, was drawn into the mix as evidence of Satanic cult activity by its critics (e.g., Tipper Gore and her Parents Music Resource Center, which led to actual Senate hearings).

Fueled by free-floating anxieties, a subculture of accusers developed from this soup of imagined influences and an unholy alliance was formed among three elements—law enforcement, therapists, and clergy members (genuine and ad hoc)—to mount a new Inquisition, really more akin to the witch-hunters of the Protestant school, which went to war against those who they believed were part of a vast Satanic conspiracy. What started as a delusion ended up being a lucrative (and for them, fun-filled) cottage industry for members of the professions involved in the "investigation." Just as in the European witch-hunts, when a witch was "found out" and executed, his or her property was confiscated and divided three ways: to the prince, to the church, and to the "finder." A similar triad developed in the Satanic Panic—also for the sake of profit. The problem is that many innocent lives were ruined by their false accusations, and real victims of the kind of crimes they were supposedly investigating were ultimately discredited and forgotten. The conspiracy of evil did exist, but it was in the hearts and minds of the accusers— Grandier was burned for the sake of the evil lurking in the hearts of his accusers.

Ironically and most tragically, the evidence of the past few years has shown that ritual child abuse really *was* taking place— except that it was not Satanists who were the perpetrators, but rather the clergy of establishment churches, members of which had first engendered the original Satanic panics in the Middle Ages!

Cults and Covens

It appears that the dynamic at work in the generation of the Satanic Panic was one involving a triangle of persecution in which church-based interests, therapists, and law enforcement forged an alliance targeting largely imaginary boogeymen (since no one was really doing these things, then everyone could be suspected of such activity with little to no evidence). It was a true return to the days of the witchcraft trials. The new "inquisitors" or "witch-finders" were the therapists ("psychologists") who became very facile at implanting false memories in their "patients" (or victims, or marks). This usually involved subjecting the victim to stress and suggesting certain things to them. Quite often the images or patterns the victims of therapy would dredge up out of their unconscious minds were ones originally experienced while watching horror films such as the ones discussed in this essay. They were then "believed" as being "recovered memories." It is a cultural pattern we thought we had put behind us historically. But sadly, this has proven not to be the case.

No other group of films generated greater aftershocks than the films of Satanic cult activity spawned by *Rosemary's Baby* in 1968. It was the United States and a few countries in the Anglosphere (Canada, UK, Australia, South Africa, etc.) that became the hotbeds of the Satanic Panic during the 1980s and into the early 1990s. The Salem witchcraft trials and their spirit of mass hysteria and delusion spread once more, just as they had three hundred years earlier. There were certain structural similarities between the events of Salem (1692–1693) and the USA generally between 1980 and 1992. One would have to be blind to cultural trends not to notice that the age of the Satanic Panic coincided with the years in which more politically conservative regimes (Reagan-Bush) were in power in the United States, and that the characterization of "the Other" vis-à-vis the political establishment changed with the Clinton administration from "devil worshipers" to gun-toting militia men with outright governmental attacks on Ruby Ridge and the Branch Davidians in Waco in 1992 and 1993, respectively. Both regimes focused in this regard on an "inner enemy," but the fervor with which the government itself attacked this inner enemy intensified after the

Rosemary's Baby (1968)

Satanic Panic, and after the fall of the Soviet empire. In favor of the Clintonista approach, at least the militia men actually *existed*, as opposed to pure inner fantasies of medieval origin being projected onto entirely innocent people as was generally the case during the Satanic Panic. Also, in 1992 an FBI investigator, Kenneth V. Lanning, issued a report entitled *Investigator's Guide to Allegations of "Ritual" Childhood Abuse*, which generally concluded that the whole phenomenon was a hoax with no credible evidence for its existence. After that, the triangle of persecution—clergy, therapists, and law enforcement—quickly began to dissolve. America would soon enough move on to another ancient enemy of Christendom: Islam.

X

Hanns Heinz Ewers

Horror from the Inside

Hanns Heinz Ewers [pron. EY-verss] (1871–1943) is a man whose presence is said to have frightened Aleister Crowley, who himself was reputed to be the "Wickedest Man in the World." H. P. Lovecraft lauded Ewers's work in his essay *Supernatural Horror in Literature* (1927). Despite all of this, Ewers remains a relatively unknown figure in the world of horror literature or filmmaking—which should be surprising since Ewers was a pioneering master of both the written word and the early transposition of ideas to the screen. The reason for his obscurity lies in the fact that he joined the National Socialist German Workers Party, the Nazis, in 1931. However, he gained no advantage from this as he was soon thereafter spurned by them due to his record for "decadence," open bisexuality, and even avowed "Philosemitism." But his reputation was ruined for any postwar reception or widespread appreciation in academic circles due to his Nazi connection. This leaves him as a wanderer in the gloom—one of the greatest spiritual Outsiders of all time.

I was first exposed to Ewers by reputation only through a passage in Gabriel Ronay's 1972 book *The Truth about Dracula*, which painted a very sinister and lurid image indeed:

> The writings of Hans-Heinz [*sic*] Ewers reflect most clearly the close link between the blood-fixated mysticism of the literary precursors to National Socialism and the vampire Dracula conjured up by Bram Stoker. . . . His horror trilogy, completed around the First World War, contained all the dark, shapeless Nordic mysticism and exultation of Teutonic blood rites that were to become so dear to the ideologists of the Nazi order. It also incorporated elements of barbarous cruelty—conspicuously missing from Stoker's horror fiction—which bear the hallmark of the historical Dracula. (Ronay 1972, 157)

I had discovered Ronay's book upon my return from Germany in the early 1970s and as I briefly renewed my interest in vampires and vampire lore in the wake of the publication of *In Search of Dracula* by McNally and Florescu. This stimulus set me on a quest to find out more about Ewers. My ever-reliable resource, the library of the University of Texas, provided many answers. I began to read some of his work in German, and in the early 1980s acquired some translations of his work from used booksellers (these early English translations were sometimes slightly edited to soften some of Ewers's words). The wonderful 1992 biography of Ewers by Wilfried Kugel, *Der Unverantwortliche* (The Irresponsible One), opened many more doors, and in 2000 I published an anthology volume of his stories entitled *Strange Tales*. This also contains a short biography and analysis of Ewers's life and some aspects of his philosophy. I refer the reader to that book for many more general details on Ewers.

Ewers is unique in the history of the writing of horror and its production for film. He appears, both to himself and to others, to have been a horror villain, a monstrous soul—but who was really a misunderstood genius. His genius still largely defies comprehension by most. Ewers is horror *from within*; he provides insight into the *subject* of horror, that is, to the mind that *produces* horror, and even that *is* horror. His work has been found

Hanns Heinz Ewers photographed by Atelier Eburth, 1920.
(Laufenburg collection)

to have an unsettling effect on the reader (or viewer) in a manner similar to, yet in character entirely distinct from, that of H. P. Lovecraft. The genius of Lovecraft is that he shows a skeptical non-participant in the uncanny slowly coming to realize that the incomprehensible horror is real, whereas Ewers is an enthusiastic participant in, and generator of, the horror in a realistic way. This characterizes both Ewers himself in his personal life as well as his alter egos, such as Frank Braun or Jan Olieslager, in his works of fiction.

Ewers: Author and Screenwriter

Ewers was a very popular writer in Germany in the first half of the twentieth century. He earned his doctoral degree in law, and hence often bore the title "Doctor." Ewers never actually practiced law but rather became a creative writer who specialized in the uncanny. Dr. Ewers wrote hundreds of short stories and seven major novels. But what interests us above all for our present study is his involvement in the filmmaking industry. Ewers was an early pioneer in the field of the cinema. As early as 1907 he began writing seriously about films and the experience of the movie theater, called *Kintopp* in the Berlin dialect of his day. (He may have even invented the term *Kintopp* himself.) From an early phase in the history of filmmaking, he acted as a creative force, interested in the narrative advantages that special effects in films might make possible. Ewers enthused over the educational and recreational possibilities the future of motion pictures would bring. He would be active in one capacity or another in the production of well over twenty films between 1913 and 1935. His role was usually that of screenwriter, but he also dabbled in production.

During the years before the United States entered World War I, Ewers was living in New York and traveling around the country. These travels included trips to Mexico to try to encourage Mexican invasions of the U.S. to detract American attention from what was occurring in Europe and so keep the U.S. out of the war on the Continent. This phase of his life forms the backdrop to his novel *Vampir*. At this time, he also worked with the famous magician Aleister Crowley on the journal Crowley edited in New York called *The International*. The Englishman was agitating against his homeland in favor the Irish at the time, so the two men had common political cause. About a year after the U.S. entered the war, Ewers was arrested as an enemy agent

Bromoil photographic print of Ewers
by Rudolf Dührkoop and Minya Diez-Dührkoop, ca. 1907.

and sent to an internment camp in Georgia (Fort Oglethorpe). He spent about a year there and was released after the war had been over for about six months in July of 1919. He returned to an economically and spiritually shattered Germany. This circumstance motivated him to become more political and he drifted in the direction of the National Socialists. As Hitler was a longtime fan of Ewers' work, he was admitted into the Party with the membership number 659,057 upon a handshake from the *Führer* himself on November 2, 1931—two years before the Nazis actually came to power in Germany. Ewers wrote two Nazi-related novels that appeared in 1932: *Reiter in deutscher Nacht* (English edition: *Rider of the Night*, also 1932) and *Horst Wessel*, both of which take place within the "Brown Shirt" and *Freikorps* culture of the Nazi movement before it seized governmental power at the end of January 1933. Within the Nazi Party itself, Ewers had many enemies due to his decadent writings and lifestyle. His bisexuality was well known, and he was even on the death list for the Night of the Long Knives, when supposed homosexuals, left-leaning Brown Shirts, and so on were purged from the Nazi Party between June 30 and July 3, 1934, but Ewers managed to escape with his life. However, his works were banned in that year. This effectively brought his writing career to an end. He died in 1943 in Berlin, and his apartment was destroyed by Allied bombs a few months later.

Ewers was an extremely popular author and figure in German culture for about thirty years between about 1904 and 1934. The acknowledged Ewers masterpieces are novels that make up the "Frank Braun Trilogy": *Der Zauberlehrling oder Die Teufelsjäger* (1909), *Alraune* (1911), and *Vampir* (1920). However, he is also very well known for his many volumes of collected short stories. Ewers was extremely prolific during his productive years and was broadly creative in the new technologies of the early twentieth century. Although of his three Frank Braun novels, only *Alraune* was ever made into a film, the whole trilogy is worth looking at in synopsis form, in order to understand the world of Ewers a bit better.

Der Zauberlehrling oder Die Teufelsjäger (The Sorcerer's Apprentice, or The Devil-Hunters, 1909) was translated into English as *The Sorcerer's Apprentice* in 1927. Some critics panned the book as being too outlandish to be believed, not realizing that the events were actually based on fact. Ewers relocated the village in question to Italy, whereas the actual events on which the story is based occurred in the Swiss mountain village of Wildisbuch between 1817 and 1823. In this story, a young Frank Braun travels to Italy and encounters a village where the inhabitants are in the throes of a fanatical Christian sect. Through techniques of psychological and magical manipulations he transforms the Christian cult into an extremist Satanic sect. After creating this dangerous situation, he barely escapes with his own life. Nowhere else does Frank Braun better demonstrate his self-designation of "the irresponsible one."

The second part of the trilogy is the best known, and the one that has been the subject of several film adaptations. *Alraune* (1911; English edition, 1929) is widely considered to be Ewers's masterpiece. The story begins with Frank Braun accompanying his uncle Jacob ten Brinken to the house of the Gontram's, a wild and Bohemian estate, where a gaggle of children run amok, including a little boy, Wölfchen, and the young girls Frieda and Olga. Ten Brinken entertains everyone with stories of his experiments with lower life forms, transplanting organs from one species to another. During the party an antique mandrake root (Ger. *Alraune*) falls off of the wall and injures a maid. The legend of the mandrake is recounted whereby it is said to spring from the semen of hanged criminals, and to scream when it is ripped from the earth. The root brings power and wealth to the house where it is kept. Frank gets the idea to use the semen of an executed criminal and artificially inseminate a prostitute who is a purely lustful wench and who would represent the Earth. He suggests this to his uncle, encouraging him to take up the experiment. They find such a woman in a brothel in Berlin and sign her to a contract to bear a child under false pretenses. When she gives birth, the child is already screaming before it is fully born, and the mother dies in childbirth. Ten Brinken raises the little girl himself and names her Alraune. The Ten Brinken household grew wealthy in Alraune's childhood. The little girl took delight in torturing her playmates and inflicting all sorts of cruelties, especially on Wölfchen. As she grows up, she develops in a rather androgynous fashion, which makes her attractive to both men and women. But it is said that her victims have to still have their "blood" (i.e., be interested in sex). She seduces men and the boy Wölfchen (whom she dresses as a girl, while she herself often dresses as a boy). In making love, Alraune is fond of biting her lovers' lips and tasting their blood. Soon even her "father" is lusting after her. The Ten Brinken house has its luck turn and Ten Brinken is threatened with prison for all of the swindling he has done—charges even include child-rape because he has taken out his unrequited sexual lusts on a tinker's daughter. In the face of disgrace, and having to leave the country and Alraune behind,

Ten Brinken hangs himself. At that point, Frank Braun returns to help take care of business. He and Alraune begin a passionate love affair in which all of their perverse desires are expressed. Their lovemaking includes vampiric elements. Frank is on guard, aware as he is of Alraune's true nature. Frieda, who also lives in the house, pines for Alraune's love. Eventually, Alraune's vampiric nature finds full expression and Frank tries to break the spell by destroying the old mandrake root, which he burns. This causes Alraune to become delirious, and she begins to dance naked on the rooftop, as if in a trance, beneath the full moon. Frieda calls out her name loudly and leaps toward her; both fall to their deaths. Thus, Frank is off to other adventures.

The events of *Vampir* (1921; English edition: *Vampire* [1934]) take place during the years of the First World War. We find Frank Braun in New York living in high society. He once more meets with his old lover, Lotte Lewi, whom he first encountered when she was fifteen years old. Now she is thirty and very wealthy. The bulk of the narrative of the novel is rather autobiographical concerning the events of the author's life during the years of WWI in America. The vampiric element is melded with ideas of the Jewish and Germanic races. Lotte is of Jewish heritage and Frank is struggling with his Germanic identity. Their erotic exchange of blood is symbolic of the relationship Ewers sees between the German and Jewish peoples in the early twentieth century. Lotte ends up sacrificing her life's blood to Frank that he may live, and that Germany may live. The whole work is a fascinating study of the time and attitudes to be found in pre-Holocaust Germany.

The Sorcerer's Apprentice is a study in guided and manipulated hysteria. There we find Frank Braun as a practitioner of the arts of manipulation of the mass mind. His experiment takes place in the "laboratory" of a small Italian village already given over to fanaticism. It is his idea to transform that fanaticism from one pole, that of Christian superstition, into its polar opposite— orgiastic, diabolical sadomasochism. He succeeds all too well and the results are frightening. The work is an artistic demonstration of the kind of thing that would actually happen in the political landscape of post-WWI Germany with fanatics moving from the Communists to the National Socialists in droves.

Ewers seems to have been well ahead of all other authors on the subject of vampirism. His representation of the concept in the novel *Vampir* reflects realistic and practical activities in connection with the idea that seems to represent what may have been actual activities engaged in by the author. Like no other vampire fiction of the day, Ewers appears to be on the same wavelength as contemporary members of the "vampire community" in Western culture. The exchange described between Frank Braun and Lotte Lewi is both a matter of actual blood and psychic powers at the same time. This combination of visceral organic reality and ephemeral symbolism is emblematic of the approach to life exemplified in Ewers' work.

Throughout Ewers's writings many themes recur. He is concerned with ideas of androgyny of the body and soul. Alraune

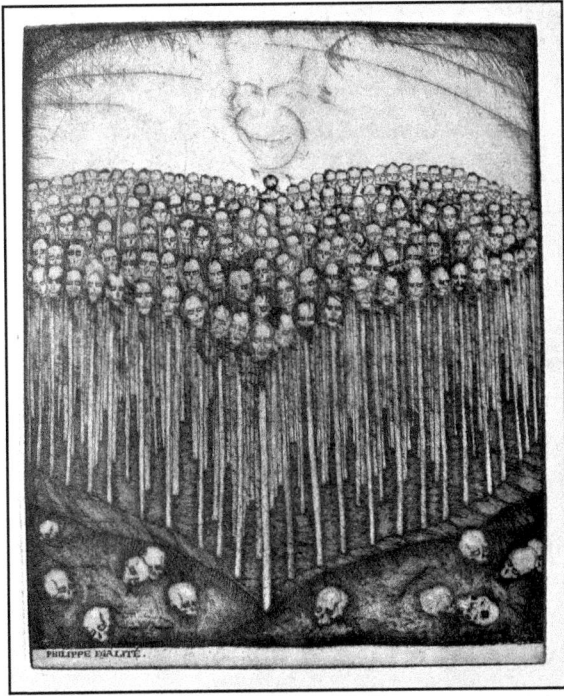

Etching by Stefan Eggeler illustrating Ewers's
Die Herzen der Könige (The Hearts of Kings, 1922).

is depicted as sexually irresistible because she embodies elements from both sexes. Apparently, the ideal woman for Ewers was one with a boyish figure and very small breasts. Lotte Lewi is described similarly in *Vampir*.

The symbol of blood was central to stories written by Ewers. Themes of the physical blood with its supposed mystical and psychological properties, as well as the aesthetics of blood being spilled, recur many times. This was naturally associated with the theme of vampirism.

Clearly, Ewers was influenced by the ideas of vitalism and monism as expressed by the scientist Ernst Haeckel who was so popular in the age of Ewers. Although one might say that there was an element of eugenics in his ideas, he was no purist when it came to race. His nationalism was rooted in culture and in the idea of *greatness*. Great men and great cultures were the ones worthy of support and continuance.

It is an unfortunate accident of history which has led to the circumstance that the ideas, aesthetics, and philosophy of Hanns Heinz Ewers never made it to the screen intact, and now never will. In the beginning these ideas were too extreme to be depicted, and now they are too politically incorrect.

Ewers and the Cinema

Although Ewers was primarily a writer of fiction, his creativity spilled over well beyond those limitations and at one time or another he was involved with radio programs, stage plays, musicals, and (of course) motion pictures. His creative involvement with films spanned from 1913 to 1935, so although most were in the silent age, he was also active in the early sound period. His main involvement was in the writing of the screenplays, and he even did a few for English-language projects.

The cinematic legacy of Hanns Heinz Ewers is best known through two film titles: *Der Student von Prag* (The Student of Prague; 1913, 1926, 1935) and *Alraune* (1918, 1928, 1930, 1952). As can be seen by the dates following the titles, each of these stories was filmed and/or modified for sound release more than once. In the early years of German cinema, films were often

Der Student von Prag (1926)

remade due to constantly improving cinematic technologies as well as for commercial reasons. The most critically acclaimed version of *Der Student von Prag* is the 1926 silent production. The 1935 version was produced after the time when the National Socialists had control of the German film industry, and for this reason films made during this period are often not viewed entirely objectively by critics. The 1913 production was hailed as the first true "artist's film"—a film written and conceived of by an established artistic writer, and based on Edgar A. Poe's story "William Wilson." It included the cinematic special effect of the reflected double (*Doppelgänger*) of the main character appearing to step out of a mirror into the room after the man had sold his soul to the Devil.

It is interesting to take a look at the story of "William Wilson" by Poe, first published in 1839, which is acknowledged as the inspiration for *The Student of Prague*. Poe's tale concerns a man of noble descent who hides his true identity behind the pseudonym "William Wilson." We learn of his boyhood at a school in England. There he meets another young boy who has the same name and a very similar appearance. He and the other boy even share the same birthday: January 19—which is also E. A. Poe's actual birthday. Critics have pointed out that in certain ways this tale is somewhat autobiographical. This other boy dresses like William and acts like him, but is only ever heard to speak in a whisper. The other boy is always whispering vague advice to William, which he resented. One night William sneaks into the other boy's room and gets a good look at his face, which he sees as resembling his own. William then withdraws from the school and so does the other boy. In time William attends both Eton and Oxford, becoming ever more "debauched." Examples of his bad behavior include cheating at cards to win money. Over the years William is haunted by his double, who thwarts efforts by William that are driven by ambition, anger, or lust. At one point William is attempting to seduce a woman during Carnival in Rome but is stymied by the double. In a rage, William forces the double into an adjoining room, although the other one does not attempt to resist, and stabs him repeatedly in the chest. William then notices the presence of a large mirror in the room and he is confronted with his reflection, which is that of the double, seeming to be dead, yet he spoke, and no longer in a whisper. He proclaims in the final words of the story:

> "You have conquered, and I yield. Yet, henceforward art thou also dead—dead to the World, to Heaven and to Hope! In me didst thou exist—and, in my death, see by this image, which is thine own, how utterly thou hast murdered thyself."

Poe's story found an enthusiastic reception in Germany, which very much took a liking to the idea of the double—or, as

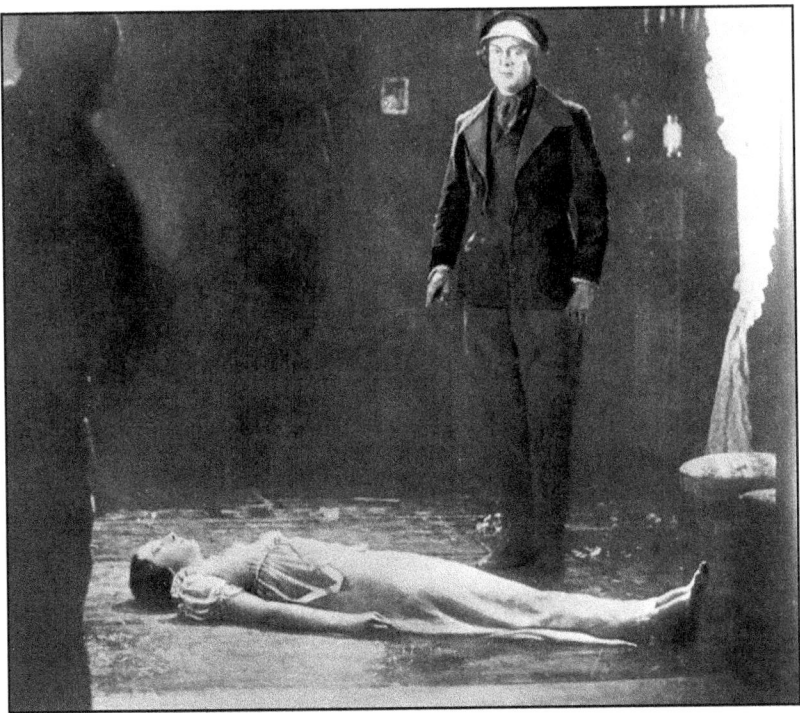

Conrad Veidt as Balduin in the 1926 version of *Der Student von Prag*.

it came to be called there, the *Doppelgänger*. This word, current in English, was first used in German in the late eighteenth and early nineteenth century by Romantics such as Jean Paul and E. T. A. Hoffmann.

The Student of Prague

The first version of the story was made in 1913. This film is marked as the first "artist's film" in any genre, and certainly the first true full-length horror film of all time. The length of the film (85 minutes) and the thought that went into the story provided by the already famous writer, Hanns Heinz Ewers, coupled with the special effects used in the production, all distinguish this film in the history of cinema. The film stars Paul Wegener, who must be considered the screen's first true "horror star." It tells of events from around 1820, where we learn of a poor young student named Balduin who is rambunctious and a great fencer.

Fencing is the major sporting activity in the fraternities at German universities. Balduin is infatuated with the Countess Margit, whom he has saved from a near drowning incident. He feels he cannot pursue her because of his poverty. A sorcerer who is lurking about, one named Scapinelli, offers Balduin 100,000 pieces of gold in exchange for an unspecified item in the student's room. Balduin readily agrees. He owns nothing close to that value. To his amazement Scapinelli calls out Balduin's reflection from a large mirror in the room. Balduin's double steps forward out of the mirror leaving Balduin without a reflection—and without a *soul*. As the student attempts to court the Countess, he is constantly pestered by the appearance of his double. Balduin is challenged to a duel by a rival suitor for the Countess. Balduin secretly makes an agreement with the father of the countess not to kill the other suitor, but the double intervenes and kills the suitor. When Balduin steals into Margit's room, their romantic interlude is disturbed by the double and she faints from shock. Balduin goes to his room to obtain his pistol, shoots the double, but as a result he himself drops dead.

A second version of the story was made in 1926 with some significant changes. Again it is set in 1820 and Balduin is a wild student, and master at fencing, but has money problems. Scapinelli, apparently a moneylender, offers a low interest loan to Balduin, which he rejects. Next we see Scapinelli out in the countryside where he whips up a storm through sorcery to cause the horses being ridden in a fox hunt to head into the party where Balduin is present. His purpose is to bring Margit, the daughter of the count, together with Balduin. She falls off of her wild horse, but is saved from the fall by the gallantry of Balduin. As a reward, he receives an invitation to a ball at the count's estate. There he realizes the depth of his poverty in comparison with Margit and her fiancé, a baron. Scapinelli appears that night in Balduin's room and offers him a contract for 600,000 florins in exchange for anything the sorcerer wants in the student's room. After the money is provided, Scapinelli leaves the room with Balduin's reflected image, which steps out into the room from a large mirror. The film then goes on to show Balduin enjoying a fortunate and lavish lifestyle, but he is plagued by the fact that his double is also on the loose and is committing various acts for which Balduin is naturally blamed. Balduin finally faces off with the double and he shoots the reflection, but in so doing only causes his own death. The film ends with a shot of Balduin's grave stone with the inscription: *Hier liegt Balduin. Er kämpfte mit dem Teufel und verlor* ("Here lies Balduin. He fought with the Devil and lost"). The clear implication is that Scapinelli was, in fact, the Devil.

The 1935 production of the film was the only sound version ever made. It is set in the late nineteenth century in Prague where we once again meet Balduin, a serious student who excels in fencing. In an inn frequented by students, they are celebrating the birthday of Lydia, a barmaid. She is secretly in love with Balduin. Unexpectedly, a great opera singer, Julia, enters the inn. One of the students gets fresh with Julia and attempts to kiss her. Balduin intervenes with his saber and, impressed with Balduin's gallantry, she invites everyone to her next performance. A certain dark figure called Dr. Carpis, a former lover of Julia, looks at the growing relationship between Julia and Balduin with misgivings, and tries to get her to come back to him. Balduin expresses his admiration for Julia, but she seems unapproachable. The student begins a conversation with his own reflection in a mirror; he refers to the reflection as a "young dreamer." Suddenly, Dr. Carpis appears and puts a black veil over the mirror and declares he will have more success this way. Balduin at once demonstrates his newfound luck at gambling. One night in a dream, his reflected image appears to him as an ill omen. Nevertheless, he goes to a costume ball with Julia. Carpis sees them and is angry; Julia is apprehensive, but Balduin dismisses her concerns. Balduin kisses Julia and Carpis brings in Balduin's lost reflection, whom Balduin begins to pursue, but gets into a confrontation with Baron Waldis, whom he challenges to a duel. Julia begs Balduin to spare the Baron in the duel. But when Carpis lets Balduin know that Julia still loves the Baron and then when the *Doppelgänger* additionally arrives on the scene, it is all too much for the student, who flies into a rage and stabs the Baron with his sabre. At that point Balduin realizes he is losing his sanity and must do something. Everywhere he goes, his *Doppelgänger* is there! He returns to his room and rips the black veil off of the mirror, and the mirror image enters the room. Both stand before the mirror, side by side. Balduin shoots the reflected image, the mirror shatters and both Balduins fall down, mortally wounded.

In general, Ewers combines the myth of the *Doppelgänger* with that of Faust. The selling Balduin's soul, and with it his reflection or image, in exchange for some sort of power (money or luck) is a benefit of short duration. In a way, Ewers is scoffing at the student, who is poor and only good at fencing. Ewers himself was a part of the student culture at the Universities of Berlin and Bonn and was an avid fencer, with the *Schmisse* ("smites") to prove it. These are the dueling scars that decorate the faces of German fraternity members, who fight duels with unguarded blades to the point of drawing blood. The scars are badges of courage—one may have lost the duel, but the scar proves one's willingness to fight for honor. In this regard also, these scars were considered by many women to be signs of virility and made men more attractive to them.

Ewers with his fencing scar.

The theme of the *Doppelgänger* is one that runs deep in the works of Ewers. He has a short story entitled "Der Tod des Baron des Jesus Maria von Friedel" (1908) in which the main character has a contra-sexual, female *Doppelgänger(in)*! This is further testimony to another theme common in his works: that of *androgyny*. Another novel by Ewers is one called *Fundvogel* (1929), which is perhaps the first major work of fiction to address the topic of gender reassignment or transsexuality. Such medical procedures and treatments were just beginning at the experimental stage in Dresden and Berlin during the 1920s.

Poster for a Berlin screening of the (now-lost) *Alraune* film from 1918.

Alraune

Alraune is the literary work for which Ewers is best known in Germany and the several films made from the idea also kept his reputation alive at least into the 1950s. A short synopsis of the book has already been provided, the films made from the book often veered off from some of the basic ideas, as we will see. The main idea that a girl is engendered using the semen of a hanged criminal artificially inseminated into a prostitute is a constant feature. The girl is a *femme fatale* of unnatural dimensions. She is also a great source of power to those who *possess* her.

The 1928 production of *Alraune* starring Brigitte Helm and Paul Wegener is considered to be the best adaptation of the Ewers novel. It must be said, however, that neither it, nor any other, adaptation comes close to the depravity of the original novel. The film opens with a dramatization of the retrieval of the mandrake root from under a gallows where a man is hanging. Professor Jakob ten Brinken specializes in genetics and artificial

Alraune (1928)

insemination. He takes the sperm of an executed sex-murderer and inseminates a prostitute procured by his nephew Frank Braun for the purpose. Braun tries to dissuade his uncle from the experiment, but Ten Brinken persists. The product of the experiment is a girl he named Alraune (mandrake). He has her raised in a cloister school, from which she runs a way with a boy she incited to steal a sum of money from a bank. Alraune ends up in a circus where she performs with a magician. The professor finds her and persuades her to return home with him, where she can live a life of luxury. Ten Brinken continues to record the events of Alraune's life scientifically. She finds this record and discovers the secret of her origin. At first, she plans to strangle the professor during the night, but then decides to instill in him a sexual obsession for her and proceeds to do this in a calculated fashion. She inflames unbearable jealousy in him with her promiscuous behavior. At a casino Alraune has a winning streak, but then leaves the professor in the middle of it, and he loses everything. At home Alraune is packing her things to leave him. Ten Brinken begs her to stay or to go away with him to a new place. She tells him she is going, but not with him. In a jealous rage, he chases her around the house with a knife. Just then Frank shows up to whisk Alraune away to lead a normal life, free of her cruel tendencies. In the meantime the professor is condemned to a life of loneliness and insanity.

Alraune was remade for a final time in 1957, but this version suffered from a weak script and was far more reserved in its contents than the original story demands. This film is also known as *Unnatural*.

Ewers had an enduring fascination with the diabolical. In the years around 1910 he held a series of lectures, sort of "one-man shows," entitled *Die Religion Satans* (The Religion of Satan). These presentations were largely based on the works of the Polish-German writer Stanisław Przybyszewski, especially his seminal little book *The Synagogue of Satan*. Despite being urged to do so, he never turned his lecture/show into a book. Rather, he used material from this project repeatedly in the body of his fictional works. Another significant influence on Ewers was the philosophy of the mystical eugenicist Maximilian Ferdinand Sebaldt von Werth (1859–1916).

On occasion Ewers described himself as a *decadent*. In general, this term is most precisely applied to certain writers working mainly in the French language toward the end of the nineteenth century, most iconically Joris-Karl Huysmans in texts such as *Là-Bas* (Down There) and *À rebours* (Against the Grain or Against Nature). The French word *décadence* implies a "falling away" or "decay" from a well-established or classical standard. For the average French citizen of the late nineteenth century, this meant the teachings of the Roman Catholic Church. Those who actually believed these teachings, yet despite this engaged in acts and held beliefs contrary to these ideas, were truly *decadent*.

They were "sinners" and sinned despite their beliefs. This is in stark contrast to the Romantics, such as the circle around Lord Byron, who were pioneers of the idea of going beyond good and evil. They aimed to be supermen and rejected cultural norms as Satanic rebels. Huysmans and the Decadents were different. But Ewers liked to dabble in the idea of being "decadent." He cleverly described the decadent as the full, perhaps overly full, final development of anything: for example, an oak tree might be seen to be a "decadent phase" of an acorn.

An important theme of *Alraune* is the concept of the *femme fatale*, which was a regular obsession of Ewers. His most famous story, and the one mentioned by Lovecraft in his *Supernatural Horror in Literature* (1927), is "The Spider" (1908). Clearly, given Ewers other works, this is an exercise in pure Expressionism. The objective story would probably appear as a seductive woman who erotically displayed herself through her window and drove her young male victims to suicide. As experienced through the narrative of the story she appears as a girl spinning at a spinning wheel, who is slowly transformed into a spider. The story revolves around a man who is trying to solve the mystery of why men who live in Room 7 at a boarding house keep hanging themselves— and he ends up falling victim himself to the same process as the others. Another outstanding example of this theme is found in his story "From the Diary of an Orange Tree" (1905), in which a young student falls under the spell of a *femme fatale* figure and comes to believe that he has been transformed into an orange tree by her power. The whole motif of the *femme fatale* was important to the late nineteenth- and early twentieth-century German culture. The most famous example of it is immortalized in Josef von Sternberg's iconic film *The Blue Angel*, starring Marlene Dietrich, and based on Heinrich Mann's novel *Professor Unrat* (1905). This tells of a respected teacher reduced to being a slave of a nightclub performer named Lola. Ewers identified this archetype as Lilith.

When it comes to the works of Hanns Heinz Ewers, we have all the material needed to make a truthful and insightful interpretation of his oeuvre—but so often prejudices of the

Poster for the Swedish release of the 1928 *Alraune* film under the title *Vampyren* (The Vampire).

interpreters and considerations of political correctness interfere with the production of a truthful picture of the man and his output. He was full of apparent contradictions and internal conflicts. It is my supposition, however, that these appearances are only outward forms, and that from his own authentic perspective, he was expressing an internally coherent and well-developed—if highly individualistic—philosophy of life. Certain aspects of this philosophy are discussed in more detail in my introduction to *Strange Tales* (2000).

Some of the most recent critical treatments of Ewers place heavy emphasis on his *racism*. While on the one hand this should not be denied, it hardly distinguishes him from the majority of his contemporaries, and therefore it is neither very interesting nor even meaningful as such. It becomes more fascinating when we study the roots of these ideas in the esoteric ideologies of the day. It should be added that Ewers's opinions of most other countries, cultures, and peoples did not come from merely reading books about them, as he traveled the world and interacted with peoples of all races and backgrounds during the course of his life. One of the most ironic factors of his experience is that although he actually joined the National Socialist party, he was *not* an Anti-Semite, but rather called himself pointedly, and in print, a Philosemite—a lover of Jewish culture. Here I present a slightly abridged version of Ewers's fateful essay on his Philosemitism, which was published in *Book of the Exile: Souvenir of the Bazaar and Fair Held Under the Auspices of the Peoples' Relief Committee for the Jewish War Sufferers, March 1916.*

WHY I AM A PHILOSEMITE
Hanns Heinz Ewers

Every sentiment that is called forth by the contact with a foreign race is, in the last instance, a matter of nerves. All logical thought, all processes of the mind, come to a halt when not accompanied by instinct. If this theory holds good for men in general, how much more is it applicable to the artist, particularly to the artist who does not work with his brain alone, but his blood—i.e., his nerves.

This physical attraction or aversion, which possibly is based on chemical conditions and the physical transmission of which we cannot yet explain, is, nevertheless, a fact, and may be observed in a smaller measure in associating with members of one's own race. Yet, because no explanation for this physical attraction has been offered, and because its true origin has not as yet been recognized, thoroughly matter-of-fact people, whose brain has become only a table of figures, have tried to deny the existence of physical sympathy and have fanatically fought for the democratic equality of races. Every true artist is an aristocrat, Heaven knows, not in a political sense....

And this certainly applies to his attitude towards foreign races. Now the physical sensation which one race bears to another is almost always a very pronounced one, and the dissenting attitude of a few individuals has but little effect on the whole condition. The Germanic race (Germans, Britains, Scandinavians, etc.) instinctively feels a strong aversion towards the African, while this feeling is not so intense among the Roman peoples....

Lord Beaconsfield (Disraeli), a Jew, has ... given expression to the thought that only two races are worthy of ruling the world: the Jewish tribe of the Semitic race and the Germanic peoples of the Indo-Germanic race....

Of what benefit has it been that Chamberlain announced in the House of Commons that a government of the world, and everlasting peace, could only be possible under a community of three Germanic peoples: Germany, the mother; England, the daughter; and America, the grandchild. Of what benefit has it been that his celebrated namesake, Houston Stewart Chamberlain, seeks to further antisemitism through his propaganda of Pan-Germanism?...

It is remarkable how many intelligent Jews exist, who possess Germanistic tendencies, although they are exponents of National Jewish Zionistic thought. How many prominent Germans, English, and Scandinavians marry Jewesses, and it will be found that on both sides they are artists. . . . What is the reason for this? Only one. Purely physical attraction. Why is this attraction greater for a member of a foreign race than for one's own? Because the ordinary must necessarily have a dulling effect on superior natures and because the contrast and the novelty charms. It is the aristocratic principle of life. And this principle does not only apply to the sex problem, it appears in all phases of life. What cultured Jew of the present time does not count among his best friends Germans, English, or Americans? And, therefore, I love the Jews and am obliged to love them, because I belong to the Germanic race and because I am an artist. (Lubarski-Debalta 1916, 36–38)

Hanns Heinz Ewers was and remains the consummate Outsider. He became a lawyer, but pursued art. He was a cosmopolitan, but became a member of the Nazi Party. He was a member of that party, although he himself was a Philosemite. His status as an Outsider pursued him everywhere, even beyond death. In so many ways, Ewers is a prefiguration of the Postmodern Man. Certain themes permeate his work: androgyny of the body and soul; the idealization of beauty; the focus on the idea of *greatness* as the criterion for the salvation of the soul; an obsession with blood (both as a metaphor for race and a vital bodily substance); and the power of art to sanctify that which is repugnant to the masses.

As compared to the level of his original impact on popular culture, Ewers had very little in the way of aftershocks in the world of horror. He faded from memory for several decades following the Second World War. A few of his stories were kept in print in mass-market paperbacks in Germany but little else. Because his novels had all been translated back in the 1920s and published in important and often lavishly illustrated editions, Ewers was fairly well known for a time in the English-speaking world as well. The fame Ewers worked so hard to develop faded

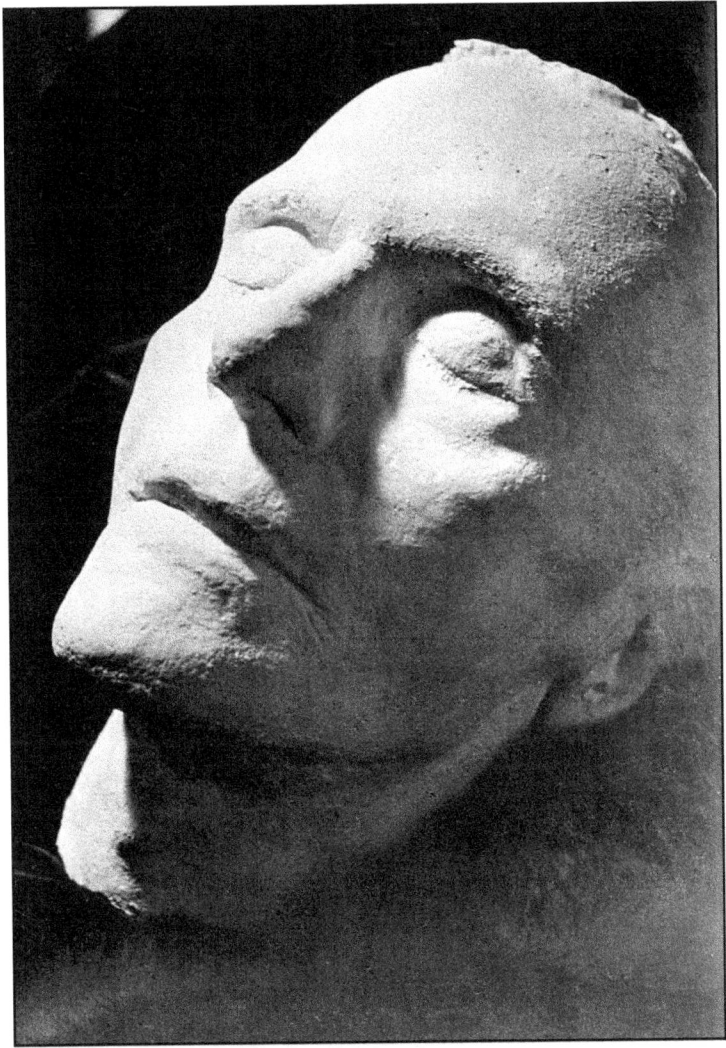

Ewers's death mask, 1941.
(HHE collection, Heine Institut, Düsseldorf)

first in National Socialist Germany, which rejected him for his decadence, and then by the postwar West for his membership in the Nazi Party. It is all too obvious to declare that the life of Hanns Heinz Ewers is a "complicated" one, and his works reflect that complexity.

More recently, Joe Bandel has undertaken the task of retranslating Ewers's otherwise hard-to-find novels and short stories and making them available in digital editions. These new translations are often more explicit than the sometimes "censored" versions found in the early English versions, but perhaps do not give Ewers his literary due. However, the big breakthrough for Ewers worldwide came along in the wake of Wilfried Kugel's informative biography, *Der Unverantwortliche*. The title, which translates to "The Irresponsible One," comes from a self-designation of Ewers's alter ego, Frank Braun, in the novel *Vampir*, referring to his modus operandi in spreading mischief in the world of international intrigue. It seems that Ewers played a similar role in the mentalities of his readers, and that this was his artistic plan at work. In my view, it is time for the work of Hanns Heinz Ewers to return to some level of popularity. New films, more aware of, and sympathetic to, the mentality of Ewers could be produced today in ways impossible before now. Yes, he was a member of the NSDAP, but his gravitation toward them was motivated by the same reaction to injustice and oppression that moved millions of other Germans to go in that direction due to the living conditions caused by the unjust and counterproductive terms of the Treaty of Versailles. He was also a Philosemite, LBGT activist, and—first and foremost—an artist. Perhaps he was irresponsible, but this stemmed from his underlying human *complexity* and *greatness*, which still harbors a number of mysteries.

XI

William Castle
Moviegoing as Ritual and Rite of Passage

As the introductory essay of this book shows, William Castle was an important part of my early initiation into the world of horror movies. His films always had a certain "something" that set them apart. His style, themes, and storylines had a personal stamp. Castle was a latecomer to the horror genre, but he left a mark on the world of the horror film matched by few others. He made the moviegoing experience something akin to the idea of "legend tripping" for a select generation of monster kids. No other filmmaker so pointedly and repeatedly exploited—even if for only a few years—the cultural reality of horror films as true rites of passage.

In our small North Texas town of Denison there were two downtown movie theaters in the 1950s and 1960s: the State and the Rialto. The State often seemed to show the movies of a bit less prestige, or "class," than the Rialto. I can't remember where *13 Ghosts* showed. But I do remember that my father took me to see the movie in the afternoon. On the walk home, I asked him about the number "thirteen." I got nothing that satisfied my curiosity. My father was himself uninterested in anything having to do with "horror" or "monsters"; he seemed more interested in

William Castle at his desk in 1946.

the courage his boy showed in confronting the horror on screen. In retrospect, since he took me to see these pictures when I was around six years old, the whole experience constituted some sort of rite of passage. Certainly something *mysterious* was conveyed to me in those theaters, something which has stuck with me my whole life.

This film, *13 Ghosts*, was certainly one of the most memorable. It was made all the more memorable because you got to take something home with you after viewing the film: the "Ghost Viewer." The Ghost Viewer was a piece of cardboard with two slots—one filled with blue cellophane, the other with red cellophane. In the film, ghosts would be invisible if you looked at the screen through the blue slot, but would be revealed if you looked through the red one. The use of this and other "gimmicks" was what set Castle apart from other producers of his time. This object was handed out at the theater to each moviegoer. It acted—if all too temporarily—as a talisman. Such objects too often get lost over time, but their meanings remain fixed in the mind. The possession of the object was an enduring sign that the initiate had made the journey to the forbidden land and returned alive to tell the tale. Few, if any, of my first-grade classmates seem to have shared in this experience, so my reports about what I had seen there usually fell on deaf ears. But the Ghost Viewer was the sign that I had been somewhere *other*. The magician behind the creation of this talisman was William Castle, who became a living icon of the horror genre in the late 1950s and early 1960s.

Castle was born William Schloss in New York City on April 24, 1918. His family was of German-Jewish heritage. He was teased about his last name as a child—a name which translates to "castle" or "palace" in German. So he changed it to "Castle" as a teenager when he first started working in theater. Both of William's parents died before he was twelve years old and the inheritance he received when he turned twenty-five allowed him to pursue his passion for show business. But the years between twelve and twenty-five were lean. Castle claims to have met Bela Lugosi backstage at the stage production of *Dracula* in 1927. From this time on, he pursued his dreams with vigor and self-salesmanship. Castle did some bit acting work in Hollywood as early as 1937, but his first serious foray into being a showman appears to have come in 1938 with his purchase of the Stony Creek Theatre in Branford, Connecticut from Orson Welles. Welles would display more than a little showmanship of his own through the year—most notably for our purposes, his sensational broadcast of October 30, 1938 on the Mercury Theater radio program in which he adapted H. G. Wells's *War of the Worlds* and created, or so legend goes, widespread panic among listeners, who thought it was not a radio drama but a news broadcast!

Experience in the theater provided Castle with opportunity to hone his skills as a showman—skills which he took with him out to Hollywood in 1939. His directorial debut was in the 1943 feature for Columbia entitled *The Chance of a Lifetime*, a crime drama. Over the following decade and a half he learned the crafts of directing, writing, and producing feature films. These were adventure stories, Westerns, crime stories, and dramas. He was competent but had not made any sort of big breakthrough.

Castle was inspired to expand his level of showmanship after seeing the French horror-thriller *Diabolique* (1955) with its publicity stunt surrounding the idea of telling the moviegoers not to reveal the ending of the film. The fact that the "monster craze" was gearing up for its greatest phase made his timing perfect. In October of 1957 the syndicated package of pre-1948 classic horror films was released to independent television stations around the country and soon thereafter Forrest J Ackerman published the first issue of *Famous Monsters of Filmland* in February of 1958. These events helped inaugurate the "Monster Kid" craze of the early 1960s.

In a series of six films over three years—*Macabre* (1958), *House on Haunted Hill* (1959), *The Tingler* (1959), *13 Ghosts* (1960), *Homicidal* (1961), and *Mr. Sardonicus* (1961)—Castle left his indelible mark on the world of horror films by creating mechanisms for the projection of celluloid events out into the world beyond the screen. He also made good use of his roots in show business by coming up with various gimmicks to sell tickets.

For *Macabre* he devised an "insurance policy" insuring moviegoers for $1,000 if any of them were to die of fright during the picture. A "beneficiary agreement" was handed out to theater patrons. It worked very well (no one collected). Castle went from town to town to promote the picture as he displayed the insurance policy. In a barnstorming publicity campaign, he appeared in a coffin and a black cape at the local premieres. The film, based on the novel entitled *The Marble Forest*, tells the story of an unpopular small-town doctor who gets a phone call that his young daughter has been kidnapped and has been buried alive—with only a few hours of air. The town turns out to help the doctor find his daughter, likely buried in a plot in the cemetery. In the end a small casket is opened and reveals the mummified corpse of a child—which causes the doctor's father in-in-law to

Macabre (1958)

die suddenly of a heart attack. As it turns out, this was all a hoax perpetrated by the doctor and a co-conspirator in order for the doctor to inherit the father-in-law's estate of ten million dollars. The co-conspirator shoots the doctor and the little girl is discovered sleeping safely in the doctor's office. The gimmick and the hoopla surrounding it proved more impactful than the film itself. The publicity gained by *Diabolique* and *Macabre* did seem to influence one Alfred Hitchcock to try his hand at a low-budget shocker—*Psycho* was the result.

For Castle's next foray into magic of cinematic marketing he brought the film off the screen and right into the audience with a gimmick he dubbed "Emergo." 3-D films had been around since *The House of Wax* in 1953, but for *House on Haunted Hill*, Castle wanted to bring the physical reality of the film directly into the

House on Haunted Hill (1959)

theater. The story is of a wealthy man, Frederick Loren (played by Vincent Price), who invites a number of people to a house, reputed to be haunted. He offers each $10,000 if they stay and survive the night. In the end, it is revealed that Loren's wife and her lover (among the guests) are both plotting to kill him, so he kills them in self-defense—by putting them in a vat of acid. Loren strings a skeleton to a marionette-type contraption and manipulates it from a hidden corner to force his wife into the vat. It is at this point in the film that a real life, full-sized human skeleton came out on a wire into the theater audience in the "Emergo" effect.

William Castle

House on Haunted Hill was Castle's first major success. He followed this up six months later with what is perhaps his masterpiece: *The Tingler*. Vincent Price again stars, this time as a doctor/coroner named Warren Chapin who has discovered the existence of a tentacled creature that develops in the spinal column when humans experience extreme fear. If the subject screams, the entity is neutralized and shrinks. However, if it is allowed to grow it will crush the spine, killing the host. Chapin meets a mild-mannered man named Ollie Higgins, whose recently executed brother-in-law has just been autopsied by the doctor. Ollie runs a classic movie theater, owned by his deaf and mute wife, Martha. When Chapin reveals his discovery to Ollie, the wimpy husband uses it to frighten his wife to death. But because she cannot scream, the creature remains developed and alive in her body. Chapin extracts it as a living thing, which he dubs "the tingler." As an independent entity, it can crawl around and kill those it makes contact with. Chapin determines to return the tingler to Martha's body as a way of destroying it. He goes to the theater, but the thing escapes its container and gets loose in the building. What happens next is the heart of *The Tingler*.

The tingler enters the projection booth and crawls in front of the projector. The film appears to break and we see the tingler's shadow crawl across the screen, seemingly thrown by projector. At this moment, the theater goes dark—the tingler that was crawling loose in the theater on screen, has broken through the fourth wall and is crawling loose in the very theater in which the audience watching *The Tingler* is sitting. In the darkness, Vincent Price's voice is heard:

> *Ladies and Gentlemen, please do not panic. But scream, scream for your lives!*
> *The tingler is loose in this theater. And if you don't scream, it may kill you.*
> *Scream! Scream!*
> *Keep screaming! Scream for your life!*

It was at that moment the great gimmick was employed—*Percepto*. Castle had seats in the theater wired with vibrating devices which were set off at this crucial moment, not only ensuring that there would be even more screaming, but also convincing those who were physically "shocked" that the tingler was surely making intimate contact with them directly.

As the screaming settles, Vincent Price speaks again:

> *The tingler has been paralyzed by your screaming.*
> *There is no more danger.*
> *We will now resume the showing of the movie. . .*

I am sure many of the theaters showing *The Tingler* absolutely erupted in screams. I remember well the Casa Linda Theater in Dallas packed to capacity with preteen boys and girls exploding into screaming fits during many scenes. The screams were usually more shocking than what was actually on the screen. (Girls, at least, manifested the same kind of psychosexual cathartic release over their latest teen idols, and this was clearly seen in 1964 when the Beatles came to the US.)

Not only is *The Tingler* an effective horror film with a science-fiction edge, but Castle's gimmick was a masterstroke as well. Perhaps somewhat inspired by the way *The Blob*, released a year earlier, had suggested that action did, or could, actually take place in the theater where the audience was watching the film, Castle contrived a story which did bring the theater audience right into

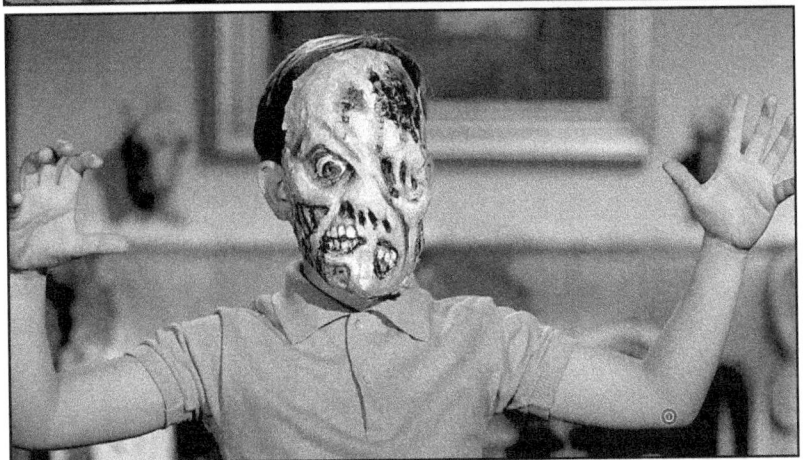

Two stills from *13 Ghosts* (1960).

the film. "Emergo" had projected elements from the film into the theater in a rather crude manner, but *The Tingler* brought the theater audience into the film on the screen on two levels.

Again, Castle followed up *The Tingler* with a new film and a new gimmick, "Illusion-O," in his notable foray into real supernatural horror: *13 Ghosts*. Most of Castle's films were thrillers with gruesome and macabre features; the horror involved was of a psychological sort. The supposed ghosts or supernatural events were tricks played by a character in the film on the other characters, or delusions of some mentally unbalanced character.

Although the psychological element is present in *13 Ghosts*, this time there were also *real* ghosts.

13 Ghosts tells the story of the family of Cyrus Zorba. They inherit a house from Cyrus's uncle, Plato Zorba. The old Zorba had collected ghosts from all over the world and brought them to this house with the aid of his medium, Elaine. The ghosts eventually mutilated and killed him. The catch to Zorba's inheritance is that he and his family have to live in the house and cannot sell it. So the family moves in, and begins to experience ghostly phenomena right away. Dr. Zorba had developed a viewer by which people can see the ghosts, and the theatrical gimmick was that moviegoers got a Ghost Viewer themselves with two colored pieces of cellophane, one blue and one red. If they wanted to see the ghosts on the screen, they used the red part; if they wanted them to disappear on the screen, they looked through the blue part. The plot twist was that the family was being scammed by a shyster lawyer playing the part of a ghost to try to scare the family away from the house so that he could search it for the cash the old doctor had hidden somewhere in the structure. In the end, Buck finds the stash of money and the ghosts rise up and kill the lawyer. The Zorbas can now happily and comfortably live in the formerly(?) haunted house.

A wonderful angle Castle used in *13 Ghosts* was the casting of Margaret Hamilton (1902–1985) as Elaine Zacharides, Dr. Zorba's assistant and medium. Hamilton had become the face of *the* witch to the previous three generations of moviegoers—as she played the Wicked Witch of the West in the iconic 1939 film *The Wizard of Oz*. In a way, this casting move was a pure "Castle-ism" in that he was bringing what the viewers took as a sort of real-life character and brought it into the filmgoing experience. It is even alluded to in the script where the little boy protagonist, Buck, asks Elaine, "Are you a *real* witch?" She responds: "Ask me no questions, and I'll tell you no lies."

Yet another twist for Castle was the inclusion of a small boy, about the same age as I was when I saw the movie in 1960. Although I had no trouble relating to the older men of the horror universe, the inclusion of such a character did make an

A publicity shot for *Homicidal* (1961).

impact on me. I had a similar experience with the film *Dinosaurus!*, which was released just one month after *13 Ghosts* and featured a boy named Julio. He even had two Marx-manufactured dinosaur figures just like I had! There was a dinosaur-craze in the late 1950s and early 1960s that many young boys participated in—it went right along with the monster-craze.

In the wake of Hitchcock's culturally impactful *Psycho*, Castle made his vaguely derivative *Homicidal* (1961). Castle never overtly mentions *Psycho's* influence, but it appears obvious, although some contemporary critics thought the Castle film was better than *Psycho*! *Homicidal* tells the story of a woman who leads a double life as a man in order to be able to inherit his/her

father's fortune—as the will stipulates the estate can only go to a male heir, the man's daughter was raised in secret as a boy by his nanny. The "homicidal" aspects come to the fore as a result of the desire of this would-be heir to kill everyone who is privy to her/his secret. The most interesting aspect of the film is that the male and female characters were both played by the actress Joan Marshall (who worked under the stage name "Jean Arliss" for this production). The gender-bending dimension of the film was provocative for the times. Just about ten years earlier Christine Jorgensen had become the first widely publicized person to have undergone gender reassignment surgery in Denmark. (The script of *Homicidal* mentions characters having lived in Denmark, perhaps as a kind of popular culture "code.") The particular gimmick used in *Homicidal* was the "Fright Break." In the climactic moments of the film, Castle's voice announces that the audience members have sixty seconds to leave the theater and go out to the lobby for a refund of their ticket price. Because some smart-alecks were just sitting through the film a second time and getting up at this point to get their money back, Castle instituted a stipulation that the refund came with a coward's walk of shame along a yellow stripe on the floor to a cardboard set-up called the "Coward's Corner" where a yellow-clad "nurse" would take the coward's blood pressure and make him sign a yellow card that read: "I am a bona fide coward." There was also a recorded voice announcing that these people are cowards. Few tried to scam Mr. Castle after he put in that "stipulation"!

Mr. Sardonicus (1961) tells the story of Sir Robert Cargrave, a much-decorated physician from London, who gets a message from his past lady-love, Maude. She beseeches him to come to her aid and to that of her husband, the Baron Sardonicus far away in "the region of Gorslava in Central Europe." Upon arriving, Sir Robert discovers Maude is virtually held captive by Sardonicus in his castle, also inhabited by his faithful one-eyed servant, Krull, and a maid, or what the Germans would call a *Mädchen-für-Alles*, Anna. He learns that Sardonicus has been horribly disfigured—his face frozen into a hideous grin, unable to open his jaw, ever since he saw his dead father's face as he dug up his grave to recover a winning lottery ticket buried in his pocket. In search of a cure, the cruel Sardonicus allows his loyal manservant, Krull, to use the maid in all sorts of painful, yet fruitless, experiments involving leeches, among other things. At one point Krull is discovered hanging Anna by her thumbs, forcing her to stand on tiptoes, while Krull applies leeches to her feet. Eventually, Sir Robert does cure Sardonicus, and the doctor and Maude are allowed to leave the castle. But in revenge Sir Robert informs Krull that despite the ruse he played in scientifically uncovering a cure, Sardonicus cannot open his mouth due to purely psychological factors. Krull now holds his master's life in his hands: will he tell him or not? At this point, the moviegoing

Mr. Sardonicus (1961)

audience is brought in on an interactive gimmick called the "Punishment Poll." Each member of the audience was issued a placard with a "thumbs-up" or "thumbs-down" indication. At the crucial moment in the film, Castle himself appears on screen and asks the audience to indicate their choice: should Sardonicus live or die? He looks over the votes and makes a show out of seeming to count them. The vote was always for "no mercy." It is said that no alternative ending was even filmed for an eventuality in which the audience ever voted for "mercy." An example of democracy in action.

After this string of box-office successes in horror, Castle's magic seemed to wane for a while. He did score another hit with the help of the star-power of Joan Crawford, fresh off of her success with Bette Davis in *What Ever Happened to Baby Jane?*, in the psychological thriller *Strait-Jacket* (1964). But Castle's final triumph came with his work as the producer of the classic *Rosemary's Baby* (1968) directed by the young and up-and-coming Roman Polanski. This success as producer was, however, fraught with what Castle himself thought was a "curse" of misfortune cast over all who were involved with this culturally taboo film.

The Meditation

It has been noted that horror films represent a new kind of fairy tale or folktale in our culture. These stories were originally perhaps incorporated into rites of passage or rites of transformation. These are rites used in cultures to mark and facilitate the transition of a person from one state of being to another: from child to adult, for example. Horror films, such as those created by William Castle, acted as virtual initiatory rites of passage for a select generation.

Folklorists have identified a phenomenon known as "legend tripping." Legend tripping usually refers to an adolescent practice of making pilgrimages to sites thought to be haunted, the location of some horrific tragedy, and so on. *The Blair Witch Project* is a great example of this kind of thing. What William Castle did was to make the moviegoing experience itself a sort of legend trip. People (especially kids) entered the theater alone, with friends, or most preferably perhaps with a girl- or boyfriend. They would enter the theater, or cave of initiation, it would become darkened, the ritual elements and ordeals orchestrated by Mr. Castle would play themselves out, and perhaps the kid would leave the theater in some profound (or modest) way *changed*. Perhaps it was because he was able to survive watching the horror of a skeleton *coming right for him* in the theater, or maybe it was because he got his first feel of just the *side* of his girlfriend's breast (or was she wearing "falsies"?). The avuncular Mr. Castle made the fright somehow safer, and gave it more of a family feel, much akin to the way in which the Grimms' Fairy Tales functioned in times past when they were first told, and later read, to kids by their mothers and grannies.

Moviegoing had been an American and European ritual since the 1920s. The movie theater was the cultural temple of the Western world from the 1920s through the 1940s. These ritualistic and experiential dimensions of events in the theater were pointedly created with full intention by the German artist Richard Wagner in the nineteenth century. He created what he called the *Gesamtkunstwerk*—the "total work of art." His purpose was to transform the audience by the experience of his theatrical and musical creations. He invented the idea of darkening the theater during performances so that the audience could only focus on the events happening on the stage. The experience of his work was to be an initiatory, rite of passage into his vision for a utopian future rooted in art. Wagner set an artistic template that would never be superseded and which every artist that followed him would try to match.

Castle introducing the "Ghost Viewer" gimmick for *13 Ghosts*.

Despite the erroneous belief that we today, in the twenty-first century, are somehow all "connected" via the digital and social media, we are actually more fragmented and atomized than ever before. The apex of American Mega-Culture (1950–1980)—in which the vast majority of the American population was connected by common experience, myth, and media—was probably during those golden years of William Castle productions. The Castle mystique could have functioned in no other environment. *Everyone* knew who Elvis was or who the Beatles were, but today the "top-selling artist" in the music industry can be named—and more than half the country will respond: "Who? Never heard of him/her/it/them." Of course, this situation is driven by a political agenda (divide and conquer), but for our purposes here it is only interesting to note how the culture of the 1960s was able to deliver common experiences to a whole generation. Among those experiences were the "legend trips" to see a William Castle production.

Conclusion and Aftershocks

William Castle will be best remembered for his signature masterpieces of the late 1950s and early 1960s. He stands alone at the summit of showmanship that he himself pioneered and mastered. In a present-day world in which the body and actual experience is increasingly divided from the consumption of media, Castle represented the last gasp of the carnival combined with the rise of cinematic showmanship. He created a scene, perfected it, and then the scene departed from this world. His form of audience involvement—insurance policies against death-by-fright, vibrators under theater seats, coward's corners—were all things the lawyers would eventually not stand for. These ritualistic aspects of Castle's approach to the filmgoing experience brought them ever closer to the realm of rites of passage and legend tripping—aspects which at this point seem to be a lost experience belonging to a bygone age. There would be films that caused great excitement on release (e.g., *The Exorcist*) but none that were part of a self-created carnival atmosphere such as William Castle was able to garner.

XII

Caligarism and the Trapezoidal Cinema

For many years, I was obsessed with the idea of the Trapezoid—the Order of the Trapezoid, the Shining Trapezohedron, and the "Ceremony of the Nine Angles." These interests grew out of the same vague childhood visions generated by watching films such as *The Black Cat* (1934). As it turns out, these boyhood visions and dreams are not as far off the mark as skeptical observers of my interests—such as my parents—might have thought.

The word "trapezoid" indicates first and foremost a geometrical figure:

The Trapezoid

A trapezoid is described in Euclidean geometry as a convex, four-sided figure with at least one pair of parallel sides. This is called a trapezium outside North America. The parallel sides are called "bases," while the other two sides are referred to as "legs," betraying the origin of the word from Greek *trápeza*, "table." A scalene trapezoid is one that has no sides of an equal measure.

Lovecraft used a variant of the word, "trapezohedron," which is a solid made up of trapezoidal faces, to give a name to one of his imaginary sinister magical organizations—the Order of the Shining Trapezohedron from his 1936 story "The Haunter of the Dark." Although many configurations are possible, a trapezohedron might appear as:

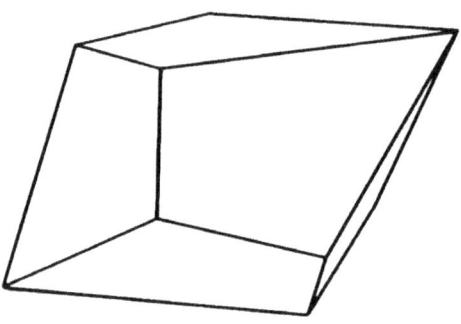

A Trapezohedron

Another version of a trapezohedron is clearly visible in the image of the "ball" attached to the chain of the inmate in Caligari's asylum (see next page). For Lovecraft, the idea of the trapezohedron was supposed to convey the principles of a non-Euclidean geometry that resulted in "obscene angles" disorienting the human mind. Lovecraft was a writer who was able to produce the same effects as the trapezoid ostensibly does by means of obscene angles in semantics. For example, there is no way the two words "obscene" and "angles" can be rationally juxtaposed in a normal adjective-noun phrase. Angles cannot be *obscene*. It does not make sense, yet there it is, and it has its psychological effects on the reader, regardless of whether his grammatical sense is outraged or not. Such Lovecraftian formulas are frightening to

Caligarism and the Trapezoidal Cinema

Caligari's asylum in *The Cabinet of Dr. Caligari* (1919).

the uninitiated mind, and absurd to the grammatical pedant—but to the initiate, they are a form of trapezoidal poetry.

The twentieth-century American Satanic philosopher Anton Szandor LaVey (1930–1997), fascinated by the same body of material, studied and speculated on the principles of the trapezoid and "obscene angles." He eventually came up with his infamous "Law of the Trapezoid." This law states that figures or spaces made up of obtuse or acute angles (those less or more than 90°, respectively) have an unsettling effect on the mind unless they are recognized as such—whereupon they can be empowering and energizing. This definition was first made explicit in print in Anton LaVey's article "The Law of the Trapezoid" in *The Cloven Hoof* in 1976.

Quite independent of Lovecraft, and preceding him by several years, a line of German artists, thinkers, and occultists came up with many similar ideas. In their case, the concepts seem directly rooted in the applications of non-Euclidean geometry and the idea of a fourth dimension of space pioneered by men such as Carl Friedrich Gauss and Johann Karl Friedrich Zöllner. Did these ideas find their way into what Robert E. Howard would imaginatively call *Unaussprechlichen Kulten* in Germany?

One of the roots of the Trapezoid's heritage slithers its way out of the German Expressionist cinema and the genre of the *Schauerfilme* (horror films) produced especially between 1919 (the date of *The Cabinet of Dr. Caligari*) and 1933 (the date when Hitler took control of the German government). This body of film work is touted as a significant influence on Anton LaVey. His artistic vision of such sources helped to shape a distinctive esoteric school. But a question remains: Was there any actual connection between the German magical scene and the films of the period? Or were these images merely the products of the filmmakers' imaginations? We are very much used to seeing uninformed mumbo-jumbo on the screen in more current films purporting to deal with the dark arts. Was it all that much different then? There are those notable exceptions to this general state of affairs: *Dr. Dracula* (1978), *Rosemary's Baby* (1968), and even *The Asylum of Satan* (1972) and *The Devil's Rain* (1975). In those cases, the sources are sometimes given credit and it is easy to separate the wheat from the chaff.

Was LaVey's understanding of the practical magical precepts that he discerned in these films another example of his genius seeing things that were perhaps not consciously intended, or

The Cabinet of Dr. Caligari (1919)

intended only in some lesser magical way? Another example of this process would be his transformation of William Mortensen's "Command to Look"—which was, after all, mainly intended as an effective way of composing photographs—into a greater magical principle. Or were these images the visible reflections of some "Black Order" of Satanists working in Germany at the time?

The story of LaVey's first exposure to these films, which were to shape much of his vision of the Trapezoid, is ambiguously and *mythically* recorded in the now rather rare 1974 biography of Anton LaVey entitled *The Devil's Avenger* by Burton Wolfe:

> During the summer of 1945, one of Tony's [LaVey's] uncles was hired by the Army as a civilian engineer to reconstruct air strips in

Obscene angles in *The Cabinet of Dr. Caligari* (1919).

Germany. Since the uncle had just been divorced, he had a family visa opening that was to have been filled by his wife. Instead, Tony went with him.

One day at the command post in Berlin where his uncle was stationed, Tony attended the showing of some German films confiscated from the Nazis' motion picture production office. The movies that interested Tony the most were the *schauerfilme* such as *The Testament of Dr. Mabuse*, about a mad hypnotist and depravity in high and low places in pre-Hitler Germany; and *Metropolis*, about a wizard-scientist named Rotwang who confounds a revolt of slave like workers by sending a humanoid to double for the Joan of Arc type of woman serving as the workers' leader. One of the *schauerfilme* told the story of an effete young man, the scion of a multi-millionaire family of munitions-makers, who entertained his friends with Black Masses. The particular Black Mass favored by this wealthy young German made use of a trapezoid suspended from the ceiling, a revolving pentagon of mirrors, creepy electronic organ music, and electric lights buzzing through his black chapel. A German interpreting the films for the viewing Army brass explained that what they were seeing was not merely fiction, but an authentic representation of a ceremony performed by the Black Order, a secret society of Satan worshippers. Did such people really exist? (Wolfe 1974, 27–28)

Indeed! Did such people really exist? The question is not answered clearly elsewhere. Later in the same text, it is said with regard to LaVey's early assessment of Aleister Crowley: "Crowley, in some parts of his books, seemed to be the nearest living facsimile to the Black Mass celebrants depicted in the German *schauerfilme* Tony had seen in Berlin" (Wolfe 1974, 32). The tenuous connection between Crowley and these films may prove more meaningful in due course. One significant problem remains as to the identity of the exact film in which this Trapezoidal Black Mass is supposed to have appeared. The best research to date indicates that either no such film exists or, if it did exist, it has not survived. However, it is certain that LaVey made contact with the emerging Trapezoidal magical current through expressionistic films—at least by his own account.

The glaring question persists: "Did such people actually exist?" In order to get the answer one would obviously have to have intimate knowledge of the German occult scene during the years in question. This is a difficult task for anyone not associated with it at that time, as the German magical culture has tended to be considerably more secretive than its Anglo-American counterpart. However, any solid connection between the self-consciously magical culture and that of the film industry (especially the creative forces behind the set designs) would be a good start. This beginning has been provided, I believe, in the person of one Albin Grau (1884–1971).

Schatten (1923)

Grau, with the magical initiatory name Frater Pacitius, was the "Master of the Chair" and "Master of the Orient Berlin" of an order calling itself the Pansophical Lodge of the Light-Seeking Brothers, Orient Berlin. This lodge was constituted in 1921. Its Grand Master was Heinrich Tränker (Frater Recnartus) and its General Secretary was Gregor A. Gregorius (= Eugen Grosche). In 1925, a sort of "secret conference" was called at Weida in Germany. The purpose of this conference was to decide whether or not to follow the Law of Thelêma proclaimed by τὸ μέγα θηρίον ("the Great Beast," as Crowley styled himself). The uttering of this Word, Thelêma (θέλημα, "will"), and the philosophical motto "Do what thou wilt shall be the whole of the Law" was supposed to usher in a new age in the history of mankind. The Weida conference was attended by Tränker and his personal secretary Karl Germer, Grau, Gregorius, Crowley, Lea Hirsig, Martha Küntzel, and Norman Mudd.

The conference was split and eventually Tränker and Grau (and thus the Pansophical Lodge) decided not to follow the Law of Thelêma. On the other hand, Gregor A. Gregorius accepted the "New Æon," and eventually in 1928 founded a Thelemite order known as the *Fraternitas Saturni* (Brotherhood of Saturn). The FS was (and is) Thelemite, but was nevertheless

Caligarism and the Trapezoidal Cinema

independent of Crowley's personal authority. This order has many sinister angles—among them the only references I have seen in older traditional occult literature to Tesla energy and the use of electrical apparatus in magical workings.

So who was this Albin Grau? A review of the credits of major *Schauerfilme* of the period reveals that he was artistic visionary responsible for such films as *Nosferatu: Eine Symphonie des Grauens* (1922), and *Schatten* (Warning Shadows, 1923). Grau also provided the storyline for the latter film, which involves a magician who hypnotizes people, and who then "entices their shadows from them causing them to perform the roles inspired by [his] shadow play, acting out their subconscious impulses in a collective dream" (Barlow 1982, 95). Previously, Grau had envisioned the world portrayed in the film *Nosferatu*. At one point, Count Orlok is shown to hold a set of documents in his hands—an analysis of these documents clearly shows them to be magical pages produced in the tradition of the Fraternitas Saturni (see my book *The Fraternitas Saturni* [Flowers 2018], 26). Beyond this, the appearance of the vampire in *Nosferatu* bears an uncanny resemblance to the egregore, the GOTOS, used by the Fraternitas Saturni to make and maintain contact with the praeternatural sponsor of the order.

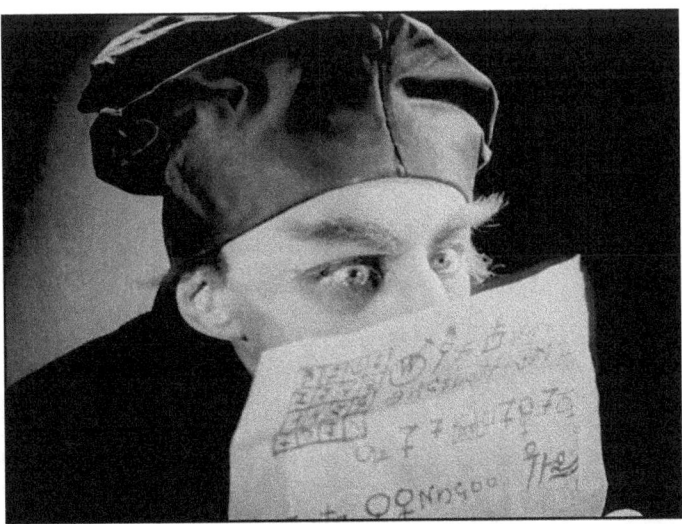

Count Orlok with a magical document in *Nosferatu* (1992).

The main point, from our perspective, is that a positive and definite link is established between the world of the makers of the *Schauerfilme* and the occult elite of Germany of that time. Whether as a glorification or vilification, these portrayals put on the screen by these filmmakers can be trusted to reflect some actual magical practice. Usually, these Satanic illustrations are meant to condemn the factions being portrayed in that light. However, some of the people working on the films must have known something about the nature of this underground. If LaVey was guessing that occult secrets were displayed on these flickering screens, it can certainly be said that he was correct.

The set designers or architects who worked on the expressionist films such as *The Cabinet of Dr. Caligari* were, it is known, deeply interested in things very similar to what Anton LaVey espoused in the Law of the Trapezoid. In Germany, as well as pre-Soviet (and even very early Soviet) Russia, expressionist artists developed theories about how distorted and illogical angles and dimensions could have a disorienting effect on the mind. This theory, and its practice, was tailor-made for the idea of expressionism. The term "expressionism" is one that is often heard, although many people may not know exactly what it means. Briefly, it is a school of art, spanning visual, literary, dramatic, musical, and cinematic forms most popular in the early twentieth century, and its artists are characterized as follows in

Left: Max Schreck as Count Orlak in *Nosferatu*.
Right: A sculptured bust of the GOTOS of the Fraternitas Saturni.

Caligarism and the Trapezoidal Cinema

The Cabinet of Dr. Caligari (1919)

The Oxford Dictionary of English (2010):

> Expressionists characteristically reject traditional ideas of beauty or harmony and use distortion, exaggeration, and other non-naturalistic devices in order to express emotional states. The paintings of El Greco and Grünewald exemplify expressionism in this broad sense, but the term is also used of a late 19th and 20th century European and specifically German movement tracing its origins to Van Gogh, Edvard Munch, and James Ensor, which insisted on the primacy of the artist's feelings and mood, often incorporating violence and the grotesque.

So, an expressionist work *forces* the viewer/reader to participate in the *subjective universe* of the artist—no matter how insane, subjective, or unusual that universe might be. As a technique, this idea remains popular today: if a character in a film imagines his dead friend is talking to him and the actor playing that friend is right there appearing as real as anything else in the scene, the viewer is *forced* to see the friend as the other character imagines him to be. That is expressionism. The inner world of the artist is *pressed out* ("ex-pressed") into the objective world.

The Cabinet of Dr. Caligari is a textbook example of expressionism on all levels. And, as is perhaps to be expected, there is a strange story behind it. The background story on this film is told is some detail by Siegfried Kracauer in his seminal work *From Caligari to Hitler* (1947, 61–76). The year is 1919. Germany is in upheaval; the Great War has just been lost (although it is unclear to most Germans as to why or how), and their world has been turned upside down. Two young visionary artists, Hans Janowitz and Carl Mayer, planned out an expressionist film in which the world would be shown to be a disorienting place and ruled by madness. This was actually rooted in a radical political stance, whereby consensus reality was deemed to be madness. Their film script is the original vision of *The Cabinet of Dr. Caligari*. The production company (Decla) and the experienced director assigned to do the picture, Robert Wiene, altered the script to show that the whole film was a story as seen through the eyes of a madman. The film begins with him sitting with another man on what might be a park bench. He says he has a story to tell... then the film proceeds in all its madness, visual and narrative. In the end, it is revealed that the man is in an insane asylum, and that the whole thing has been a vision of insanity from his perspective. The original vision of Janowitz and Mayer was more politically radical, but Wiene's version was more artistically potent and illustrative of the universal and eternal message of expressionism. The young enthusiasts actually believe the world is mad, whereas the more mature artist knows that he is a magician casting visions into the world.

One of the most potent images from *The Cabinet of Dr. Caligari* is of an insane criminal who has been locked up in a cell and attached to a sort of ball and chain. Except this "ball" is not spherical, but rather angular—and actually appears to be

Caligarism and the Trapezoidal Cinema

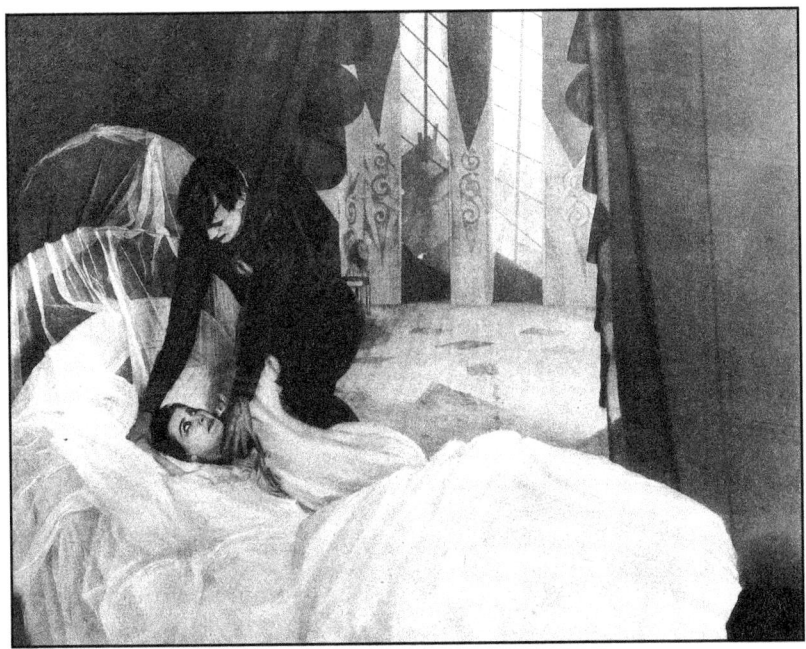

The Cabinet of Dr. Caligari (1919)

a trapezohedron! In so many ways, this is an image of the mind of the individual ensnared by the Law of the Trapezoid, being ignorant of its effects and thus being doomed to be disoriented by these very effects. There can be no doubt that the German artists of Weimar Era Berlin were aware of the psychological effects of non-Euclidian geometry, and that they attempted to implement these ideas in many of the films of the time.

The theories of expressionism, encapsulated in the Law of the Trapezoid, dictate that the absence of awareness leads to insanity, and that our inner responses to external stimuli can either be enlightening or enslaving, depending on our state of mind and awareness. Geometrical shapes and spaces remain one of the most misunderstood aspects of life, and the work of expressionists of the early twentieth century remains one of the most fascinating windows into that world.

There is still plenty of room for further research into the lives and possible occult backgrounds or connections of other set designers or architects who worked on these films, including the fairly well-known Hans Poelzig (*The Golem*), Hermann Warm (*Caligari*), Robert Dietrich (*Homoculus*), Otto Hunte (*Metropolis* and the Mabuse films). For a deep-level study of the mysteries of the trapezoid in myth and magic, see Toby Chappell's *Infernal Geometry* (Inner Traditions, 2019).

The original 1919 Caligari film was one of the true innovations in the history of cinema. No one ever has tried to remake it. Two films have been inspired by its legacy: a 1962 production called *The Cabinet of Caligari* and *Dr. Caligari* (1989), an attempt at creating a campy pornographic-horror take, which is a general failure.

XIII

Ed Wood's
Plan 9 from Inner Space:
The Visions of the Outsider

Plan 9 from Outer Space has been deemed one of the "worst movies ever made." Its shortcomings are many and often detract from the deeper underlying message, which may have been lost in translation. To understand the *Plan*, one has to understand the man: Ed Wood (1924–1978).

Edward D. Wood, Jr., was born on October 10, 1924, in Poughkeepsie, New York. He saw his first horror movie when he was about seven years old: *Dracula* (1931) starring Bela Lugosi. Four years later he was gifted his first movie camera for his eleventh birthday. At seventeen he enlisted in the Marine Corps and participated in heavy battlefield operations in the South Pacific, where he was wounded several times. He lost his front teeth in hand-to-hand combat. According to his own report, he was already practicing transvestitism—wearing women's undergarments beneath his fatigues while doing battle with the Empire of Japan. After the war, Wood joined a carnival and played the part of a half-man/half-woman in the sideshow. But his dedication to film brought him to Hollywood in 1947. There he did a bit of everything: writing, directing, acting, and doing stunt-work (at least once in drag). This work all took place within

Plan 9 from Outer Space (1959)

the lowest echelons of the film industry. Ed's transvestitism was a deeply held and essential part of himself that he had kept secret all of his life until he made the film *Glen or Glenda* (1953). It was shortly after meeting Bela Lugosi, who had been a personal hero of his, that Ed made this great personal leap in filmmaking. *Glen or Glenda* was a semi-autobiographical effort about a transvestite/transsexual. Throughout the film, Lugosi plays the part of a godlike figure expounding the laws of nature, perhaps manipulating them with his cosmic chemistry set, as he utters the enigmatic words: "Pull the string, pull the string!" This, like all of Ed's movies, suffered from poor production values and often abysmal acting. But it was a serious effort at expressing the idea of the individual's need to be understood and accepted,

Ed Wood's Plan 9 from Inner Space

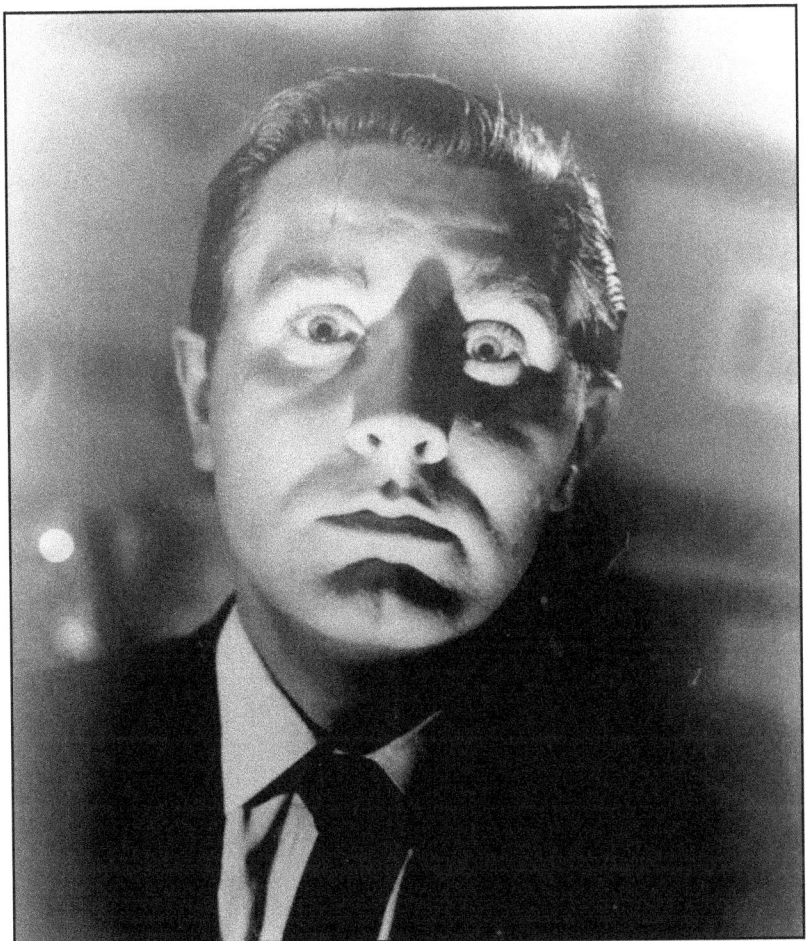

Edward D. Wood, Jr. (1924–1978)

especially by those whom he loved. Ed had held his secret all his life; now he expressed it and projected it onto a screen for the whole wide world to witness. With his first significant picture, Ed made clear the underlying nature of his secret—he was a sexual Outsider.

The films for which Wood became best known were those most widely viewed on television in the 1960s (i.e., *Bride of the Monster* and *Plan 9 from Outer Space*). Because these were among his least obvious as far as a sexual theme was concerned, this aspect of Ed Wood's art form was often overlooked. But he began his creative legacy with *Glen or Glenda* and ended it with hardcore sex films, erotic novels, and a how-to course in sexual techniques. Sandwiched between *Bride of the Monster* and *Plan 9* is a little-seen film entitled *The Bride and the Beast* (1958), which reaches the zenith of sexual subversion. The narrative structure of this film is quite simple. In the first segment we meet Dan, a big-game hunter, who has just married a woman, Laura. They go to his secluded estate on their wedding night. There she is introduced to a captive gorilla, named Spanky, which Dan keeps in a cage in his basement. There is an immediate sexual attraction between the woman and Spanky. Late in the night, he escapes from his cage and attempts to become romantic with Laura.

The Bride and the Beast (1958)

Dan, of course, then shoots and kills his lifelong ape-buddy. Dan's friend, a physician named Dr. Carl Reiner, hypnotically regresses Laura and it is revealed that she herself was a gorilla in a "past life." The second part of the film shows Dan and Laura on their honeymoon taking a safari in Africa. There Dan kills and traps various animals, and Laura seems to enthusiastically participate. This part of the film is reminiscent of other movies about Africa of the period, such as *Hatari* (1962). At this point we are wondering about Laura's simian proclivities, but we don't have to wonder much longer. The third and final chapter begins with a gorilla who comes sauntering up to the camp, seemingly summoned telepathically by Laura. After exchanging longing glances with the woman, the ape snatches her away. She seems to go quite willingly. He carries her off to a cave, where they are soon joined by some other gorilla pals. Dan finds her and the gorillas. He fights the apes, but is knocked out by one of them, who takes Laura off deeper into the jungle. We see images of the gorilla carrying his willing and happy human bride. In the final scene, Dan commiserates with Dr. Reiner about the wife he lost to the apes in Africa. The doctor claims he had noticed certain animalistic characteristics in her earlier, due to her previous existences or incarnations. He then concludes: "I believe she's gone, Dan—gone back to where she came from."

There appears to be something of the Kharis/Anankê theme in *The Bride and the Beast* as well. We have seen in the mummy mythology (essay II) that the "romantic" tension is set up between individuals exemplifying two forms of immortality: the static and the dynamic. Spanky has remained "unevolved" in his static and archaic level of being, whereas Laura has undergone evolution through many lifetimes, all the way back to the time when she was a simian. All of this is, of course, a popular and nonscientific understanding of Darwinism, but in keeping with the common understanding of the "theory of evolution" from ape to human.

Wood was unlikely to have been familiar with the ideas of Jörg Lanz von Liebenfels (1874–1954), one of Europe's great eccentrics of the early twentieth century. This ex-Cistercian monk from Austria held that humans of today are actually a mixture of a divine race of mankind, marked by blond hair and blue eyes, and a dark simian race of subhumans. A book by Liebenfels, entitled *Theozoology* (1905), is perhaps the most politically incorrect text ever penned. Liebenfels was obsessed with the kind of themes and images present in *The Bride and the Beast* (and many other Hollywood productions from *King Kong* [1933] to *The Shape of Water* [2017], which show the sexual interaction between beautiful women and beastly creatures, usually of the ape family). Probably the best of these is *Murders in the Rue Morgue* (1932), discussed earlier. What sets *The Bride and the Beast* apart from other horror films with this theme is that Wood is totally sympathetic with the position of the ape and the woman he loves. The apparent, if subtle, villain in the story is a "great white hunter" who tries to stand between them. In most scenarios the "hero" defends the woman from the "monster," but Wood, like many another genius of the horror genre, has demonstrable sympathy for the monster in this paradigm. Here the Great White Hunter tries to defend his woman but loses her to the ape.

Bride of the Monster (1955)

Ed Wood's Plan 9 from Inner Space

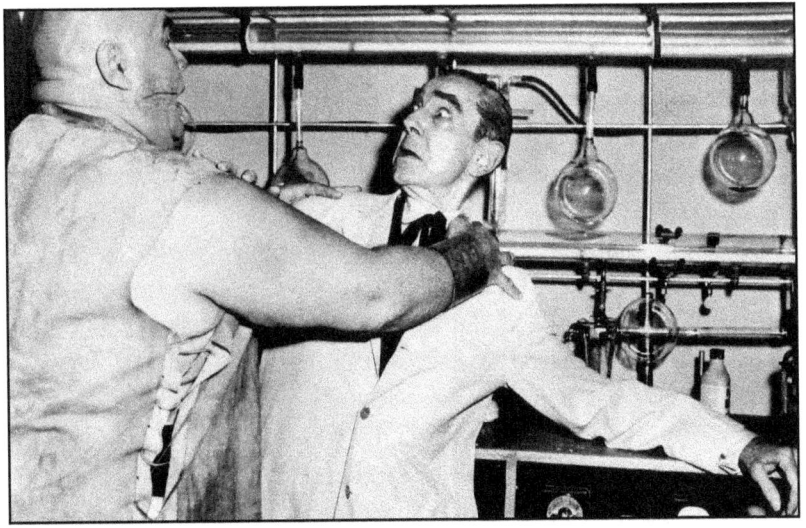

Tor Johnson and Bela Legosi in *Bride of the Monster*.

One of the most important aspects of Ed Wood's career is his relationship with the legendary Bela Lugosi at the end of the veteran horror star's life. Wood and Lugosi became friends and collaborators on the younger man's projects. Their most complete project was a film shot under the title "Bride of the Atom," but released as *Bride of the Monster* (1955). It was filmed in 1954, after which Lugosi committed himself to a hospital for his longtime addiction to morphine. A month after the release of *Bride of the Monster*, Lugosi died. Among Wood's horror films, *Bride of the Monster* is by far his most polished work. One of this film's great assets—and something often lacking in a Wood production—is some competent and even compelling acting for the role played by Bela Lugosi. Lugosi adds that touch of "dragons' breath" that takes the movie over the edge from divine schlock into the realm of Hollywood magic.

One of the most famous scenes in the film (and one that is given prominence in the Tim Burton film *Ed Wood*) is the short speech written for Bela by Ed. Bela apparently loved it, and it is, in a sense, a philosophical statement on the part of Edward D. Wood, Jr. to the world:

Home? I have no home. Hunted, despised. Living like an animal. The jungle is my home. But I shall show the world that I can be its master. I will perfect my own race of people. A race of atomic supermen which will conquer the world!

This is a statement by the Outsider who feels rejected by the world, but who is not running from it to hide under a rock. Rather, this Outsider declares his intention to master the world, and to do so in the company of others like him, or of his own creation. Ed Wood was an Outsider in the film industry, as well as in other avenues of life. But his films are often a testimony to his desire to enter into the Insider world—which is why he always tagged his films with the phrase "Made in Hollywood, USA."

Wood moved in a world of people who lived what would later come to be called "alternative lifestyles." Most of these individuals were in one way or another people like Ed: Outsiders. They were sexually or professionally in a sort of liminal state—mostly misunderstood or unappreciated in some way, yet full of life force. These included struggling actors, fake psychics, wrestlers, gays, and the only female horror host of the pre–Shock Era: Vampira (= Maila Elizabeth Syrjäniemi = Maila Nurmi [1922–2008]). Vampira, famous for her seventeen-inch waist and vampiric persona, was the first horror hostess who had her own show on a local Los Angeles television station, KABC, from 1954–1955. The show was popular but was cancelled for mysterious reasons. Clearly, the idea of having local personalities assume horrific characters to host the films of the Shock Package released by Screen Gems in 1958 stems from Vampira's act at KABC in Los Angeles. Unable to hire actors in a more conventional manner, Wood tended to cast these colorful friends in his films. These people were all in fact *performers* in life in one sense or another, just not in the conventional Tinseltown sense. This casting, too, gives Wood films a certain quality of "otherness."

In November of 1956, the first scenes of "Grave Robbers from Outer Space" were shot, but it would take Ed almost three

Ed Wood's Plan 9 from Inner Space

Vampira in *Plan 9 from Outer Space*.

years to get the support to finish and release the film. Legend had it that to appease religious investors who thought the idea of "grave robbing" was too sacrilegious, Wood retitled the movie *Plan 9 from Outer Space* (1959). In fact, Wood changed the name on his own after the film was finished and the investors claim to have made no such demand. This was to be his "masterpiece"— or at least the film for which he is now best known.

The complex and difficult business environment of mainstream American filmmaking was something Ed just could not, or would not, master. Although by the end he was involved in one way or another in the making of around thirty films, the difficulties of translating his ideas to the screen proved just too great. Wood was also a writer and he took great pride in the dimension of his creativity. After 1963 he increasingly devoted his efforts to producing books. These were often novels set in a seamy underworld of perversion, carnivals, prostitution, and sadism, mixed with horror. Titles of these works include: *Black Lace Drag*, *Side-Show Siren*, *Devil Girls*, *Death of a Transvestite*, *Raped in the Grass*, *The Sexecutives*, *Carnival Piece*, *To Make a Homo*, and *Death of a Transvestite Hooker*. But Wood also wrote

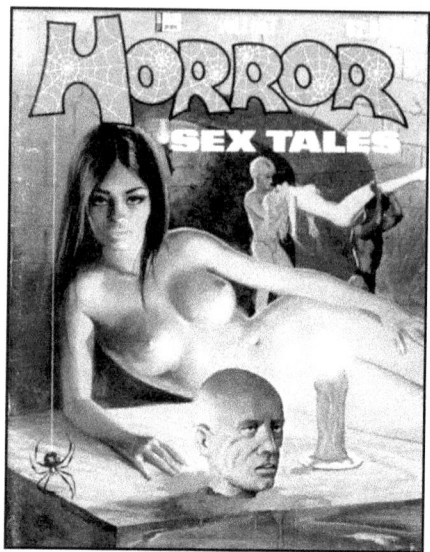

One of the many publications to which Wood regularly contributed his short stories.

many nonfiction books about sexuality and the world of the occult such as: *Bloodiest Sex Crimes of History*, *The Perverts*, *Love of the Dead*, *Sex Museum*, *Sexual Practices in Witchcraft and Black Magic*, and *A Study of Fetishes and Fantasies*. He even produced a whole "Sex Education Correspondence School" in 1975. This was a combination of twelve 120-page books issued each month along with an 8mm film illustrating the lessons! By the time of his death, Wood had written around seventy-five books between the years of 1963 and 1978. Additionally, he wrote hundreds of short stories and articles for magazines. An extensive bibliography and filmography of the works of Edward D. Wood, Jr., including those he wrote under several pseudonyms, are listed and discussed in the Feral House classic *Ed Wood: Nightmare of Ecstasy* (1992) by Rudolph Grey.

From the mid-1970s onward, Ed Wood sank into a deep alcoholic depression. All of his money was spent on liquor, and eventually he and his wife were evicted from their shabby apartment in Hollywood and they had to move in with a friend. Three days later on December 10, 1978, he was found dead in bed, following a drinking binge.

Although Ed Wood was no doubt a sufferer of what we call today Post-traumatic Stress Disorder (PTSD), rooted in his experiences in heavy and bloody combat in the South Pacific during WWII, it is reported that he was already a transvestite at that time, wearing women's underthings under his fatigues. So evidence shows that his sexual proclivities have little to do with his war experiences. But Wood's interest—or even

Ed Wood's Plan 9 from Inner Space

obsession—with matters of sexuality went well beyond his own transvestitism, as his activities at the end of his life show.

Some might wonder about the how and why of Ed Wood's descent into depression, alcoholism, and eventual death at the early age of fifty-four. Perhaps this was rooted in his lack of success in Hollywood. But in general he was continuing to create things right up to the very end—writing, dreaming, and even creating his "Sex Education Correspondence School." From my experience as a kid living in the 1960s, where most of our fathers were WWII veterans, I noticed that the vast majority of the men who had seen any real action in the war were very badly affected by it. Many of them were alcoholics and had some really weird behaviors. We now know this to be PTSD, but at the time it was little recognized except in those for whom the symptoms were just too extreme to miss. (Back then it generally was referred to as "shell shock.") Although PTSD may have greatly contributed to his self-medication, it does not account for his sexual interests, since the latter seem to predate the major causes of his stress disorder. Based on my childhood observations, I put these psychologically damaged war veterans into three categories: the Good, the Bad, and the Sad. I knew men from all three categories. The Good, like Ed Wood seems to have been, turned the pain inward on themselves; the Bad took it out on others; and the Sad seemed to muddle along as best they could.

The aforementioned theme of the Outsider again comes to the forefront in the story of *Plan 9*. Invaders from another planet are, of course, the ultimate sort of Outsiders. They have come to our planet and want to communicate and make themselves understood, yet they cannot even gain recognition for their existence, as exemplified in the following iconic scene from the film. Here the extraterrestrials are confronted regarding their malevolent intentions toward Earth. We cannot let the significance of the character's name go unremarked—Eros the Greek god of sensual love:

> **Eros:** "I? A fiend? I am a soldier of our planet. I, a fiend? We did not come as enemies. We came only with friendly intentions. To talk. To ask your aid."
> **The Colonel:** "Our aid?"
> **Eros:** "Yes. Your aid for the whole universe. But your governments of Earth refuse to even accept our existence. Even though you have seen us, heard our messages, you refused to accept us."
> **The Colonel:** "Why was it so important to contact the different governments of Earth?"
> **Eros:** "Because of death. Because all of you of Earth are idiots."

This sequence of dialog is really the heart of *Plan 9*. The film, like the rest of Wood's cinematic endeavors, is a reflection of the sentiments expressed here by Eros. Everything that Wood did was an effort to communicate from his outré world, from his alternative universe, to the world of consensus reality sitting in the movie theaters of America. Perhaps also he was reaching out to the other kindred spirits to be found here and there in those audiences, to let them know that they were not alone in the universe. Certainly, the theme of the extraterrestrials coming to Earth to teach the childish human race how to be better citizens of the universe is not unique or new. This is one of the major themes of science-fiction films of the 1950s, most perfectly expressed perhaps in the classic *The Day the Earth Stood Still* (1951). What is meaningful in Wood's treatment of the theme is that he clearly identifies with the aliens, and that the alien world is identified—if only secretly—with his personal subculture of misfits and alternative-lifestyle types. If we take this further, we see that he is referring to the world of the liberated—those who have come to accept and express their own personal uniqueness, versus the world of the bound—those who follow the conventions of the ordinary, often in ways that are opposed to their true wills and natures. The famous English mage Aleister Crowley (1875–1947) expressed a similar philosophy through his Aeonic Word *Thelema*: "True Will."

Rudolf Grey's biography *Ed Wood: Nightmare of Ecstasy* (1992) was used as the basis for Tim Burton's 1994 film *Ed Wood*. This movie provides us with one of the best examples of an interesting subgenre of films: movies *about* the making of horror films or the literature upon which they are based. This is also remarkable as a subgenre. Are there films about the making of Westerns, gangster movies, or other genres? No, not really. But there are a number of films about the making of horror movies or the people who made them. Besides *Ed Wood* there is *Shadow of the Vampire* (2000), *Matinee* (1993), *Gods and Monsters* (1998), and *The Man of a Thousand Faces* (1957). We could extend this into the literary field with Ken Russell's *Gothic* (1986), which in a Romantic fashion tells the story of that haunted summer when Mary Shelley conceived of the writing of *Frankenstein*. There is also the campy and self-referential *How to Make a Monster* (1958), which is a horror movie set in the studio world of horror-movie makers in the late 1950s at American International, and *Madhouse* (1974), a film about rival personalities in the horror-film industry starring Vincent Price and Peter Cushing as fictional characters. I am sure there must be more, but those

Plan 9 from Outer Space (1959)

are the ones that immediately spring to mind. Many of these films, *Ed Wood* included, take considerable liberties with the facts about the subject, but most of them also represent fine examples of storytelling. Their quality speaks to the depth and complexity of the worlds they portray. These are special worlds, full of magic and magicians.

For those who might be feel that I am overthinking the all-too-banal subject of Ed Wood and his creations, it is worth mentioning that there is actually exists a *Church of Ed Wood* led by Reverend Steve Galindo. Far from being a celebration of absurd and discordian elements like those things expressed in the Church of the Subgenius, the teachings of the Church of Ed Wood are fundamentally linked to the ideas contained in Wood's underlying philosophy of life and art. Additionally, there is a very interesting and useful book by Bob Craig entitled *Ed Wood: Mad Genius* (2009). This book treats Ed's creations as if they were fine works of philosophy, cinematography, and social criticism, which they may well be—albeit unconventional ones. Craig, like myself, is interested in the ideas behind the work rather than the details of the craft from a purely cinematic perspective. Craig, perhaps correctly, sees Wood's three obsessions as sex, death, and resurrection.

Famously, the film critic and conservative pundit Michael Medved deemed *Plan 9 from Outer Space* by Ed Wood to be the "worst movie of all time." I am here to tell you that it is categorically *not* the worst film of all time, and in fact it has a number of redeeming elements. No matter how much technology is poured into the special effects for today's sci-fi action films, the vacuity of the ideas animating them often betrays films that are far worse than Wood's *Plan*. *Plan 9* has an idea, a point of view, and a higher purpose—it is executed in the most incompetent ways imaginable, but that's all just a superficial consideration. Here and now I call on the powers that be in Hollywood to remake *Plan 9 from Outer Space*! Make it the way Ed Wood would have liked to have made it, if he had had a competent screenwriter and a budget for special effects! After Hollywood has insanely tried to "remake" films such as *Psycho*, a virtually perfect film the first time, it makes far more sense to remake films which *need* to be remade—or made the way they should have been made in the first place.

Ed Wood is the artistic Everyman. Any and all who feel themselves to be Outsiders (most of us have felt that way at one time or another) and who have something to say about themselves and the world around them—something that they wish the rest of humanity could only understand—can relate to Ed Wood. These people can see themselves somewhere in his vision. Despite his reputation as a bad filmmaker and as a colossal incompetent, Edward D. Wood, Jr. has inspired more people than this image would normally allow. In that there is some magic.

XIV
Sci-Fi Theater
(Preview of a Coming Attraction?)

The problem of dividing films that belong to the horror genre from those that belong to science fiction has already been mentioned and explored to some extent in the introductory section of this book. Fans of one genre tend to be fans of the other, especially in the classical era. This was further promoted by the fact that the filmmakers and screenwriters often used patterns found in one genre in works of the other. The root of the "problem" goes back at least to the time of Mary Shelley's *Frankenstein*, which could just as easily be called a work of science fiction as one of Gothick horror.

For our purposes here, I will discuss the elements of science fiction as belonging to four categories:

1. Nature Out of Control
2. Man's Misuse of Science
3. Invasion by Other Worlds
4. Exploration of Other Worlds

These categories can and do easily cross-fertilize one another. The cinematic archetypes of these four categories are:

1. *King Kong* (1933)
2. *Frankenstein* (1931) [1818]
3. *War of the Worlds* (1953)
4. *Forbidden Planet* (1956)

A feature often found in science-fiction material, both literary and cinematic, is that of unknown or newly imagined technologies. This aspect often becomes a "character" unto itself. These are most often modes of communication and transportation. It is truly amazing how much of this imagined technology in science fiction has actually become science fact in recent years.

A series of essays similar to the type found in this volume could be developed about a wide spectrum of specifically science-fiction films. This too would be focused on works made before the mid-1970s. At that time, as grown-up Monster Kids such as Steven Spielberg and George Lucas began to make their own creations, their sense of self-awareness and self-reference tended to limit the sort of patterns in the genre that had been previously active and which were the result of naive upwelling from the unconscious, whether individual or collective. For example, the Star Wars narrative was acknowledged to have been consciously influenced by the scholar of mythology, Joseph Campbell—especially in the form of his book *The Hero with a Thousand Faces* (1949).

In this special essay, I will not be able to delve into the films on the same level as in the other essays, and many great films will have to remain unmentioned. The main purpose here is to establish a certain typology of science-fiction films and interpret those types as such. Just as with the horror genre, the classic science-fiction films before the mid-1970s were very often based on older literature created by such writers as H. G. Wells and Jules Verne. These literary backgrounds by visionary individuals provided the philosophical framework that gave the genre its gravitas in the early days.

Sci-Fi Theater

1. Nature Out of Control

The relationship of man to nature has always been an ambiguous one, fraught with fear and danger. Because man is an incomplete creature—a spiritual and intellectual being in a world of tremendous and often dangerous natural forces as well as many beasts, some of them friendly and others deadly—humanity has often had to fear and control nature in order to survive. From the earliest times, human beings have studied, analyzed, and classified nature for its useful aspects and its dangerous ones. Occasionally, humans discovered previously unknown beasts that posed great danger. Today we call the discovery and description of unknown beasts the "science" (although most would call it the pseudoscience) of cryptozoology.

The so-called Father of History, the Greek writer Herodotus, had notes about the bones of dragons having being found in the deserts and elsewhere. One of the most popular forms of literature in the Middle Ages was the bestiary: these were catalogs of fantastic creatures such as unicorns and basilisks, as well as human oddities such as "unipeds"—one-legged men who hopped about. Such works were taken seriously by the establishment thinkers of the day because they had no reason to doubt that the world was so large and therefore must contain many as-yet-unseen wonders.

When I was a kid, one of my favorite books was *The Maybe Monsters* (1963) by Gardner Soule. It recounted the usual monstrous cryptozoological wonders—the Loch Ness Monster, Sasquatch, and sea monsters, among many others. Without having to stretch reason *too* much, it was easy to believe that if we delve deep enough into the Earth or explore far enough into the remotest parts of our planet, we will discover things previously *unknown*. In our present-day world of satellites and computers, more of the world has become known so that we can spy on even the most remote and inaccessible parts of the planet by these technological methods. This has meant that that many of the imaginative scenarios of an H. Rider Haggard, Jules Verne, or Arthur Conan Doyle (whose works posited unknown realms in remote areas of our globe, and which seemed more plausible until more recent developments) have now been pushed off into the sphere of pure fantasy. Even as late as the 1950s, the child's mind could admit to the possibility that there were some remote areas of South America or Africa that might house still-living dinosaurs! Other planets, too, remained mysterious, and we could still believe in the canals on Mars.

Movies featuring cryptozoological terrors abound, especially in the 1950s. Most of these, however, belong in some sense to our next category because these creatures' unusual size was caused by man's misuse of science—most usually *atomic* science. The archetype of cryptozoological horror is his royal highness from Skull Island—King Kong. The 1933 film was a cultural sensation. The level of pathos generated for Kong is on a par with that achieved by Karloff in *The Bride of Frankenstein*.

The naturally occurring zoological wonders of surviving dinosaurs or creatures from approximately their Jurassic Age of evolution were only dangerous to the civilized world when

A French poster for *King Kong* (1933).

members of that world entered their remote realms, or when the creatures were somehow brought into the civilized world where they did not belong. *King Kong* was probably originally inspired by Arthur Conan Doyle's *The Lost World*, first made into a film in 1925 with Willis O'Brien's stop-motion animation (which was also used in *King Kong*). The idea of finding some remote part of the world where prehistoric animals have survived was greatly enhanced in its plausibility with the discovery of a living specimen of the coelacanth—a species thought to have been extinct for sixty million years—off of the coast of South Africa in 1938. (The coelacanth even has a starring role in the 1958 film *Monster on the Campus*.)

One of the most popular (fictional) prehistoric beasts in the history of film was Universal's gill-man movies in the *Creature from the Black Lagoon* series (1954–1956) of three films. Besides the original there is *Revenge of the Creature* and *The Creature Walks Among Us*. The Academy Award–winning film *The Shape of Water* is directly inspired by these *Creature* films—specifically in a manner so as to consummate the implicit sexual element in the original films. In *The Creature Walks Among Us* the gill-man is brought to civilization and surgically transformed due to burns he received in his (re-)capture.

Perhaps more common than natural survivals of species from the Jurassic or Cretaceous Ages are creatures that are jarred back into existence through human intervention or interference. One of the first of this genre was *The Beast from 20,000 Fathoms* (1953), in which a dinosaur is freed from its hiding place in a volcano by atomic testing. The most famous of all of these creatures is Godzilla (Japanese: Gojira), a dinosaurlike beast that has greatly gained in size and has become equipped with the ability to project a sort of atomic flame-thrower from its mouth. The original Japanese version, *Gojira*, was released in 1954. But in 1956 an English-language version was released featuring an American actor (Raymond Burr) to make the film more "relatable." Perhaps one of the worst examples of this kind of film is the Danish-produced *Reptilicus* (1961), in which a piece of a prehistoric creature is dug up in a mining operation in the frozen tundra, and when it is warmed, it replicates itself. The most interesting aspect of this Nordic effort is that the creature is actually a dragon of the kind described in ancient Norse sagas—it does not breathe fire but rather spits an acidic venom that can melt anything.

A whole monster archetype unto itself is found in the "giant-bug" pictures that seemed so common in the 1950s. Here creatures that should have remained fairly harmless are caused to be giant-sized, frequently under the influence of radiation. By far the best and most classic of all of these films is *Them!* (1954), in which giant ants from the desert around the atomic bomb testing sights begin to interact with humans in a deadly way. Another film belonging to this genre is *Tarantula* (1955), in which scientists use radiation to modify food to produce a super-nutrient. They hope to be able to end world hunger, but a tarantula gets into it and mayhem ensues. Both *The Black Scorpion* (1957) and *The Deadly Mantis* (1957) feature giant creatures released from below the earth through a naturally occurring volcano.

But it must be noted that it was not just bugs and other such creatures that were subject to size modification in the context of horrific and wondrous events. Humans, too, could be manipulated in this manner on the silver screen. Notable examples are *The Amazing Colossal Man* (1957), *War of the Colossal Beast* (1958), *The Incredible Shrinking Man* (1957), and the most terrifying of all—*Attack of the 50 Foot Woman* (1958). In this last film a wealthy heiress troubled by a philandering husband has a close encounter with an extraterrestrial of huge size in his spacecraft out in the desert. This causes her to grow to the billed stature and take vengeance on her two-timing husband. Several interesting feminist themes are found in such movies.

A notable exception to the frequent role of radiation causing all of the woes is the 1972 film *Frogs*, which shows the repercussions of the prolonged misuse of pesticides by a family of toxic white plantation owners. Despite the title it is not only frogs that appear to organize and rise up in rebellion against their

Godzilla (1956)

oppressors, as even the butterflies try to get in on the revolution. This particular cinematic trend reached its final and most absurd conclusion in that same year with the release of *Night of the Lepus* about giant rabbits caused by genetic experiments. This particular film has been deemed an (unintentional) comedy in subsequent years. This last example is one of just picking the wrong creature to try to make into a villain.

This type of film, divided as it is between the naturally occurring giant beasts and the ones manufactures by human agency, also betrays two different interpretations. The first type consists of films depicting a scenario in which science has been misused or used in an irresponsible manner to unintentionally create these monsters. Such films fall into the category of the Golem or Frankenstein typology. The other type of "nature out of control"–narrative expresses man's sense of wonder at the power of nature and his anxiety over tampering with her in order to control his environment. Such attempts are often fraught with unintended consequences. In our lives in the modern Western world today, we discover that many people are killed by the power of current medical technologies intended to cure them—the medical technologies and pharmaceuticals are so powerful that they can both heal and harm in ways unimagined in the past. Also, we see that despite our attempts to control nature and dominate her, she maintains the capacity to revolt against her misuse and abuse, to rise up and do unexpected and dangerous things. This paradigm has assumed the level of a new modern mythology, and it is not unlikely that we often misinterpret events or phenomena as the result of man's misuse of technology, when in fact they may be the result of nature's actions—which are so immense we cannot comprehend them.

2. Man's Misuse of Knowledge

One of the oldest themes both in horror and science fiction is the idea of man's misuse of science, previously often referred to as *magic*, and how this unwise use will lead to unforeseen consequences that will be detrimental to man's survival and happiness. The archetype of this can be found in the Golem legend and in the story of the Frankenstein's Monster. Its deepest roots are found in the myths and legends of magic and sorcery. The principle is wonderfully illustrated by Disney's presentation of Mickey Mouse as the Sorcerer's Apprentice in the film *Fantasia*. Simply put, man—or certain men (or mice)—can sometimes evoke powers and events that he does not have the wisdom to design or to control once success has been initially gained. In a great collective sense, this type of narrative is also exemplified in the genre we can call dystopic—portraying a future political, cultural, and technological world of our own creation that has gone terribly wrong. Some would argue that we have already entered into just such a dystopia, while others feel that some sort of utopia is right around the corner. The greatest dystopic vision of the silent-screen era is *Metropolis* (1927), which does manage a hopeful conclusion. The most famous dystopic narratives are perhaps Aldous Huxley's *Brave New World*, George Orwell's *Nineteen Eighty-Four* (1949), and H. G. Wells's *The Shape of Things to Come* (1933). The latter two were made into films fairly

Frontispiece illustration for the 1831 edition of Mary Shelley's *Frankenstein*, showing the scientist's horror at his new creation.

early. Wells actually participated in the film project *Things to Come* (1936), and *Nineteen Eighty-Four* was first filmed in 1956, with a later version in 1984 starring John Hurt. By far the most powerful and practical view of the "future" is Orwell's novel. The title *1984* was really a code for 1948—the year he wrote it, for he saw so many of the things he "predicted" as already

Island of Lost Souls (1932)

happening. Like all mad experiments, dystopias begin and are carried forth in the fervent belief that the creation of the "brave new world" is a *good* thing. But the questions always persist: Are you wise enough to design a new world? Are you sure you have accounted for all the variables? Are you sure there will be no unintended consequences? The answers to these questions are categorically "No." The attempt to design a "new culture" or a "new politics" is going to end badly. The twentieth century is littered with the wreckage and corpses of sinister and misguided "-isms"—demonstrating that when each is taken to its extreme conclusion, a dystopia ensues.

On another level humankind, either individually or collectively, can be seen to hatch various technological wonders, which again have the predicted unintended consequences. Films such as *Them!*, *Godzilla*, and *The Invisible Man* (1933) illustrate this point. One of the most powerful films belonging to this group is the too-often-overlooked *Island of the Lost Souls* (1932), based on the H. G. Wells novel *The Island of Dr. Moreau* (1896). Here we see our "mad doctor" engaged in a program of using "plastic surgery, blood transfusions, gland extracts, and ray baths" to create a synthesis of human and beast, and then trying to mate them with humans to create a new race. The good doctor comes to a nasty end in his own "House of Pain."

All of these narratives belong to the golem-type of story in which the creator is destroyed by his creation and this destruction ensues because he did not take responsibility for his creation and its success exceeded his ability to control or understand it. When technology is applied to a degree beyond humanity's moral and intellectual capacity (wisdom) to deal with its effects, that technology will tend to be destructive. We learn that lesson today in different realms of life, from "social media" to artificial intelligence, to the internal combustion engine. The story of *Frankenstein* is a perhaps the most iconic representation of this phenomenon.

3. Invasion by Other or Hostile Worlds

Most often when people think of science fiction, the first sorts of things that come to mind are flying saucers and missions to other worlds. Stories about invasions from hostile planets in the cosmos are highly dramatic and make for excellent action and adventure in narratives. They are also opportunities for the use of great special effects—but if the filmmaker does not have the capacity for this, the possibilities for disaster are also considerable. Some of the best of the genre belong to the category of *invaders from space*.

In the United States the media accounts of the first rash of sightings of so-called flying saucers fueled the imagination of the public and the first science-fiction film titled obviously enough *The Flying Saucer* appeared in 1950. It is probably not a coincidence that a cluster of sightings of UFOs came around areas of the country where experimental aircraft—most especially captured Nazi technology, which is said to have included flying saucerlike craft—might have been tested, such as Washington State (home to Boeing and its facilities) and the deserts of New Mexico. These sightings occurred especially in the year 1947. UFO mania and the spreading of the idea that they were "alien technology" was probably a misdirection maneuver concocted by the intelligence services to confuse the Soviets. We did not want them to know what sorts of technologies we had captured.

Growing up I saw one after another of these kinds of movies on television. When I was in the fifth grade, there seemed to be an explosion of interest in UFOs and the popular news magazines of the day—*Life*, *Look*, and so on—did major photographic spreads on the phenomenon. I remember being so inspired as to get my parents' Browning box camera and go out one night with a friend hunting for flying saucers. It would be thirty more years before I was ever to see a real "UFO." But that's another story.

The greatest archetype of this "invaders from space" genre is H. G. Wells's *The War of the Worlds*. The 1897 novel was widely read but was not made into a major motion picture until 1953. The "modernized" setting of the film made it less effective than if it had remained in the "steampunk" world of H. G. Wells. In the novel, the Earth is invaded by Martians, who are absolutely invincible in military terms. However, they are overcome by

The War of the Worlds (1953)

The Thing from Another World (1951)

Earth pathogens, against which the Martians have no immunity. One of the most famous aspects of this story involves its use by Orson Welles in a Halloween episode of his radio program *The Mercury Theatre on the Air* (broadcast October 30, 1938). For this episode he presented a story based on *War of the Worlds* that made use of a narrative technique imitative of actual news broadcasts on the radio. This resulted in some people believing

Sci-Fi Theater

that the Earth had actually been invaded by Martians. The scale of the panic was exaggerated in newspaper reports. But the use of media to cause a panic was a portent of things to come.

In 1951 two iconic films were produced that told of the invasion of Earth by extraterrestrial beings, each with a very different agenda. *The Thing from Another World* told the story of a military outpost in the Arctic where an alien spacecraft has crashed into the ice. The men subsequently come under attack by the inhabitant of that craft. It is unclear as to what the Thing wants, or even if it is the only one of its species. The men hold off the attacks, despite the attempts at betrayal by a Lenin-esque scientist who wants to communicate with the Thing, until they are finally able to kill it with electricity. A reporter who was on the scene concludes his news conference about the events with the famous words: "Tell the world. Tell this to everybody, wherever they are. Watch the skies everywhere. Keep looking. Keep watching the skies."

The vicious hostility of the Thing is in contrast with the well-intentioned threats of domination and behavior-control delivered by Klaatu in *The Day the Earth Stood Still*. He warns mankind not to misuse the newly developed capacity for atomic warfare, or the robotic enforcers of nonviolence—in the form of machines such as his "companion," or commissar, Gort—will annihilate us.

An altogether more oddball visitor also came to the screen that same year in the super-low-budget effort by Edgar G. Ulmer: *The Man from Planet X*. This tells of a spaceship landing from a previously unknown planet now passing through our solar system. The pilot of the ship is a diminutive man in a spacesuit, who is in distress. Two scientists (Professor Elliott and Dr. Mears) and a reporter, John Lawrence, try to communicate with him. This fails initially, but the conniving Dr. Mears figures out how to communicate through musical tones and attempts to force the alien to provide the formula for the metal used in his spaceship. Mears then detaches the breathing apparatus from the visitor, trying to kill him. But he survives and begins to take captives from among the townspeople. It is learned that the spaceship is

The Man from Planet X (1951)

a forward operation for a planned invasion from Planet X, which is a dying world. Such an invasion will be launched when the planet reaches its closest point to Earth. Therefore, the military is ordered to destroy the spaceship, including the unscrupulous Dr. Mears. Planet X cannot launch the invasion and passes out of our solar system harmlessly. Some see an autobiographical vision of Ulmer himself in this plot. Ulmer remained somewhat of a "stranger in a strange land" after his immigration from Weimar Germany.

Perhaps the first and one of the most effective tales of alien mind control is *Invaders from Mars* (1953), a classic film rooted in the psychological realities of children. It tells the story of how a little boy named David witnesses events of the Martian invasion as a craft descends into sandpits near his house. In the aftermath of the landing, he notices that his parents are "different" and have come under the influence of the invaders. (What child has not realized that his or her parents are "different"—and this difference is even more exaggerated when the kid is not in the room.) In the end, we are relieved to discover it was all a dream—or was it a premonition of things that are about to happen? Once David has learned "it was all a dream," he goes back to bed and looks out his window and sees the flying saucer once more descend into the sandpits. He's wide awake now, so all he can do is say: "Gee whiz!"

There were several other films with similar concepts. One of the most implausible creatures ever seen on screen—the shape of which was perhaps suggested in *Forbidden Planet*—is found in Roger Corman's *It Conquered the World* (1956). In this instance the extraterrestrial uses batlike flying entities to implant the mind-controlling elements into people's necks. This last film was "remade" in 1966 on an even lower budget and seen only on television—*Zontar, the Thing from Venus*. Another film often cited as belonging to this type is *It Came from Outer Space* (1953). Upon closer examination, we see that the motivations of the extraterrestrials here are more akin to those found in *E.T. the Extra-Terrestrial* (1982), in that they appear to be here by accident and are only trying to leave Earth and get back home. The original story treatment for this film was done by the great Ray Bradbury.

One of the most effective films ever made on this topic is the 1956 version of *Invasion of the Body Snatchers*. There were no monsters or tentacled things from another world—rather, it was an unseen power or force contained in an otherworldly plant that sprouted pods, by means of which the bodies of targeted earthlings could be replicated with new and compliant minds—compliant to what, or to what purpose, is left unknown. From the robotic and emotionless result, we can guess that we are once more dealing with a metaphor for the gray and humorless world of the East Bloc. An important factor is that the victim of the

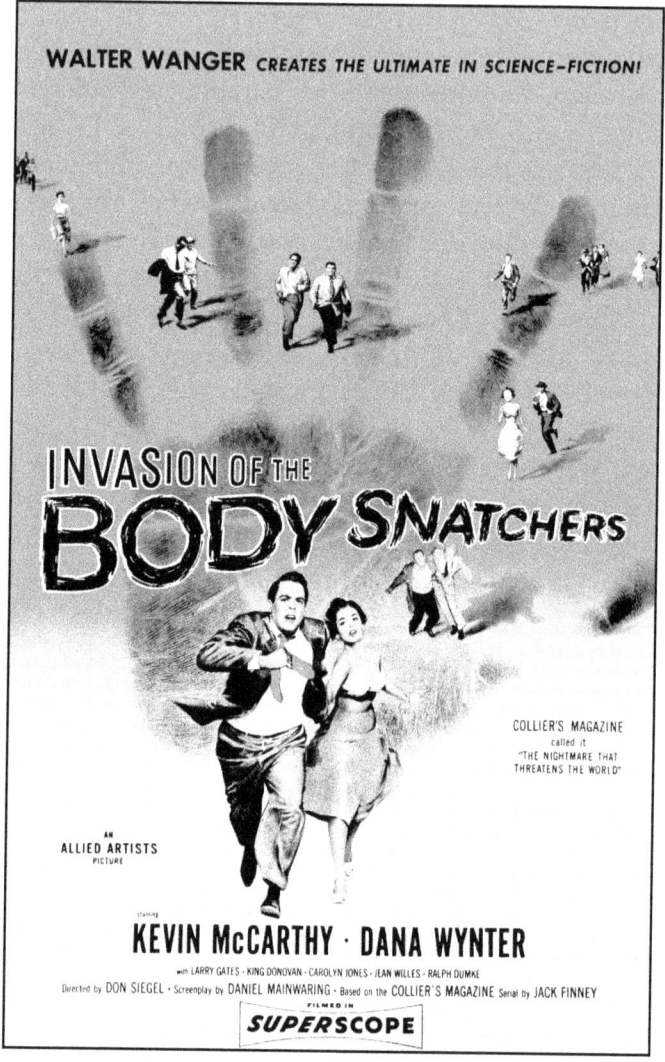

Invasion of the Body Snatchers (1956)

process has to *go to sleep* (become unaware) before the pod can do its work of replicating and replacing the individual.

The fear of invasion by hostile forces is as old as humanity and human consciousness. The human community—family, clan, tribe, or village—has always been vulnerable to hostile incursions and even utter destruction by more aggressive, bellicose, and militarily superior neighbors. It is to this cosmic fear, to this age-old human anxiety, that these films and stories speak. Once it became a generally accepted idea that the universe might be full of Earthlike planets, upon which a variety of sentient beings might exist, man's fear of invasion from these unknown planets became plausible. On the other hand, the most widely accepted and popular interpretation of most of these films is that they are crude metaphors for an irrational (?) American anxiety over being "invaded" by Soviet agents and that the absurd idea of *socialism* might somehow find its way into the American brain resulting in a mind-numbing *sameness* of acceptable thought patterns. Gee whiz!

4. *Exploration of Other Worlds*

This type of narrative involves the exploration of new—usually hostile—realms, ones that are something other than our normal, mundane existence. These are often other planets, but this is not the only possible scenario. For example, the stories could show an interaction with other temporal realities (time travel), dimensions (fantasy), or previously unknown and/or unexplored areas of our own world (deep under the sea, under the Earth's surface, unexplored regions of the Earth, etc.).

The origins of this kind of mythic narrative lie in our ancestral migratory patterns. In the most ancient times our ancestors, the Indo-Europeans, were a semi-nomadic people who came out of Central Asia around six thousand years ago. The history of these events is complex, but the reflections of this way of thinking form a persistent part of our mentality: we instinctively want to travel, to see what is over the next hill, even to invade and colonize other territories. "Frontierism" is in our blood—the idea was ever present in the 1960s when JFK called his agenda the "New Frontier" (a part of it was the space program) and each *Star Trek* episode began with the words: "Space, the final frontier . . ." From the Stone Age onward, our ancestors sought to discover new frontiers and find new opportunities in new lands. This impetus is behind the American colonies and the westward expansion of Europeans in North America. For Indo-Europeans, their homeland can be anywhere and they are culturally happiest when forging new frontiers. With this as a deep, mythic background, the science-fiction genre of the discovery and exploration of new worlds is quite natural.

I can well remember time spent as a child in the early 1960s, sitting in front of the TV in the morning before school and watching the various launches of the Mercury program. Alan Shepard was launched into space on my eighth birthday in 1961. In this time period, we kids saw a new world opening before us—it carried both hopes and nightmares.

The masters of science fiction in the nineteenth century delivered several narratives about transportation of humans beyond the confines of Earth: Jules Verne (*From the Earth to the Moon* and *Around the Moon*) and H. G. Wells (*First Men in the Moon*) both provided important blueprints for future film ventures. The earliest film to be inspired by these works was the 1902 fantasy production of Georges Méliès called *Le Voyage dans la Lune* (A Trip to the Moon). Perhaps the first serious film about space travel was Fritz Lang's often-overlooked *Frau im Mond* (1929), which was well researched as far as the practicalities of space travel at the time. The film showed such features as: the rocket named *Friede* ("Peace") is built in a tall building and moved to the launch pad; the rocket blasts off after a countdown from ten to zero; in flight the rocket ejects a first and second stage; the crew rests in horizontal chairs to minimize g-force effects; and foot-straps are used to hold the crew down in zero gravity. All of these details would become a part of space exploration as engineered by many a German scientist in America and Russia. The German rocket scientists Hermann Oberth and Willy Ley acted as advisors for the film, and those in the Wernher von Braun circle at the Verein für Raumschiffahrt (Society for Space Travel) were big fans of the film. They even painted the logo from the film on the tail of one of the infamous V-rockets.

Among the most iconic films about the discovery of new worlds are *Forbidden Planet* (1956), *The Angry Red Planet* (1959), and *First Men in the Moon* (1964). The last of these was based on the H. G. Wells book of the same name published in 1901, which is also an important piece of literature in this vein.

Sci-Fi Theater

A frame from Georges Méliès's *A Trip to the Moon* (1902)

Arthur C. Clarke and Stanley Kubrick showed us the way beyond the fear-based view of both the exploration of space, as well as visitations from beyond in his works *Childhood's End*, *The Sentinel*, and others which were used to create the narrative of one of the greatest science-fiction films of all time: Stanley Kubrick's *2001: A Space Odyssey* (1968). This is a film about both the intrusion of extraterrestrial life on Earth and man's exploration of space to take humanity to a higher level. Kubrick intentionally leaves the film open to a variety of interpretations, but certain things appear most probable in the meaning of the film. On one level, it is about the evolution of consciousness. Actual transitions from one species to another are shown: from pre-human to human, when the apes make contact with the monolith on Earth, and then when humanity is capable of leaving the confines of Earth and makes contact with a monolith on the moon and another one orbiting Jupiter—triggering a new level of evolution, symbolized by the fetus of the new species hovering over the Earth, ready to take possession of it. These fit with both

Zoroastrian and Nietzschean philosophies—hence the use of symphonic music by Richard Strauss: *Also sprach Zarathustra*.

Although the exploration of other heavenly bodies is the most obvious example of this type of science-fiction adventure, a subgenre to it should be recognized as the terrestrial version of the same idea. Here explorers discover strange realms in our terrestrial sphere—under the water (*20,000 Leagues Under the Sea* [1954]), below the Earth's crust (*Journey to the Center of the Earth* [1959]), or somewhere in a remote location on the Earth's surface (*The Lost World* [1925, 1960] or *The Mysterious Island* [1961]). To this can also be added a "journey" into another dimension of reality altogether (e.g., *The Time Machine* [1960]). Such stories convey to us a sense of the immediate presence of the "other," a feeling that extraordinary experiences might be found not all that far away from us. These films instilled a sense of wonder surrounding nature and could give the feeling to a child, or to the part of each of us that remains a child, that "another world" might be found just around the corner, or in a creek-bed in the neighborhood.

At first glance, this theme of the discovery of new worlds should have a more optimistic viewpoint. Such discoveries are, after all, heralded in human history as being among the greatest achievements of mankind. However, the narrative is to a great extent held hostage for the purposes of the films and stories, which are meant to present a message of danger and hostility lurking in areas beyond man's "normal" range of existence. In many ways, this mythic paradigm is akin to the fairy-tale mythology in which the woods or forested regions, lying beyond the limits of the village fence or the well-trodden roads, are fraught with danger of both a natural and a supernatural character. The stories warn especially children to stay where it is safe and not to venture too far beyond the bounds of normal life. Because the narrative requirements of storytelling are based on conflict and the resolution of that conflict in favor of the conventional forms of reality, stories about the exploration of things beyond our ken took on themes of horror and tragedy. What in actual historical experience has been characterized by a force of attraction, a sense of mystery, and a feeling of hope is turned into one of repulsion, apprehension, and fear. But this seems to have been done out of convention, sometimes necessitated by compliance with censors—either official censors or mere feelings of what is "acceptable" to the audience.

In recent years, the horror genre has become dominated by stories of glamorous vampires and torture-porn slasher movies, whereas the science-fiction genre seems to have developed in a more sophisticated direction. The older, more classic science-fiction narratives do seem to fall into the categories outlined in this essay, and this likewise holds true for the literature by authors such as H. G. Wells and Jules Verne, upon which so many of the vintage science-fiction films were based. The enormous contemporary attraction to science fiction seems to be drawn from the fact that much of what ancient myths and sagas used to be able to do in people's minds—create a landscape of infinite possibilities where magic rules the world—only seems plausible, or syncretically true, in the world of science fiction, dominated as it is with seemingly miraculous forms of technology.

Afterword
The Light Grows Dimmer

The horror films of old still shine with an unearthly glow—a black flame and a white light dance on a silver screen to convey their secrets over the decades. The deeper significance of these films should not be lost or scoffed at by smug pseudo-intellectuals, for by doing so our culture will have been made all the poorer. The essays in this book have attempted to open the doors of insight and act as exercises in the reflective study of these cultural artifacts in a spiritually meaningful way. At least that has been my intention and hope.

At present, more horror films are being produced and they are making more money than ever before. They are receiving honors and awards at an unprecedented rate, yet they do not hold the iconic role in the culture they once did. This probably stems from the fact that society has changed—as have the films themselves. Horror films are also much more respected today than they ever were in the past. A Monster Kid, Jonathan Demme, directed the first horror film to win an Academy Award for best picture, while garnering best-director honors for himself, in 1991 with *The Silence of the Lambs*. This was an accomplishment matched by Guillermo del Toro for his gill-man film, *The Shape of Water*, in

2017. In his acceptance speech for the Oscar, del Toro thanked "the monsters" for saving him. Certainly, the genres of horror and science fiction have vindicated themselves historically. At the same time, with all the gains, something has been lost. But the fantastic news is that because the classic material has been saved and is easier to access than ever before, it is still there to inspire generations to come. This book is an exercise in that resurrection of the dead, whereby we may continue to interact with our old friends in ever deeper ways.

Advances in special effects—either using sophisticated prosthetics or employing computer-generated images—have allowed filmmakers to show any sort of transformation or dismemberment in all the details that were often only suggested or alluded to in the classic era. Just as erotic films or pornography went from often being stories with explicit sexual scenes to merely scenes of nothing but sexual content, many horror films appear to be frameworks for the demonstrations of gory details.

This being said, probably some of the best horror movies ever made were produced after 1975, to be sure. The levels of insight, knowledge, and sophistication far outshine what could be done in the early period. The one aspect that remains generally unmatched from the older time is the art of cinematography and set design. This art could be matched today, but the audience for it would not be sufficient to warrant the investment, I am sure.

One of the major shortcomings of the whole horror genre today is the lack of great horror stars. Lon Chaney, Bela Lugosi, Boris Karloff, Peter Lorre, Lon Chaney, Jr., and finally Vincent Price brought greatness to the genre and in turn have been blessed with a kind of immortality few film performers have ever received or ever will receive. The closest thing to these today was perhaps Johnny Depp. The torch could have been passed, or may indeed have been passed, from Vincent Price to him during the making of *Edward Scissorhands* (1990), but he seems not to have fully embraced the role—yet.

An important reduction in the importance and function of the horror film as a rite of passage was caused by the movie rating system introduced in the late 1960s. Before this system was put into place, horror films tended to be seen by much younger audiences: prepubescent and pubescent kids. The average age went up for the typical audience member after the rating system was implemented. The earlier system allowed horror films to fulfill a function that stories, such as the often-gruesome "fairy tales" of the Brothers Grimm, fulfilled in times past. Young kids could be scared, and their courage tested, but within a safe and friendly environment. I think this is why the films of the 1950s and early 1960s effectively featured older, avuncular men (Karloff, Lorre, Price), with whom the Monster Kids were able to identify and love. These films functioned as rites of passage at the correct time in the child's development. Once the typical viewer was an older teenager, the time of this effective function was past. In the classic horror film, children tended to be absent whereas they take center stage in the mid-1970s "slasher" films.

Up until the mid-1970s, horror films were things loved *by* kids, but they were not things that were particularly or necessarily made *for* kids. Once they started to be made almost exclusively for younger audiences, the genre literally and figuratively turned on the kids and showed them being victimized in the most cruel ways imaginable. The brutal victimization of attractive, sexually active, and popular teenagers becomes a centerpiece of the horror film.

This turn of events may be consciously rooted in the ancient Greek philosophy of Aristotle. It is easy to conceive of the horror film as a subgenre of *tragedy* (as opposed to *comedy*). In the part of his work *Poetics* devoted to the Tragedy, Aristotle famously defined this art form as "an imitation of an action that is serious, complete, and of a certain magnitude; in language embellish with each kind of artistic ornament, . . . through pity and fear effecting the proper purgation of these emotions" (VI, 2). Pity is aroused by witnessing "unmerited misfortune," and fear is excited by that misfortune occurring to a "man like ourselves" (VIII; trans. Butcher).

This "unmerited misfortune of a man like ourselves" essentially means that by looking at an artistic representation of bad things happening to people with whom we identify, we feel pangs of sympathetic pain—and *horror*—due to this identification. We assume that the obverse of this, *comedy*, would work by reversing the formula. I say "we assume," because Aristotle's second volume of *Poetics*, "On Comedy," is lost. The Italian semiotician Umberto Eco elaborately speculated as to why and how it was lost in his medieval crime novel, *The Name of the Rose*. He speculated that the Christian monks responsible for copying these ancient works in order to preserve them for posterity omitted the work "On Comedy" because they did not support laughter: if man is permitted to laugh at all, he may one day laugh at God, and that must be prevented at all costs.

In any event, comedy would be the misfortune of those with whom we do *not* identify. Hence an unsympathetic character is produced, and we see bad things happen to him and we laugh. Historically, clowns have been men unlike ourselves, or men in whom we do not see ourselves. Their misfortune is merited in that they are idiots or perhaps even unlikeable characters.

The typical horror film after about 1978 is what has come to be called the modern slasher movie. To be sure, this genre of film had its very early antecedents—*M* (1931), *Psycho* (1960), *Peeping Tom* (1960), *Homicidal* (1961), *Torso* (1973), and *Black Christmas* (1974). This last film was directed by Bob Clark, who also directed one of America's most beloved films: *A Christmas Story*! The most explicit prototype of the slasher film was made in 1971 by the Italian master Mario Bava, entitled *A Bay of Blood*. But after the mid-1970s, gore could be shown in ways never before possible. However, the more significant trend was toward the casting of very young people as the victims of the horror. This appears to be a direct application of the aforementioned Aristotelian formula. If you want to scare kids, make kids the victims of misfortune (e.g., decapitation, dismemberment, evisceration). By the same token, there developed a comedic edge to this trend as well, equally rooted in the Aristotelian formula. The underlying archetype of such films is: popular, good-looking kids go to a remote location intent on having sex, and they are beset by a serial killer who disposes of most of them in a gory fashion before being foiled in the end (usually by a female

Afterword: The Light Grows Dimmer

protagonist). The formula was originally intended to exploit the Aristotelian formula of showing bad stuff happening to kids with whom the audience was supposed to identify. Things went a bit haywire in the reception, though, because, as it turned out, most of the youths in the audience were not the kind that were going out the lake to have sex—they were at the movies, not out at the lake with the popular kids. So, when "Chad" or "Ashley" gets eviscerated, it is seen in a virtually comical framework with a certain pornographic appeal by the average nerdy "outsider" sitting in the audience. The great news for slasher filmmakers is that it works at the box office either way!

Another major disadvantage from which the horror film of today suffers is the result of the unbridled freedom that the filmmakers have to show scenes of gore and splatter. This freedom in many ways diminishes the artistic value of the genre. The limits that were imposed upon horror films by censorship actually forced the level of art to be of a higher order in the older films—with the exception of the arts of special effects, of course. It is sometimes hard to realize how limits and rules lead to greatness in art. To take an example from another field of human endeavor, sports, it is as if football were being played with no rules. The only object is to get the ball across the goal line. With no rules, one side may bring bats and knives to the game—the skills of athletic superstars would have no opportunity to be manifest and would be lost to the experience of fans of the sport. Art and virtuosity thrive on rules and limitations. Without these, everything quickly descends into a mechanism for feeding the appetites of the undiscerning.

As with the stories of werewolves and vampires, about whom it is said that they return to make victims of those they love the most, the horror film was similarly made the victim of those who loved them most. The Monster Kids grew up, were given special powers, and returned to make victims of that which they loved best. Perhaps now the victims are in the process of rising from their graves and in the future, we will be gifted with an even greater mythic universe. In the world of the human imagination, anything is at least possible.

Appendix A:

Best Classic Horror Films 1913–1975

In this age with a fascination for such lists, those purporting to contain the "best" horror films abound. Each list created by individuals will be full of biases. Mine is no different. My biases are toward the supernatural, the Gothick, and toward those films that have had some sort of wider cultural impact. Also, most of mine are American because comparing the horrors produced by and for other cultures can cause asymmetrical conclusions. To be included in a list of the best, a film has to have a certain degree of cinematic quality or innovation. Many films discussed in the essays of this book are not on this list because their quality was not high enough (e.g., *Plan Nine from Outer Space*). This does not mean that these films do not have a certain greatness of their own, it is just that they cannot be included in the Hundred Best list because of these deficits. But certain others are included despite some glaring problems due to their cultural impact or importance to the genre (e.g., the 1940s *Mummy* series).

There are many films that are on the edge between horror and science fiction, such as *Invasion of the Body Snatchers* (1958) or, most importantly, the *Creature from the Black Lagoon* series. The apparent extraterrestrial origin of the antagonist in the former and the "freak of nature gone wild" aspect of the latter shift them to the science-fiction category.

In certain cases, a whole series of films—such as the Universal *Frankenstein* series—will be included as a single entry, but with each title counted separately.

Silent Era

The Student of Prague (1913, remake 1926)
The Cabinet of Dr. Caligari (1919)
The Golem (1920)
Nosferatu (1922)
Warning Shadows (1923)
The Hunchback of Notre Dame (1923)
Waxworks (1924)
Phantom of the Opera (1925)
The Unknown (1927)
Alraune (1928)

1930s

M (1931)
Dracula (1930)
Dr. Jekyll and Mr. Hyde (1931)
Frankenstein (1931)
    Bride of Frankenstein (1935)
    Son of Frankenstein (1939)
    Ghost of Frankenstein (1942)
The Mummy (1932)
Freaks (1932)
Old Dark House (1932)
Vampyr (1932)
White Zombie (1932)
Murders in the Rue Morgue (1932)
Island of Lost Souls (1932)
The Black Cat (1934)
The Werewolf of London (1935)
Mad Love (1935)

1940s

The Mummy's Hand (1940)
    The Mummy's Tomb (1942)

Appendix A

The Mummy's Curse (1944)
The Mummy's Ghost (1944)
The Wolf Man (1941)
Frankenstein Meets the Wolf Man (1943)
    House of Frankenstein (1944)
    House of Dracula (1945)
Cat People (1942)
    Curse of the Cat People (1944)
The Leopard Man (1943)
The Seventh Victim (1943)
I Walked with a Zombie (1943)
The Lodger (1944)
The Picture of Dorian Gray (1945)
The Spiral Staircase (1946)

1950s

The House of Wax (1953)
Night of the Hunter (1955)
Les Diaboliques (1955)
The Black Sleep (1955)
Curse of the Demon (1957)
The Curse of Frankenstein (1957)
The Horror of Dracula (1958)
The Tingler (1959)
House on Haunted Hill (1959)

1960s

Eyes without a Face (1960)
Peeping Tom (1960)
Psycho (1960)
Black Sunday (1960)
Fall of the House of Usher (1960)
Mr. Sardonicus (1961)
The Innocents (1961)
Carnival of Souls (1962)

Whatever Happened to Baby Jane? (1962)
The Haunting (1963)
The Birds (1963)
The Masque of the Red Death (1964)
Black Sabbath (1963)
The Haunted Palace (1963)
Hush... Hush, Sweet Charlotte (1964)
Repulsion (1965)
Hour of the Wolf (1967)
Rosemary's Baby (1968)
Night of the Living Dead (1968)

Early 1970s

The Devils (1971)
The Abominable Dr. Phibes (1971)
    Dr. Phibes Rises Again (1972)
Simon: King of the Witches (1971)
Last House on the Left (1972)
The Wicker Man (1973)
The Exorcist (1973)
Don't Look Now (1973)
Black Christmas (1974)
Texas Chainsaw Massacre (1974)
Jaws (1975)
Deep Red (1975)

Appendix B:

Best of the Rest 1976–2022

Carrie (1976)
The Omen (1976)
The Tenant (1976)
Suspiria (1977)
Eraserhead (1977)
The Dark Secret of Harvest Home (1978)
Halloween (1978)
The Shout (1978)
The Brood (1979)
The Changeling (1980)
Dressed to Kill (1980)
The Shining (1980)
The Fog (1980)
The Howling (1981)
Wolfen (1981)
Poltergeist (1982)
Cat People (1982)
The Hunger (1983)
Videodrome (1983)
A Nightmare on Elm Street (1984)
The Company of Wolves (1984)
Angel Heart (1987)
Near Dark (1987)
Jacob's Ladder (1990)
The Silence of the Lambs (1991)
Twin Peaks: Fire Walk with Me (1992)

Bram Stoker's Dracula (1992)
In the Mouth of Madness (1994)
Interview with the Vampire (1994)
The Ring (*Ringu*) (1998)
    American adaptation: *The Ring* (2002)
The Sixth Sense (1999)
The Blair Witch Project (1999)
The Ninth Gate (1999)
The Others (2001)
The Devil's Backbone (2001)
Call to Cthulhu (2005)
Let the Right One In (2008)
The Conjuring (2013)
The Babadook (2014)
The Witch (2015)
The Shape of Water (2017)

Appendix C:

Twenty Guilty Pleasures

These are personal favorites, sometimes because of the time period in my life when I saw them, and partly due to the themes contained in the films. In all cases, however, they are defective in some way or another which prevents them from being included in list of the truly best films.

Mystery of the Wax Museum (1933)
Robot Monster (1953)
Bride of the Monster (1956)
From Hell It Came (1957)
Curse of the Faceless Man (1958)
How to Make a Monster (1958)
Plan 9 from Outer Space (1959)
The Hypnotic Eye (1960)
The Leech Woman (1960)
The Lost World (1960)
Dinosaurus! (1960)
Curse of the Werewolf (1961)
Reptilicus (1961)
Die, Monster, Die! (1965)
The Fearless Vampire Killers (1967)
The Dunwich Horror (1970)
Count Yorga, Vampire (1970)
The Mephisto Waltz (1971)
The Asylum of Satan (1972)
The Devil's Rain (1975)

Appendix D:

Fifty Must-see Classic (Pre-1975) Science-Fiction Films

Frau im Mond (1929)
Metropolis (1927)
Island of Lost Souls (1932)
King Kong (1933)
The Invisible Man (1933)
The Invisible Ray (1936)
Things to Come (1936)
The Invisible Man Returns (1940)
Doctor Cyclops (1940)
The Man from Planet X (1951)
The Thing from Another World (1951)
The Day the Earth Stood Still (1951)
Invaders from Mars (1953)
War of the Worlds (1953)
It Came from Outer Space (1953)
Them! (1954)
Creature from the Black Lagoon (1954)
20,000 Leagues Under the Sea (1954)
This Island Earth (1955)
Forbidden Planet (1956)
Godzilla (1956)
The Incredible Shrinking Man (1957)
Invasion of the Body Snatchers (1958)
I Married a Monster from Outer Space (1958)
It! The Terror from Beyond Space (1958)
The Fly (1958 and 1986)
The Blob (1958)

Journey to the Center of the Earth (1959)
The Time Machine (1960)
Village of the Damned (1960)
Mysterious Island (1961)
Voyage to the Bottom of the Sea (1961)
Journey to the Seventh Planet (1962)
First Men in the Moon (1964)
Last Man on Earth (1964)
Alphaville (1965)
Planet of the Vampires (1965)
Fantastic Voyage (1966)
Fahrenheit 451 (1966)
Barbarella (1968)
2001: A Space Odyssey (1968)
Planet of the Apes (1968)
THX 1138 (1971)
A Clockwork Orange (1971)
The Andromeda Strain (1971)
Silent Running (1972)
Slaughterhouse Five (1972)
Westworld (1973)
World on a Wire (1973)
Zardoz (1974)

Bibliography

Apel, Johann August, and Friedrich Laun. 1810–1818. *Das Gespensterbuch*. 7 vols. Leipzig: Göschen.

Aquino, Michael A. 2013. *The Church of Satan*. Eighth edition. 2 vols. San Francisco: [N.p.].

Aristotle. 1922. *The Poetics*. Translated by S. H. Butcher. London: MacMillan.

Barlow, John D. 1982. *German Expressionist Film*. Boston: Twayne.

Belanger, Michael A. 2004. *The Psychic Vampire Codex*. York Beach, Me.: Red Wheel/Weiser.

Blake, Michael F. 1990. *Lon Chaney: The Man Behind the Thousand Faces*. New York: Vestal.

Burns, Bob, and Tom Weaver. 2003. *Monster Kid Memories*. New York: Dinoship.

Campbell, Joseph. 1949. *The Hero with a Thousand Faces*. Princeton: Princeton University Press.

Chappell, Toby. 2019. *Infernal Geometry and the Left-Hand Path: The Magical System of the Nine Angles*. Rochester, Vt.: Inner Traditions.

Cohn, Norman. 1975. *Europe's Inner Demons: An Enquiry Inspired by the Great Witch-Hunt*. New York: Basic.

Conan Doyle, Arthur. 2011. *The Best Supernatural Tales of Arthur Conan Doyle*. Selected and introduced by E. F. Bleiler. New York: Dover.

Craig, Bob. 2009. *Ed Wood: Mad Genius: A Critical Study of the Films*. Jefferson, N.C.: McFarland.

Davis, Wade. 1986. *The Serpent and the Rainbow*. New York: Simon and Schuster.

Day, A. J., ed. 2004. *Fantasmagoriana: Tales of the Dead*. St. Ives: Fantasmagoriana.

Doyle, Arthur Conan. 1892. "Lot No. 249." *Harper's New Monthly Magazine*, September issue: 525–44.

———. 1890. "The Ring of Thoth." *The Cornhill Magazine*, January issue: 1–10.

Dresser, Norine. 1989. *American Vampires: Fans, Victims, Practitioners*. New York: Norton.

Dyson, Jeremy. 1997. *Bright Darkness: The Lost Art of the Supernatural Horror Film*. London: Cassell.

Eisler, Robert. 1978 [1948]. *Man into Wolf: An Anthropological Interpretation of Sadism, Masochism and Lycanthropy*. Santa Barbara: Ross-Erikson.

Eisner, Lotte H. 1973. *The Haunted Screen: Expressionism in the German Cinema and the Influence of Max Reinhardt*. Translated by Robert Greaves. Berkeley: University of California Press.

Ellis, Havelock. 1942 [1905]. *Studies in the Psychology of Sex*. 2 vols. New York: Random House.

Davidson, H. R. Ellis. 1986. "Shape-changing in the Old Norse Sagas." In *A Lycanthropy Reader: Werewolves in Western Culture*, edited by C. F. Otten. Syracuse: Syracuse University Press. Pp. 142–60.

Davis, Wade. 1985. *The Serpent and the Rainbow: A Harvard Scientist's Astonishing Journey into the Secret Societies of Haitian Voodoo, Zombies, and Magic*. New York: Simon and Schuster.

Eisenberg, Nancy. 2016. *White Trash: The 400-Year Untold History of Class in America*. New York: Viking.

Endore, Guy. 2005 [1933]. *The Werewolf of Paris*. N.p.: Blackmask.

Ewers, Hanns Heinz. 1929. *Alraune*. Translated by S. Guy Endore. New York: Day.

———. 1917. *Edgar Allan Poe*. Translated by Adele Guggenheimer-Lewisohn. New York: Huebsch.

———. 1927. *The Sorcerer's Apprentice*. Translated by Ludwig Lewisohn. New York: Day.

———. *Strange Tales*. 2000. Translated, edited, and introduced by Stephen E. Flowers. Bastrop, Tex.: Lodestar.

———. *Vampire*. 1934. Translated by Fritz Sallagar. New York: Day.

Eyries, Jean Baptiste Benoît. 1812. *Fantasmagoriana, ou Recueil d'Histoires d'Apparitions, de Spectres, Revenans, etc*. Paris: Schoell.

Féval, Paul Henri Corentin. 1972 [1860]. *Le Chevalier Ténèbre*. Paris : Inter-forum.

———. *La Vampire*. 1865. Paris: Docks de la librairie.
———. *La Ville-Vampire*. 1874. Paris: Dentu.
Florescu, Radu. 1975. *In Search of Frankenstein*. New York: Warner.
Flowers, Stephen E. 2015. *Sigurðr: Rebirth and the Rites of Transformation*. Bastrop, Tex.: Lodestar.
Gennep, Arnold van. 1960. *The Rites of Passage*. Translated by M. Vizedom and G. Caffee. Chicago: University of Chicago Press.
Gerard, Emily. 1885. "Transylvanian Superstitions." *The Nineteenth Century* 18: 130–50.
Grey, Rudolph. 1992. *Nightmare of Ecstasy: The Life and Art of Edward D. Wood, Jr.* Second edition. Portland, Ore.: Feral House.
Guy, Gordon R. 1987. *Zacherle!* Glastonbury: Guy.
Hardy, Phil, ed. 1987. *The Encyclopedia of Horror Movies*. New York: Harper and Row.
Harms, Daniel, and John Wisdom Gonce III. 2003. *The Necronomicon Files: The Truth Behind Lovecraft's Legend.* Second edition. Boston: Weiser.
Hill, Douglas, and Pat Williams. 1965. *The Supernatural*. New York: Hawthorn.
Hoffman, Daniel. 1972. *Poe Poe Poe Poe Poe Poe Poe*. Garden City, N.J.: Doubleday.
Jones, Stephen. 2000. *The Essential Monster Movie Guide*. New York: Billboard.
Isenberg, Noah. 2014. *Edgar G. Ulmer: A Filmmaker at the Margins*. Berkeley: University of California Press.
Ketterer, David. 1979. *Frankenstein's Creation: The Book, The Monster, and Human Reality*. Victoria: University of Victoria Press.
———. 1979. *The Rationale of Deception in Poe*. Baton Rouge: Louisiana State University Press.
Kracauer, Siegfried. 1947. *From Caligari to Hitler: A Psychological History of the German Film*. Princeton: Princeton University Press.
Krafft-Ebing, Richard von. 1965 [1886]. *Psychopathia Sexualis*. Translated by Franklin S. Klaf. New York: Arcade.

Kugel. Wilfried. 1992. *Der Unverantwortliche: Das Leben des Hanns Heinz Ewers.* Düsseldorf: Grupello.

LaVey, Anton Szandor. 1978. "How to Become a Werewolf: The Fundamentals of Lycanthropic Metamorphosis; the Principles of Their Application." *Cloven Hoof* (71) 10.1: 1–4.

———. 1976. "The Law of the Trapezoid." *Cloven Hoof* (64) 8.6: 1–4.

———. 1972. *The Satanic Rituals.* Secaucus, N.J.: University Books.

Lauritsen, John. 2007. *The Man Who Wrote Frankenstein.* New York: Pagan.

Law, John W. 2000. *Scare Tactic: The Life and Films of William Castle.* San Jose: Writers Club.

Leroux, Gaston. 1996. *The Essential Phantom of the Opera.* Edited by Leonard Wolf. New York: iBooks.

Lovecraft, H. P. 1963. *The Dunwich Horror and Others.* Sauk City, Wis.: Arkham House.

———. 1964. *At the Mountains of Madness and Other Novels.* Sauk City, Wis.: Arkham House.

———. 1965. *Dagon and Other Macabre Tales.* Sauk City, Wis.: Arkham House.

Lubarski-Debalta, S., ed. 1916. *Book of the Exile: Souvenir of the Bazaar and Fair Held Under the Auspices of the Peoples' Relief Committee for the Jewish War Sufferers, March 1916.* New York: Peoples' Relief Committee for the Jewish War Sufferers.

McNally, Raymond T., and Radu Florescu. 1994. *In Search of Dracula.* Second edition. Boston: Houghton Mifflin.

Mauss, Marcel. 1952. *A General Theory of Magic.* Translated by Robert Brain. New York: Norton.

Naha, Ed. 1982. *The Films of Roger Corman: Brilliance on a Budget.* New York: Arco.

The Oxford Dictionary of English. 2010. Edited by Angus Stevenson. Third edition. Oxford: Oxford University Press.

Plato. 1963. *The Collected Dialogues.* Edited by Edith Hamilton and Huntington Cairns. Princeton: Princeton University Press.

Poe, Edgar Allan. 1845. "Some Words with a Mummy." *The*

American Review: A Whig Journal of Politics, Literature, Art and Science, vol. 1, no. IV (April 1845): 363.

———. 1935. *Tales of Mystery and Imagination*. Illustrated by Arthur Rackham. London: Harrap.

———. 1976. *The Science Fiction of Edgar Allan Poe*. Edited by Harold Beaver. London: Penguin.

———. 1996. *The Complete Poetry of Edgar Allan Poe*. Edited by Jay Parini. New York: Signet.

[Polidori, William]. 1819. *The Vampyre: A Tale*. London: Sherwood, Neely, and Jones.

Prawner, S. A. 1980. *Caligari's Children: The Film as Tale of Terror*. Oxford: Oxford University Press.

Rider Haggard, Henry. 1897. *She: A History of Adventure*. London: Longmans.

Robinson, William J. 1922. *Married Life and Happiness, or Love and Comfort in Marriage*. Fourth edition. New York: Eugenics Publishing Company.

Ronay, Gabriel. 1972. *The Truth about Dracula*. New York: Stein and Day.

Rymer, James Malcolm, and Thomas Peckett Prest. 1845–1847. *Varney the Vampire, or The Feast of Blood*. London: Lloyd.

Sargent, Denny. 2020. *Werewolf Magick*. St. Paul, Minn.: Llewellyn.

Seabrook, William. 2016 [1929]. *The Magic Island*. New York: Dover.

Shelley, Mary. 1818. *Frankenstein: The Modern Prometheus*. London: Lackington, Hughes, Harding, Mavor & Jones.

Sheridan Le Fanu, Joseph. 2013. *Carmilla: A Critical Edition*. Edited by Kathleen Costello-Sullivan. Syracuse: Syracuse University Press. [Originally serialized in *The Dark Blue* magazine 1871–1872].

Silverman, Kenneth. 1991. *Edgar A. Poe: Mournful and Never-ending Remembrance*. New York: Harper-Collins.

Skal, David J. 1998. *Screams of Reason: Mad Science and Modern Culture*. New York: Norton.

———. 2001. *The Monster Show*. Second edition. New York: Faber and Faber.

———. 2004. *Hollywood Gothic: The Tangled Web of Dracula from Novel to Stage to Screen*. Revised second edition. New York: Faber and Faber.
Soule, Gardner. 1963. *The Maybe Monsters*. New York: Putnam.
Steblin-Kaminskij, M. I. 1973. *The Saga Mind*. Translated by Kenneth H. Ober. Odense: Odense University Press.
Steinbrunner, Chris, and Burt Goldblatt. 1972. *Cinema of the Fantastic*. New York: Galahad.
Steinhauser, Monika. 1969. *Die Architektur der Pariser Oper*. Munich: Prestel.
Stoker, Bram. 1897. *Dracula*. Garden City: Doubleday.
———. 1903. *The Jewel of Seven Stars*. London: Heinemann.
Summers, Montague. 1960. *The Vampire: His Kith and Kin*. Secaucus, N.J.: University Books.
———. 1966 [1933]. *The Werewolf*. Secaucus, N.J.: University Books.
Underwood, Peter. 1972. *Karloff*. New York: Drake.
Voger, Mark. 2015. *Monster Mash: The Creepy, Kooky Monster Craze In America 1957–1972*. Raleigh, N.C.: TwoMorrows.
Völker, Klaus, ed. 1971. *Künstliche Menschen*. Munich: Hanser.
Warren, Bill. 1986. *Keep Watching the Skies!: American Science Fiction Movies of the Fifties*. Jefferson, N.C.: McFarland.
Watson, Elena M. 1991. *Television Horror Movie Hosts*. Jefferson, N.C.: McFarland.
Weaver, Tom, Michael Brunas, and John Brunas. 2007. *Universal Horrors: The Studio's Classic Films 1931–1946*. Second edition. Jefferson, N.C.: McFarland.
Webb, Don. 2021. *Energy Magick of the Vampyre*. Rochester, Vt.: Inner Traditions.
[Webb, Jane]. 1827. *The Mummy! A Tale of the Twenty-second Century*. 3 vols. London: Colburn.
Wilson, Colin. 1982. *The Outsider*. Los Angeles: Tarcher.
Wolfe, Burton. 1974. *The Devil's Avenger*. New York: Pyramid.
Wood, Jr., Edward D. 1990. *Plan 9 From Outer Space: The Original Uncensored and Uncut Screenplay*. Edited by Tom Mason. Newbury Park, Calif.: Malibu Graphics.

www.ingramcontent.com/pod-product-compliance
Lightning Source LLC
Chambersburg PA
CBHW051034160426
43193CB00010B/939